LOCATING LC

Statecraft, cit
and democ

Jane Wills

P

First published in Great Britain in 2016 by

Policy Press
University of Bristol
1-9 Old Park Hill
Bristol
BS2 8BB
UK
t: +44 (0)117 954 5940
pp-info@bristol.ac.uk
www.policypress.co.uk

North America office:
Policy Press
c/o The University of Chicago Press
1427 East 60th Street
Chicago, IL 60637, USA
t: +1 773 702 7700
f: +1 773-702-9756
sales@press.uchicago.edu
www.press.uchicago.edu

© Policy Press 2016

British Library Cataloguing in Publication Data
A catalogue record for this book is available from the British Library

Library of Congress Cataloging-in-Publication Data
A catalog record for this book has been requested

ISBN 978-1-4473-2304-4 paperback
ISBN 978-1-4473-2303-7 hardback
ISBN 978-1-4473-2307-5 ePub
ISBN 978-1-4473-2308-2 Mobi

Cover design by Hayes Design
Front cover image: Big Ben Tower © Vectomart and UK map
© Natapong Paopijit | Dreamstime.com
Printed and bound in Great Britain by CMP, Poole
Policy Press uses environmentally responsible print partners

Dedicated to

Agnes Lilian and

Eric Trevelyan

Contents

List of figures and tables

Figures

Tables

Acknowledgements

I am very grateful to the Leverhulme Trust for providing the fellowship that allowed me to complete the research and writing involved in this book. Andrea Gibbons, Erica Pani and James Scott provided invaluable research support for different parts of the project. Kerry Cable at Business Friend completed all the interview transcriptions to a very high standard. Ed Oliver has done a brilliant job in (re)producing all the figures that are used in the text. Emily Watt, Emily Mew and Laura Vickers from Policy Press have been very encouraging throughout the process of commissioning, writing and editing *Locating Localism*.

My life at Queen Mary is blessed by having a wonderful group of colleagues, some of whom have been friends for more than 20 years, and I am especially grateful to Alison Blunt, Tim Brown, Kavita Datta, Beth Greenhough (now moved to Oxford), Al James, Jon May, Cathy McIlwaine, Catherine Nash, Miles Ogborn, Alastair Owens, David Pinder (now moved to Roskilde in Denmark), Simon Reid-Henry, Adrian Smith, Stephen Taylor, Philippa Williams and Kathryn Yusoff. I am always mindful that we owe a great deal to Roger Lee, Philip Ogden and Nigel Spence for creating a collegial workplace culture before we arrived.

Over the past decade I have explored the ideas in this book with many students, but especially those studying for the Masters and Postgraduate Certificate in Community Organising which I taught between 2010 and 2015. These classes – and my learning – were greatly enriched by the quality of the students taking the course and the additional teaching provided by Jonathan Cox, Sophie Stephens, Sotez Chowdhury and Maurice Glasman. The opportunity to teach with Maurice while he was developing the ideas that came to be described as Blue Labour, and which led to his elevation to the House of Lords, has been particularly formative in the development of my work over this time. For a few years, Luke Bretherton (now at Duke University in the US), Maurice and I were collaborating in our efforts to better understand the tradition of non-partisan community organising developed in the US and its implications for the UK. We combined the insights from theology, political philosophy and geography to make sense of a new approach to doing politics, and it took each of us in different directions.

While I've been at Queen Mary, I have supervised the PhD theses of Jeremy Anderson, Anibel Ferus-Comelo, Caroline Gaskell, Paula Hamilton, Kate Hardy, Liam Harney, Jane Holgate, Amy Horton, Lina Jamoul, Andrew Lincoln, Jenny McCurry, Erica Pani and James Scott, and each has further helped me to hone some of the arguments made in this book. Albeit in very different contexts, these students have been looking at the ways in which different forms of organising can make an impact on the trajectory of communities and institutions, and the extent to which positive socioeconomic and political development can be achieved.

So too, the research conducted for this book has focused on the ways in which people attempt to make change in relation to their community, focusing on neighbourhood planning, community organising and civic capacity. I am very grateful to everyone who kindly facilitated my research and to those who agreed to be interviewed as part of the work. A full list of all those who were interviewed is given in the research appendix at the end of the book. However, special thanks are due to Tessa Dugmore and Sarah Castro from Poplar HARCA for facilitating the research into the Neighbourhood Community Budget that is reported in Chapter Three; to Anna Randle, who welcomed me into Lambeth Council in order to understand its work to become a cooperative council – documented in Chapter Four; to Tessy Britton and Laura Billings, who introduced me to the Open Works platform being pioneered in South London (also covered in Chapter Four); to Jo Hawkins, Di Boston, Dennis Kitchen, Maggie Meade-King and Rachel Allison for their help in my efforts to get to grips with neighbourhood planning as covered in Chapter Five; and to Neil Jameson and Matthew Bolton for a long-standing and multi-faceted relationship with Citizens UK, which is discussed in Chapter Six.

I also benefited from insightful interviews with Robert Rutherford at the Department for Communities and Local Government, Phillip Blond from Respublica, Steve Wyler at Locality, Justin Griggs from the National Association of Local Councils, Richard Lee from Just Space, as well as Angela Singhate and Gill Fitzhugh from Queen's Park Community Council in West London. Professor John Tomaney read over a previous draft of this book and provided extremely useful comments. Presentations given at Birkbeck College, University of London (June 2014), at an event on community planning held by The Bartlett (UCL) and the Open University (December 2014), at the School of Religions and Theology at the University of Manchester (March 2015) and at the Annual Conference of the Royal Geographical Society (August 2015) also provided additional feedback for which I am very grateful.

Localism is an idea that has always been of interest. When I was an undergraduate student in the early 1980s, I read E.F. Schumacher's *Small is Beautiful* and ended up writing a dissertation about efforts to generate power from cow dung in two Indian villages. A normative commitment to the idea of geographic community (that many would cast as romantic and unrealistic) underpinned the provision of bio-gas plants in these rural locations, as well as my own efforts to study their impact. Looking back, I now recognise that parts of my childhood explain what has been a persistent attachment to the idea that communities can develop solutions to at least some of their problems.

I grew up in a Methodist family, where my own community was all about tea, cake, singing and praying and, despite efforts to escape, I later came to recognise the virtues of what can appear to be very old-fashioned and extremely mundane. In this regard, my parents, Greta and the late Reverend N. Trevelyan Wills, taught me a lot. Rather surprisingly, they came from different geo-political points of view in relation to the question of community. My Dad was a communitarian Cornishman who clung to a romantic and oftentimes sentimental sense of the past while my Mum grew up in the North-West, with a strong belief in the power of social and spatial mobility to provide a way to escape from the past. These twin political traditions, which I later came to recognise as communitarianism and liberalism, were able to find an accommodation in our family home just as they both remain central to our national political life. Understanding the puzzle of my parents' successful marriage between a strong sense of rooted communal tradition and a less rigid commitment to opportunity has been a powerful current in my thinking for the past 30 years. It is perhaps not surprising that I decided to study geography, subsequently becoming preoccupied with understanding the continued importance of place and social relationships in a world that is subject to powerful global forces that are prompting ever-greater tides of demographic displacement and interconnection. Indeed, this book explores exactly this problematic; it considers the physical and political role of place and extant social relationships in a world that often seems very hostile to the kinds of old-fashioned community in which I grew up. My personal experiences and the research reported in the later parts of this book point to something persistent about the power of place to bring people together, albeit that there may be less tea and cake, singing and praying than there was in my past.

Outside work, I am very grateful to Jim Chapman for all his support and I dedicate this book to our daughter, Agnes, and to our son, Eric, whose disability has re-taught us the importance of relationships, the need for life to be local and the power of love.

In regard to the reproduction of the various figures included in this book I am very grateful to the Hansard Society, the Institute of

Public Policy Research, the Royal Society of Arts, the University of Chicago Press, Policy Exchange, Tessy Britton (Civic Systems Lab), David Clifford, John Mohan, Jon Wilson and Paul Whiteley for their permission to reprint their images and/or to draw on the data collected or deployed by them. These sources are indicated in the appropriate parts of the text. In addition, Chapter Five is a reworked version of material already published in the journal *Political Geography* and I am grateful for permission to reuse this work.

Introduction: the argument being made in this book

All polities have a geographical division of political power (Maas, 1959; Berry, 1987). Authority, responsibility and power over decision making are unevenly distributed across space, being attached to an institutional matrix of political decision making that reflects the history of any particular state. Over the past 30 years, for a combination of reasons, momentum has been building to revisit the inherited spatial architecture that underpins politics in the UK. There is now a growing consensus about the need for greater devolution, decentralisation and localisation.

However, re-imagining and remaking the state, and recasting the behaviour of its cadre and citizens, is a difficult thing to do, especially when the institutional infrastructure to support the decentralisation of political decision making does not yet exist. Indeed, in this context there is a danger that the wave of devolution currently underway in England will simply involve the redistribution of political power from one set of elites to another; from politicians and officials in Whitehall and Westminster to those in the town halls of Manchester, Sheffield and our other great cities (Parker, 2015). Reaching the *demos* and doing something potentially more transformative will demand the creation of new civic infrastructure and capacity at the neighbourhood scale. Although a quarter of the population – largely those living in rural areas – are covered by long-established parish councils, the vast majority of the population have no access to this tier of government (NALC, 2015, 5). Moreover, even those who do are often disappointed by the constrained and unimaginative decisions being made.

This book explores the challenges posed by the weakness of our local civic infrastructure and its attendant impact on our civic capacity and democratic life in England. The book presents the findings from four different research projects that have been conducted to explore ongoing efforts by some government-funded organisations and groups of residents to set up new institutions in urban areas. The research exposed the valiant efforts being made by unpaid volunteers who want to make improvements to their local area. In the spirit of the early parish government that emerged in England after the Reformation (covered in much more detail in Chapter Two), these emergent bodies are focused on the provision of communal services and social events, on improving the quality of the local environment and reshaping the trajectory of local development. However, the book also highlights the

1

challenges of creating this infrastructure in some parts of the country, and the paucity of knowledge about what can be done about the uneven development of civic capacity in England today.

Whereas the New Labour governments (1997–2010) sought to use the state to engage with the people, the previous and current Conservative-led governments (from 2010 to the present) have been more liberal and less prescriptive, passing permissive legislation that creates the space for citizens to act on their own terms and in their own way. However, this is unlikely to yield results in every location, and in places where the existing population lacks the capacity or interest to respond, they are likely to be left further behind by the shift to localisation. In such circumstances, non-partisan community organising has the potential to reach people, engaging them in local efforts to make a difference that simultaneously provide opportunities to develop new skills (as outlined further in Chapters Four and Six). However, this requires careful thought about the model of organising that is best able to engage local people and it demands some financial investment in the labour involved. This book argues that more needs to be done on this front.

As such, and in line with the brief of Policy Press, *Locating Localism* is focused on contemporary developments in policy and practice. However, unpicking localism also exposes the need to develop alternative ways of thinking about the political geography of England today. In trying to make sense of localism, I have been struck by the paucity of our thinking about the geography of political power and the limits this imposes on our ability to imagine other ways of organising the state and enacting citizenship. The prevailing geographical division of powers has shaped what we have come to expect; growing up in a centralised polity has limited our ability to develop an alternative geographical imagination about the operation of political power. Most obviously, we have inherited a long-established tendency to prioritise the national over the local, and, as Jim Bulpitt (1983) suggests, this has been about the 'high' form of politics located at Westminster trumping the 'low' politics of the local town hall. As outlined in Chapter Two, our geo-constitution and its attendant system of political representation has evolved to create a centralised hierarchy of political decision making such that the local is cast as an appendage of the will of the centre.

During the 20th century this centralisation has been reinforced by the operation of national political parties that fill positions at the local level in order to follow non-local national agendas (Copus, 2004; Bogdanor, 2009). In addition, however, there has also been a long-standing tendency to prioritise the role of the expert that has often reinforced the denigration of the local arena, casting it as necessarily inefficient and vulnerable to capture by self-interested folk (pejoratively described as the 'usual suspects'). Over the past 200 years, calls for expertise and efficiency have tended to outweigh the focus on nurturing democratic public engagement. As a result, the local has been cast as dangerously parochial, often associated with nostalgia and sentimentalism, and even xenophobia, and it is generally thought to be thoroughly bad (and for more on this see Tomaney, 2013).

In this context, any analysis of new trends in the political geography of English statecraft is less than straightforward. Taking localism seriously requires rethinking the fundamentals of our spatial imaginaries about political power and the role and place of government. In a situation in which the local is already dismissed as small-minded, defensive and marginal to the whole, there is little hope for granting it any importance. Thus, as it is presently constituted, the debate about our national political geography limits the space for local organisation and then further denigrates the outcomes secured, and, in this regard, it is necessary to make a prior philosophical argument about the potential of place to be other than it is currently constituted before any new thinking can really be done. In this regard, Gerald Frug (1999, 2000, 2014; Barron and Frug, 2005) has been making a strong intellectual argument that we develop a non-zero-sum understanding of political power such that we can see the potential of strong local organisation contributing to the good of the whole. Rather than setting the local against the interests of the wider polity in what he describes as forms of 'defensive localism' (and the same is true of top-down narratives about 'parochialism'), Frug advocates the development of overlapping spheres of decision making within any polity. In so doing, he draws on the example of the South African constitution, in which different spheres of government are seen as 'distinctive, interdependent, and inter-related' (Frug, 2014, 3). This constitution imagines the geography of political power to comprise overlapping spheres, none of which is fully autonomous, but each of which contributes to the good of the whole. This is a more horizontal model of political organisation and action and its successful execution would require a less partisan approach to politics whereby local agents feel able to represent their interests to a larger collective and negotiate over the outcomes, rather than being subject to rigid limits to initiative or strict party discipline that are imposed from above (Frug, 1999, 2014; see also Clark, 1984).

Warren Magnusson (2005a, 2005b, 2012) has built on this work to further argue that the city is particularly important as a site for the development of self-organisation, self-government and the generation

3

of non-sovereign political power. He argues that recognising the importance of sub-national units of political organisation – such as cities – requires recognising the co-existence of political authority beyond state sovereignty in bodies like municipalities, local councils and aboriginal groups (particularly pertinent in relation to his work in the Canadian context). While each unit has different purposes, authority and legitimacy, each contributes to the common good of the whole. By thus rethinking the geography of political power, and developing a new language around concepts such as subsidiarity and self-government, it becomes possible to remake the dominant paradigm through which we think about the geography of government and politics.[1]

This book seeks to contribute to the growing body of academic work that demands another look at the local in relation to our political life and the quality of our democracy. As the shift towards localist statecraft exposes the limits of our dominant paradigms for thinking about politics and its geography, as well as the weaknesses of our institutional infrastructure, there is an opportunity to revisit questions about the importance of place. In the context of growing concerns about anti-politics (Clarke, 2015), and its relationship to populism (Chwalisz, 2015), a growing number of people are recognising the need to foster greater popular engagement in political life. In so doing, it is the local arena that will be the site for a new round of democratic experiment and institutional change, even if those local innovations relate to changes taking place beyond the nation-state as well as things much closer to home (Smith, 2009; Bohman, 2010; Chwalisz, 2015). Thus the debate about localism necessarily involves grappling with the inheritance of our intellectual traditions, our political institutions, practices of citizenship and the role of the state. There is a great deal at stake.

In what follows, Chapter One introduces localism, explains the momentum building behind the idea and provides some scaffolding to make sense of this emerging field of policy in England today. Chapter Two situates this localist turn in relation to the much longer history of the evolution of England's geographical division of political powers and the geo-constitution. From these foundations, Chapter Three explores the way in which this geographical inheritance shapes the practice of democracy in England today, determining the way in which citizens are both able and willing to engage in political life. The rest of the book looks at four examples of localist experimentation, starting with initiatives led by the state. Chapter Three looks at the development of a Neighbourhood Community Budget in Poplar in East London and Chapter Four focuses on Lambeth Council's efforts to foster a cooperative relationship with local residents in South London. The penultimate pair of chapters focus on bottom-up efforts to craft new institutions and civic capacity, looking at neighbourhood planning in Chapter Five and community organising in Chapter Six. The final chapter brings us back to the issues raised by this research, revisiting arguments about the weaknesses of our local civic infrastructure, the need for more to be done and the importance of place.

Note

[1]   As such, the arguments in this book are in keeping with the thinking of pragmatists and post-structuralists who highlight the contingent nature of 'truth' and the performative impact of language in making the world (Rorty, 1979; James, 2000 [1907]; Gibson-Graham, 2006). Thinking about the possibilities of localism requires that we acknowledge the limits of prevailing models of thought and the impact of language on the world we purport to describe.

ONE

Making sense of localism

Broadly speaking, localism comprises a shift in policy making and practice to decentralise political power towards local institutions and local people. Thus far, localism amounts to a series of experiments in statecraft and shifting expectations around citizenship. Some of these developments – in policy, local government, planning and community organising – provide the focus for much of the detail in later parts of this book. For now, however, this chapter aims to set the scene, setting localism in its wider geo-political context.

In many ways, localism is the next logical step in a process of political devolution that began during the Blair–Brown New Labour governments between 1997 and 2010. These Parliaments championed the successful devolution of political power to Scotland, Wales and Northern Ireland. During this period, Britain's national story became increasingly focused on an alliance of four different nations with divergent trajectories, and this has continued today. The creation of the Scottish Parliament has been particularly important in facilitating the development of a new cadre of national politicians, who used the new institution and its capabilities to pioneer new policies and practices with growing support from their people. Just 14 years after its creation, this Parliament was able to vote to pursue a referendum for full independence. The subsequent referendum campaign electrified the nation and the Scottish people proved their capacity to threaten the very unity of the British state. The referendum generated extraordinary levels of popular engagement and record turnout from voters, mobilising a new generation of political activists, fuelling the ranks of Scotland's political parties and generating a stronger sense of national identity, purpose and pride. The experience of active political engagement has then, in turn, shifted the culture and expectations of Scottish political life (Featherstone, 2015).

Scotland is a nation with an increasingly assertive political leadership and a strong sense of identity, but, in the wake of devolution, some parts of the British establishment and some political activists have started to explore the potential to further increase political decentralization within the United Kingdom (UK). Moreover, while the New Labour governments had granted limited devolution to Scotland and, to a lesser extent, Wales and Northern Ireland, they were never willing to consider the thorny issue of political representation for the largest and most dominant nation within the alliance. At the time, English political representation was the issue and cultural identity that couldn't speak its name (Scruton 2006 [2000]; Kenny 2014), but in the wake of the Scottish referendum this issue has moved to centre stage. There are growing calls for English votes for English laws (EVEL) and some sort of English Parliament. Furthermore, there are growing numbers of people calling for greater political devolution and freedom below the national level. Over recent years momentum has been building for the decentralisation of political authority and responsibility to different bodies within England (and for the history of English regionalism see Tomaney, 2006). Just two months after the Scottish referendum in September 2014, a Combined Authority covering the city-region of Manchester made a successful pitch for greater powers to be devolved, alongside the election of a new Mayor for the region. Not surprisingly, politicians in other parts of the country have similarly demanded the power to retain more of the money raised in their region and to have the capacity to make more decisions over locally important issues, most notably in London (GLA, 2013; O'Brien and Pike, 2015).

Thus, questions concerning the political geography of the UK have moved centre-stage. It is more than 100 years since Westminster resounded to fractious debate about Home Rule for Ireland, and that political battle ran from 1886 to 1920 before being partly resolved. Now again, the geography of our political settlement – our geo-constitution – suddenly seems open to question. There are new political opportunities for those who want to assert their national, regional or local identity, and to make the case for new political powers to represent perceived local interests. The genie of devolution is out of the bottle and, as yet, there is no certainty as to when or where it will be put back behind glass.

However, while nations have an established narrative and a sense of a shared imagined community, however shaky and internally divided, there is much less certainty about the implications of devolution at the sub-national scale within England. Of course some geographical areas have a stronger sense of shared history, culture, identity and pride than others, but there is no certainty about the appropriate geographical areas or the institutions, to which power should and could be devolved. The geographical containers called region, city-region, metropolitan area, local authority, ward, neighbourhood and 'community' are all potential players in this re-imagining of political geography. Added to this, the demand to strengthen existing forms of representative democracy (and particularly local government) is being made alongside experiments with new forms of direct democracy and local engagement. As such, localism is an emergent field of policy, practice, experiment and contestation. I try to explain it more fully in the rest of this chapter and then consider its wider development and implications in the rest of this book.

What is localism?

Most obviously, localism is about engaging people in local civic life, but less obviously, it is also about the nature and purposes of the central state. Indeed, localism can be understood as an effort to reconfigure the geographical division of political powers across the nation by shifting power from the centre towards the localities (Maas, 1959). Although any geographical balance of powers necessarily develops incrementally and the cartography of the state is altered through ad hoc decision making and serendipity as much as through rational planning, the early 19th century was a time that began a process of ever-greater state centralisation in the UK. Our ideas about good government increasingly embraced the notion that a strong central state was essential to protecting the freedoms, rights and equality of the people. Aided by the existential threat posed by the Second World War, the development of a strong centre was justified on the basis of securing economic growth and the provision of welfare across the whole community. At its simplest, the development of localism is a reaction against this centralisation of political power. A combination of forces are now at work to challenge the established geographical balance of power.

Localism can be interpreted as an argument about the limits of central government to do what the politicians – and the people – want it to do. In an era in which people are no longer so confident that it is possible to push through a programme of government from the pages of the party manifesto down to the encounters between public sector workers and citizens, localism has developed as a way to rethink government. In particular, it is a response to widespread criticism of the centrally determined policy targets that were adopted in the early years of the New Labour governments (1997–2010). In the face of an obvious failure to solve many of the pressing social and economic problems of our times – many of which have got worse – localism represents a recognition that staff on the front line – and the local politicians that provide oversight to their employment – need to be empowered to act as circumstances demand. As such, localism is linked to the anti-bureaucratic structure of feeling that can now be found among the new generation of citizens brought up alongside the new technologies that facilitate horizontal connectivity between strangers to produce software, knowledge and shared ideas about getting things done (Gauntlett, 2011; Finlayson, 2012; Parker, 2015). In addition, the language of localism is used to describe the ways in which citizens can organise themselves to find solutions to their common concerns (Bryson and Crosby, 1992; Stone et al, 2001; Fung and Wright, 2003; Healey, 2006; Leighninger, 2006; Saegert, 2006; de Sousa Briggs, 2008). Through this lens, localism is argued to facilitate the creation of a 'Big Society' in which citizens are solving their own problems with minimal support from the state.

Thus far at least, however, English localism is best characterised as a 'top down' initiative. It is largely an elite reaction to growing popular disillusionment with the mainstream political process. There is a growing 'void' (Mair, 2013) between the citizens and the political class, and this is often articulated in a geographical lexicon: the elite are understood to be concentrated in Westminster, Whitehall and the posh parts of London and the South East. There is a popular notion that this elite have done well for themselves while the rest of the country has been left far behind (Chwalisz, 2015). The geography of electoral support for the United Kingdom Independence Party (UKIP) in many of the coastal towns that have been hard hit by economic decline, inequality and political powerlessness is particularly striking in this regard.

In the wake of the electoral threat of UKIP in England, and more widespread hostility to mainstream politicians, the main political parties have looked increasingly exposed, shorn of an emotional connection to the people and bereft of the policy solutions that are adequate to the challenges faced. In this context, all three of the mainstream political parties – Conservative, Labour and Liberal Democrat – have adopted localism as a key part of their political programme. In order to try to fill the widening 'expectations gap' between the people and their politicians (Flinders, 2012), political leaders have adopted the policy and practice of localism. In so doing, however, the irony is that the politicians are then expecting a great deal more of the citizens, in some ways widening the expectations gap on their side of the table. While the people have largely unrealistic expectations of politicians, the political class have reacted by developing a focus on localism which expects much more of the people.

As this suggests, localism comprises a shift in geographical imaginations about government. It has been developed by national politicians in the expectation that the local state and citizens will take up more of the role of government. Driven more from above than below, localism represents a challenge to the model of government and politics that developed during the 20th century and, in theory at least, it marks the development of a new phase of statecraft. This model is about a central government that devolves political power, authority and responsibility to lower-level institutions and people. Following the principle of subsidiarity, it is argued that decisions should be made at the lowest possible spatial scale – being closest to the people affected. The vision is that localism will facilitate greater initiative and creativity in public policy making as place-based publics are convened to solve local problems. In this model, the central state is there to facilitate rather than direct what happens on the ground. Localism is about a spatial and institutional pluralisation of government and agency, moving the locus of political power and decision making from a concentrated executive in the capital city towards a wider diversity of actors across the nation at large. Reminiscent of arguments in political economy about the self-organisation of the economy, localism makes a similar argument about politics; by opening up possibilities and creating new incentives for a wider variety of actors to engage in political decision making, its proponents argue that political power can be better distributed across the society, with beneficial effects for us all (Hayek, 2001 [1944]; Hoffmann, 1959; Huntingdon, 1959; Magnusson, 2012).

In this regard, localism also carries traces of the civic republican and communitarian traditions. It is the latest iteration of a long-standing normative argument that democracy requires active intermediate institutions and high(er) levels of civic engagement in order to be a success (Barber, 2003 [1984]; Sandel, 1998; White and Leighton, 2008; Pettit, 2012). However, as Clarke and Cochrane (2013) suggest, localism is also liberal – it is about 'freeing up' the local state, citizens and communities to act on their own perceived interests. As such, localism comprises a combination of liberalism and institutionalism. Localism is cast in something of a republican hue that prioritises the role of the people and the importance of place in efforts to open up spaces for democratic engagement (Lind, 2014). In distributing political power more widely, liberal localism exposes the importance of existing social institutions and people's capacity to act. It is a liberalism that highlights the role of social organisation and, in many ways, it takes us back to the traditions of social liberalism that were strongest in the years before more social-democratic models of politics became prevalent after the Second World War (Green, 1885; Hobhouse, 1964 [1911]; Dewey, 2000 [1935]).

This kind of liberal institutionalism exposes important – and unresolvable – tensions at the heart of contemporary liberal democracy and its associated culture(s).Classical liberalism is about freeing citizens from the social obligations, customs, traditions, religions and experiences that tended to underpin political virtue in pre-modern society. Yet this also makes it much harder to govern, as any successful society *requires* the distribution of key political virtues such as delayed gratification, social solidarity, compliance with majority decisions and adherence to collective tradition (Oldfield, 1990; Mansbridge, 1995). In response to this challenge, liberalism has often been fused with a recognition of the importance of strong community institutions that can provide educational opportunities to support everyday citizenship and foster the motivation to act in the interests of the wider collective. Writing from a range of perspectives, social liberals, civic republicans and communitarians are all preoccupied with the role of institutions in the creation of such political virtue in liberal and secular times (MacIntyre, 1981; Barber, [2003 [1984]; Sandel, 1998; Dewey, 2000 [1935]; Putnam, 2000). However, as with talk of the 'Big Society', there is more than a hint of wishful thinking about much of this debate. It is strongly normative and rarely grounded in empirical data, not least because much contemporary practice actually queries the arguments made for a secular citizenship that can replace the spirit of engagement on which society used to depend (as explored in more detail in Chapters Two and Three of this book).

Thus, localism is somewhat caught in the tensions between two poles of political thought. On the one hand, localism represents a cry for freedom from the central state but, in so doing, it raises an apparently contradictory demand that lower-tier organisations and local citizens should act to fill the political space. If we think of localism as an experiment in liberal institutionalism it helps to explain this combination of a call for freedom that is simultaneously aligned with the need for organisation.

In this regard, it is likely that localism will take deepest root where there is sufficient local interest and capacity to engage. This, in turn, will be more likely in some areas than others, reflecting the nature and composition of local communities, their existing organisation and activity, the presence of civic leaders and key local institutions, as well the opportunities that are presented for making a difference. The geography of existing civic infrastructure and capacity will underpin the fortunes of localism and, in this regard, greater liberalisation will expose the uneven national map of social norms and existing civic capacity. The presence of local civil-society organisations, the strength of social networks between them and the wider citizenry, has to be explored alongside prevailing forms of civic capacity, which comprise the ways in which local people are able and willing to organise around their shared interests, to raise their voice, generate a response (which can involve self-organisation as much as the official organs of authority and power) and get things done. In this regard, civic capacity also concerns the responses made by the various arms of the state and the way in which state-funded bodies (education, health, local government, police and security, for example) respond to the public (Stone, 2001; Stone et al, 2001; Lowndes et al, 2006; Jun and Musso, 2013).

In a further level of complexity, localism requires that the civic capacity of the local state will need to go beyond simply responding to the demands being made by local residents and their organisations. Rather than simply reacting to the people, localism has been cast as a way of doing government in very new ways. Partly driven by austerity and the need to save money, but also being shaped by the ideological arguments outlined above as well as the potential benefits of developing new ways of working, localism demands that the state make a 'civic offer' to work with the people. This concerns the degree to which the state (at all levels) is 'open' to forming meaningful relationships with other state-funded organisations and a diversity of interests including the citizenry, and this then shapes the civic capacity that can be generated, as well as its likely effects. As outlined in Table 1.1, localism demands rethinking the way in which the state conceives of its own scope, procedures and culture and, in turn, the extent to which

Table 1.1: The state's civic offer and civic capacity: a framework for understanding localism

The civic offer	Civic capacity
The freedom and willingness of different parts of the state to work with diverse local interests and citizens	The capacity of the local state, local organisations and the local population to respond to the civic offers being made to engage
The institutional infrastructure of state, market and civic society at multiple scales	The institutional infrastructure that exists and/or can be generated
The practices being developed to secure new ways of working	The mechanisms developed to secure ongoing relationships and engagement
The culture of relationship building	The capacity to formulate an agenda, act and make change
The emergence of vision and shared identity around collective problem solving and governance	The ability to sustain this work over different projects, over time, in place

different parts of the state and its citizens are able and willing to engage with a wide range of people in getting things done.

Using a different vocabulary, similar arguments have been made in relation to patterns of regional economic growth and the way in which the ability to tap a 'devolution dividend' from localist policy depends on regional-level institutions and their capacity to act for regional growth (Farole et al, 2011; Tomaney, 2014). Scholars have argued that the prevailing political institutions in any area shape local power relations, mediating economic processes and playing a critical role in shaping incentives for action that, in turn, set the trajectory of local culture and practice (Martin, 2010). Witnessing this is often more obvious where institutions are weak, causing 'bottlenecks' in economic activity that can involve 'poor mobilization of stakeholders, lack of continuity and coherence in the implementation of policies by institutions, institutional instability, lack of a common and strategic vision, and lack of capacity and gaps in multi-level governance frameworks' (Tomaney, 2014, 132). This strand of research highlights the importance of regional institutions but, as yet, it tells us little about the creation, operation and evolution of such important forms of organisational life.

So too, understanding the potential 'localist dividend' from the wider devolution of power at a range of spatial scales will depend upon institutional legacies and the impact they have on community organisation, social networks, power relations, the civic offer and civic capacity. As outlined in the rest of this book, the implementation and outcomes of the localism agenda rest heavily on the work of local institutions that are able to listen, represent, negotiate and act in the space between communities and different arms of the state. Local civic capacity is clearly related to the local civic infrastructure and the civic offer being made by the state, and this is the backdrop to understanding the outcomes of the localist experiments that are covered in later parts of this book.

Emergent forms of top-down and bottom-up localism in England today

As will have been evident in the material presented above, new forms of localism involve both the state and its citizens. As such, there are both top-down and bottom-up forms of localism underway in England today. On the one hand, localism relates to the devolution of political power from Whitehall and Westminster (the 'centre') to England's localities. These imagined localities potentially include a wide range of 'local' bodies including representatives from city-regions, local authorities, Local Economic Partnerships and other state-funded bodies, as well as communities. On the other hand, the term is also used to capture the ways in which people can be more fully engaged in the political process and civic life through their connections to place. In this second reading of localism, the geographic locale provides the ground on which citizens are called to new forms of agency in relating to each other as well as to state-funded bodies and local politicians. Localism is used as a term to signal and further develop people's capacity for civic enterprise and political engagement in relation to place. These two strands of localist reform are designed to work together to ensure subsidiarity whereby 'power [is] held at the lowest possible level, whether this is individuals, communities, neighbourhoods, local institutions or local government' (Department for Communities and Local Government, cited in House of Commons Select Committee on Communities and Local Government, 2011, 10).

As such, localism is about 'top down' reforms whereby responsibilities, funding and authority are to be taken from parts of government in Whitehall and passed to other bodies such as local authorities. Indeed, many proponents of localism argue that local authorities or combined authorities and/or Local Economic Partnerships should take on a greater role in areas such as infrastructure planning and spending, skills training and public health (Heseltine, 2012; RSA, 2014; Blond and Morrin, 2015; Columb and Tomaney, 2015; O'Brien and Pike, 2015). By devolving decision making to those closer to the ground, it is argued, more appropriate and more efficacious decisions will be made with greater accountability for what is done. In addition, many proponents of localism advocate greater financial freedom, such that local bodies can decide how to raise and spend the money they have without interference and control from the centre. With greater financial freedom and a larger brief, localism is about granting civic leaders the space and power to act in the interests of their local communities, thereby trying to generate the economic growth, jobs and well-being that serve both local and national interests. In so doing, it is argued, increased political engagement will follow as local citizens and interested parties have the scope to demand change and hold local politicians accountable for the things that are done. In recent years, this form of localism has been strengthened by powerful interventions from policy advocates for elected mayors in cities in the US (Glaeser, 2012; Barber, 2013), as well as from representatives of local government and their supporters who advocate a stronger role for elected bodies in the operation of democracy in England. The House of Commons

Select Committee on Communities and Local Government has made this case in a series of inquiries into the balance of power between the centre and local government (2009), localism (2011) and devolution in England (2014).

In addition, however, arguments about localism also signal a demand for more 'bottom up' forms of civic engagement. Rather than being about devolving power to more localised arms of the state, this part of the localism agenda is about tapping the capacity of citizens to engage in solving their own problems by working together, sometimes in relationship with the local state and state-funded bodies, but also on their own terms. By focusing on the ways in which people can act together to find solutions to their own concerns, this kind of localism is really an argument about community organising and its relationship to democracy. Localism is a proxy for arguments about the place of the people in democratic life. Those subscribing to this form of localism are concerned to unpack the ways in which sharing space in particular places can provide both the social relationships and the common experiences from which citizens can then engage with each other as well as with various arms of the state.

This second strand to localism has a very long pedigree in democratic thought and practice. John Stuart Mill (1890 [1861]) is still celebrated for his argument that democracy requires the opportunity for people to engage in local self-government, thereby learning the skills they need in order to practise citizenship and develop a wider sense of 'self-interest' (Pateman, 1970; Dahl and Tufte, 1974; Macpherson, 1977; Held, 2006). Since the 1960s various British governments have called for more active citizenship and community self-help, and, as outlined more fully in Chapter Three, David Cameron's call for the creation of the 'Big Society' is merely the latest instalment in a long catalogue of government efforts to get citizens to do more (Loney, 1983; Hurd, 1989; Wilson, 1999). Organisations such as local authorities, hospitals, housing associations and police authorities are now being further challenged to cede some authority and power to those living in the local community and/or those using their services. Whereas in the past there has been a tendency for civic engagement strategies to involve a rather limited offer, working to the agenda already set out by the state – to be a school governor, a friend of the library or the park, or a community champion on a local authority forum, for example – some proponents of localism are now advocating a more radical transfer of power (Local Government Taskforce, 2014).

This more ambitious localism would involve unleashing new opportunities for citizens to act on their own interests and, in so doing, to be recognised, respected and welcomed by the various arms of the state. Rather than being viewed with alarm as a bit of a nuisance, active citizens would be granted a hearing and the chance to work for change together with elected and appointed officials. If this kind of statecraft develops, it will involve new relationships between citizens and the state, with opportunities for co-commissioning, co-design and co-production (Boyle and Harris, 2010; Boyle et al, 2010; NESTA and NEF, 2010; Cooke and Muir, 2012; Slay and Penny, 2014). Should this take off, it would represent a major shift in the balance of power from the state towards its citizens and their community-based organisations. However, the empirical material presented in Chapters Three and Four indicates that this is very hard to achieve.

Challenges to localism

As outlined at the end of this chapter, new legislation and political interventions are being designed to try to foster localist experiments in England, and there is every sign that this trend will continue in the future. However, there is little clarity about the outcomes of this agenda. On the one hand, there is no certainty about the extent to which those employed by the state (including those in 'arms-length' organisations) will change their practices in order to take up the mantle of greater responsibility as well as engaging with their citizens in new ways. Over the past 100 years, the development of a more centralised state has reinforced the role of the national government over local government, and this has had cultural consequences for politicians and public alike. As outlined in the next chapter, local government has lost much of its power and its connection to the local community, and although the localism agenda is highlighting the need to reconfigure the geography of these relationships and revisit the role of local government, the legacy of centralism runs deep. Going forward, the actions of those in central government will be as important in facilitating localism as the actions of councillors and officers in local government, and both will impact on the ability to create new civic offers and to galvanise civic capacity from within and beyond the state.

In addition, there is little shared understanding of why, how and when citizens might decide to engage with government. Although many citizens endorse the view that people should have more control over local services and get more involved in helping to improve our public services and local areas, fewer people agree that they should get personally involved and even fewer actually do get involved (Table 1.2). Indeed, it is estimated that a small 'civic core' of less than 10% of the population provide the majority of the time, energy and support needed to keep local civic life functioning through volunteering, participating in organisations and donating money, albeit that a larger group of about a third of the population also contribute in significant ways (Mohan, 2011, 2012; Wilson and Leach, 2011; see also Chapter Three).[1]

As such, localism has exposed a significant 'intelligence gap' in relation to policy, practice and analysis. As outlined in more detail in Chapter Three, there is little clarity about how state bodies can work with communities in a meaningful and efficacious way; about why and how people might decide to engage; and about how to sustain such working practices into the future. While localism rests on an expectation of greater civic leadership and capacity being manifest across the state and within the population, as yet, there is limited evidence that politicians, officers and citizens really understand how this might happen, let alone being able and willing to behave in this

Table 1.2: Attitudes towards local engagement, 2010

Statement	Strongly agree (%)	Tend to agree (%)	Total (+ve)	Tend to disagree (%)	Strongly disagree (%)	Total (-ve)
People should have more control over how public services are provided locally	54	31	85	7	2	9
People should have increased control even if that increases the postcode lottery	29	34	63	17	10	27
People should get more involved in helping to improve our public services and local areas	49	37	86	6	4	10
I should get more involved in helping to improve our public services and local areas	28	40	68	13	9	22
The government is responsible for improving public services and local areas, they shouldn't be calling on the public to help	32	28	60	21	10	31

Source: Ipsos MORI and the Economist poll, on the Big Society, April 2010 (in Dorey and Garnett, 2012, 407).[2]

way (Bogdanor, 2009; Jennings, 2012; Ware, 2012). As a representative from the New Local Government Network (NLGN) put it to the House of Commons Select Committee on Communities and Local Government as part of its inquiry into localism (2011, 52), 'The UK is not yet a nation of localists'. In this regard, localism might come to be little more than another government fad, not least because the dominant trends in society towards increased inequality, ever-higher rates of population mobility and ethnic diversity, and declining membership in civil society organisations all *increase* the challenges of securing more public engagement in political life. A thriving localism would need ever-greater effort to successfully overcome the impact of these ongoing changes in order to support new political ecosystems in every town and city in England. As Ware (2012, 92) suggests, 'Being serious about localism … would involve a far more extensive, expensive and long-term policy than is being proposed currently.' The localist experiments reported later on in this book explore the ways in which people are trying to move in this direction and find new ways of working together, and there is an ever-greater need to understand ways to deepen devolution, civic capacity and citizen engagement across the diversity of England's city-regions, cities, towns and communities. If it is to be successful, localism will reconfigure the geography of the constitutional settlement away from the centre, and towards cities, communities and citizens. It should ignite greater geo-political diversity across the country and unleash much greater innovation and experiment in the way things are done.

However, in 'freeing up' local politicians, civic leaders and citizens, this form of liberal institutionalism will shed clearer light on the geography of our civic institutional inheritance and will then raise arguments about the need to build more effective civic infrastructure in some parts of the country, exposing the challenge of doing this without imposing models from above that thereby undermine the very spirit and meaning of localism. Respecting local differences and traditions means that the central state has to resist imposing a one-size–fits-all plan for increasing civic engagement that is only going to undermine the very social relations on which it depends (Scott, 1998). Being true to localism requires care in the formulation of policy, such that it doesn't undermine the delicate fabric of local civil society and community from which change can come.

As outlined in much more detail in the following chapter, localism reflects a dramatic shift in the geographical imaginary underpinning the British state. If it is to be realised, it will demand a new form of statecraft and citizenship that undoes the centralism that has developed since the early 19th century, in order to replace it with a focus on subsidiarity, local democracy, a local civic offer, civic capacity and a stronger civic infrastructure (Table 1.3). This is a lot to get used to. As represented in Table 1.3, the changes involved are much more significant than is often implied. National targets and diktat are to be replaced by local democratic decision making; long-established concerns about the need for geographic equality and the injustice of the postcode lottery are to be overturned by a freedom for localist decision making that will reflect local political capacity; a national welfare service is to be replaced, or at least augmented, by locally determined and co-produced service provision. As suggested in the Introduction, we scarcely have the intellectual resources to think about this kind of statecraft and citizenship, and it is clear that our politicians under-estimate the challenges involved, while our citizens largely fail to recognise the potential gains to be made. As yet, we are at the start of this journey and there is no certainty about where it will end.

Table 1.3: The geography underpinning statecraft in England: centralism versus localism

	Centralism	Localism
The vision	National standards and uniform delivery	Subsidiarity
The means	A national strategy, targets, audit and local compliance	Local democracy (politicians, voters, lay representatives, citizens and community)
The fears	The postcode lottery (uneven provision)	The lack of local capacity
The risks	Being out of touch and unable to meet the challenges faced; a democratic deficit	Providing an uneven and uncertain landscape for business and life; that the loudest voices determine what's done
The goals	Social and spatial equity in access, experience and outcomes of services	Locally determined and accountable activity and outcomes

The emergence of localism as a political vision for change

Since the turn of the century, a growing number of voices from across the political spectrum have made the case for this kind of devolution and civic engagement. Arguments for localism have built momentum through a stream of policy publications and government-led and appointed inquiries such as those established by the House of Commons

Select Committees for Communities and Local Government and Political and Constitutional Reform (Table 1.4). These documents all argue that, over time, Britain's political constitution has become too centralised to allow local organisations and people to take the initiative to respond appropriately and creatively to local challenges and needs. As Michael Heseltine (2012, 5–6) put it in the opening pages of his government-commissioned report into wealth generation in the UK:

> Over many decades, power and initiative have shifted under governments of all persuasions from provincial England to its capital city and its bureaucracies. Strong local leadership in our great cities created the industrial revolution and made us what we are. London did not dominate … [but overtime] local government assumed the character of Whitehall's branch offices. The private sector has a remarkably similar profile. To an extraordinary degree head offices are London based, or overseas. Regional managers have replaced enterprising leaders.

While this centralisation is argued to have squeezed the life out of local political democracy, the increased role of the central state is also argued to have squeezed the life out of local civil society, such that people rely on government rather than collective innovation in order to solve social problems and meet local needs. Moreover, localists point to the centralisation of the British state as compared with our major competitors, and, in relation to funding, only about 25% of national expenditure is currently controlled by sub-central government bodies (see Figure 1.1).

Localism has attracted support from both the left and right of the political spectrum. While it was discussed by some Labour politicians during the later years of their governments between 1997 and 2010, there were also a number of Conservative politicians who were developing similar ideas as a way to rethink their approach to government. Broadly speaking, in its more conservative manifestations localism is envisaged as a way to strengthen the local and regional economy as well as a way to ignite a Big Society in which local people will be re-engaged in civic and political life, backed up by a more accountable but much smaller state (Cameron, 2009; Kelly, 2012). In its more left-wing manifestations, localism is envisaged as a way to foster a 'relational state' in which local people work *with* the state to create social change (Glasman, 2010; Cooke and Muir, 2012; Mulgan, 2012; Parker, 2015). In both, there is a vision of a more revitalised local public

Figure 1.1 International comparison of the percentage of general government expenditure spent by sub-central government (2010)

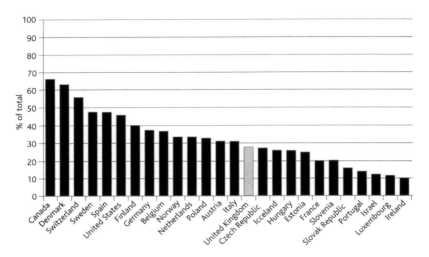

Source: Heseltine, 2012, 29. Data from OECD National Accounts.

realm in which state and citizens have the freedom to work together to launch experiments in government, economy, service provision and local activity – the civic capacity I outlined above.

Localism appeared in the manifestos of all the main parties in their pitch to win the 2015 general election. The Conservatives (2015, 13) pledged to continue their efforts to 'devolve far-reaching powers over economic development, transport and social care to large cities which choose to have elected mayors'. The Labour Party (2015, 11) likewise declared that 'we will devolve more power and control, not only to Scotland and Wales, but to our great English cities and county regions ... And we will share power and responsibility with people in their communities to help them help themselves and shape their services in response to their local circumstances.' The Liberal Democrats (2015, 26) said exactly the same, pledging to 'Devolve more economic decision-making to local areas, building on the success of City Deals and Growth Deals, prioritising the transfer of transport, housing and infrastructure funding, skills training and back-to-work support.' While the Liberal Democrats have long been associated with arguments about local autonomy, it is very significant that both the Labour and Conservative parties have moved in this direction since the late 1990s. As outlined in the next chapter, prior to this, both had contributed to state centralisation, with expectations of a reduced role for local authorities, citizens and civil society groups.

Table 1.4: Key publications advocating localism published since the turn of the 21st century

Year of publication	Author(s), title, publisher
2000	G. Filkin, G. Stoker, G. Wilkinson and J. Williams, *Towards a new localism: A discussion paper*. New Local Government Network.
2002	D. Corry and G. Stoker, *New Localism: Refashioning the centre–local relationship*. New Local Government Network.
2003	G. Clark and J. Mather, *Total politics: Labour's command state*. Conservative Policy Unit.
2003	T. Travers and L. Esposito, *The decline and fall of local democracy: A history of local government finance*. Localis.
2004	S. Jenkins, *Big Bang localism: A rescue plan for British democracy*. Policy Exchange.
2007	Sir Michael Lyons' Inquiry into Local Government, *Place-shaping: A shared ambition for the future of local government*. The Stationery Office.
2009	House of Commons Communities and Local Government Select Committee report on *The Balance of power: Central and local government* (HC 33-1). The Stationery Office. [With the government response published as Cmnd 7712, 2009]
2010	D. Boyle and M. Harris, *The challenge of co-production: How equal partnerships between professionals and the public are crucial to improving services*. New Economics Foundation.
2010	J. Norman, *The Big Society: The anatomy of the new politics*. The University of Buckingham Press.
2010	P. Blond, *Red Tory: How Left and Right have broken Britain and how we can fix it*. Faber and Faber.
2010	HM Government, *Decentralisation and the Localism Bill: An essential guide*. The Stationery Office.
2011	House of Commons Communities and Local Government Select Committee report on *Localism* (HC547). The Stationery Office.
2012	J. Wilson, *Letting go: How Labour can learn to stop worrying and trust the people*. Fabian Ideas 632.
2012	G. Cooke and R. Muir (eds,) *The relational state* (including essays by Geoff Mulgan and Marc Stears). Institute for Public Policy Research.
2012	A. Power, *The Big Society and concentrated neighbourhood problems*. British Academy Policy Centre.
2012	Lord Heseltine, *No stone unturned in pursuit of growth*. HM Government. [With the government response published as Cmnd 8587, 2013].

Table 1.4 (contd)

Year of publication	Author(s), title, publisher
2013	House of Commons Political and Constitutional Reform Committee report on *Codifying the relationship between central and local government* (HC565-I). The Stationery Office. [With the government response published as Cmnd 8623, 2013].
2013	Greater London Authorities' London Finance Committee, *Raising the capital*. Greater London Authority.
2013	M. Taylor and S. McLean, *Citizen power Peterborough: Impact and learning*. Royal Society of Arts.
2014	Local Government Taskforce, *People-powered public services* (for the Labour Party's Policy Review). Local Government Association, Labour Group.
2014	Royal Society of Arts' (RSA's) City Growth Commission, *Unleashing metro growth*. Royal Society of Arts.
2014	The Smith Institute (ed), *Labour and localism: Perspectives on an English new deal*. The Smith Institute.
2014	House of Commons Communities and Local Government Committee report on *Devolution in England: the case for local government* (HC 503). The Stationery Office.
2014	J. Cruddas and J. Rutherford, *One nation: Labour's political renewal*. One Nation Register.
2014	E. Cox et al, *Decentralisation decade: A plan for economic prosperity, public service transformation and democratic renewal in England*. Institute for Public Policy Research, North.
2015	P. Blond and M. Morrin, *Restoring Britain's city states: Devolution, public sector reform and local economic growth*. Res Publica.
2015	S. Parker, *Taking power back: Putting people in charge of politics*. Policy Press.

The development of leftist localism

In office between 1997 and 2010 the New Labour governments had a complicated approach to the geography of state power. On the one hand, they supported greater devolution to Scotland, Wales and Northern Ireland and, at times, they adopted a communitarian language about civic engagement and community leadership. On the other hand, however, they were also associated with the implementation of a battery of performance controls and targets for local service provision that were overseen by an increasingly powerful auditing regime (Clark and Mather, 2003; Jenkins, 2004; Wilson, 2012). Their regime sought to enforce nationally determined standards and practices upon local political institutions and services, requiring regular audit and disciplinary measures for those failing to act as expected (Seddon, 2014). Later coming to recognise the limits of this approach, some ministers did try to row back on their use of targets and the associated centralisation, advocating a 'new localism' that comprised 'double-devolution' down to local authorities and, from there, to communities and citizens (Rao, 2000; Blears, 2003; Davies, 2008; Stoker, 2011; although for a defence of centralism from this period see Walker, 2002).[3] As the leading New Labour politician, Alan Milburn MP put it in May 2004: 'I believe we have reached the high water mark of the post-1997 centrally-driven target-based approach ... Reforms to enhance choice, diversify supply and devolve control are all now taking hold as Government moves from a centralised command and control model to what has been called a new localism ... Public services can't be run by diktat from the top down ... accountability needs to move downwards and outwards to consumers and communities. Empowering them is the best way to make change happen' (in Stoker, 2004, 117).

However, in practice, the localist initiatives introduced by New Labour were generally about 'earned autonomy' that was granted when local politicians did the things that national government wanted them to do and, as such, this represented a 'centralised localism' rather than increased autonomy for local organisations (Stoker, 2004, 2011; Davies, 2008; Lodge and Muir, 2011; Painter et al, 2011; Durose and Rees, 2012). As outlined in more detail in Chapter Three, most of the policy attention during this period was actually devoted to fostering greater public engagement in the work of local authorities, with the state left firmly in charge.

In the wake of electoral defeats in 2010 and 2015, this legacy has been rethought and recast for the future. As indicated in Table 1.4, the Labour-supporting Institute for Public Policy Research (IPPR), the Fabian Society, the Smith Institute and the Labour Party's policy review team have all published policy documents that promote localism, and these interventions highlight the importance of local association and self-organisation (particularly in the trade union movement) and a recognition of the limitations of relying solely on the central state for social improvement. However, the Labour Party has long struggled with the tension between respect for local autonomy and the strongly held ambition to secure improved standards of welfare across the country. To achieve the latter, the Party has focused on setting centralised standards and expectations of service and, although this model of policy has been contested at various times (Cole, 1947), the desire for social improvement has been tied up in a vision of spatial equality whereby citizens have access to the same services provided to the same quality standards wherever they live (see also Table 1.3). Exemplified by the way in which the National Health Service was created in 1945, incorporating thousands of local hospitals run by local authorities, charities and trusts, the Labour vision was to avoid the dangers of moral judgement and uneven provision associated with relying on charity by providing a uniform service. As Bogdanor (2009, 253), explains, this meant that 'the principle that citizens in different parts of the country had an equal right to the nation's resources came to displace concerns about the representation of place'. Local democracy took second place to the standardisation of service.

Thus, New Labour's deployment of targets and audits was a product of this historic commitment to socio-spatial equality, even if uniformity was never realised in practice (Wilson, 2012; Parker, 2015). In this context, it is highly significant that a number of leftist commentators have started to argue that previous Labour governments were too controlling, and self-defeating in their desire for control. As Jon Wilson (2012, 38) explains, 'Like every left of centre party in the middle of the 20th century, Labour believed too much in the authority of experts to know what people wanted; in the capacity of a supposedly enlightened elite to wield power unilaterally for the public good.' In developing a new vision for Labour policy and practice, he and others now argue for a more localist form of government that would involve politicians being 'convenors, bringing people together to help them help themselves, finding solutions to their problems and improving their communities' (Cruddas and Rutherford, 2014, 36).

At least before Jeremy Corbyn took over the leadership in 2015, parts of the Labour Party were starting to rethink the language of 'postcode lotteries' in favour of 'postcode choice'. If 'local democracy' is going to mean more than the local delivery of national decisions, there is growing recognition that activity and services will have to reflect local political decisions. However, in contrast to some on the right, the Left are emphasising the need to reform rather than reduce the role and size of the state (Lodge and Muir, 2011; Cooke and Muir, 2012; Mulgan, 2012; Stears, 2012; Burden, 2013; Cruddas and Rutherford, 2014; Local Government Taskforce, 2014; The Smith Institute, 2014). Areas of state activity that rely on good-quality relationships between staff and citizens are being singled out for particular attention. It is argued that the staff who are on the front line of government in working with the public can develop more meaningful relationships through which better outcomes will happen (and for the history of this debate, see Denhardt and Denhardt, 2000; Bartels, 2013).

It is argued that these more 'relational services' comprise at least a third of current state expenditure (Table 1.5; Wilson 2012), and, as Mulgan (2012) suggests, it is helpful to distinguish those that are delivered 'to' and 'for' the public from those where there is scope for greater relationship building and even co-production with service users (Figure 1.2). Of course, this emphasis on the services that have greatest potential for changing relationships with citizens would require a particular skill-set in the staff employed by the state. As Mulgan (2012, 29) suggests, it would demand 'greater empathy, a better ability to see things from the point of view of others, stronger skills in both communication and listening, and skills of mobilisation, including particular skills in how to organise coalitions for change, particularly where the goal is to change cultures'. Public bodies would have to retrain and recruit staff to secure the social skills required for making stronger relationships if this kind of civic offer were to be made to the public.

Table 1.5: Areas and amounts of government spending 2011–12

Type of spending	Total UK £millions	Per capita	% total spending
Relational services Education; health; social services; Jobcentre Plus	£245,659	£3,945.66	36.8%
Protective services Defence; police; fire; prisons; environmental protection	£82,636	£1,327.23	12.4%
Transfer payments Pensions; benefits; credits	£178,765	£2,871.17	26.8%
Other Infrastructure; housing; aid; culture; debt; central government	£159,752	£2,565.86	24%
Total	£666,812	£10,710	100%

Source: Wilson (2012, 7)

This deployment of localist statecraft is understood to be a way to foster better and more efficacious relationships between citizens and the state as well as a potential means to unleash the social innovation needed to actually improve service outcomes. However, the extent to which this vision is practicable in large, complex, publicly funded organisations like the NHS, local government or schools is still open to debate. As Leach et al (2012, EvW133) put it in their evidence to the House of Commons inquiry into the potential codification of relations between central and local government, different categories of state activity are more or less suitable for localisation. They contrasted an area like defence, which demands centralisation, with activities where local government is an 'agent' for national policy (child protection, housing benefit, civil defence) or where it has greater autonomy (in areas like civic engagement, environment and community cohesion). As such, localism is likely to be differentially realised across government activities and it is the relational services that are most promising vehicles for localisation.

Figure 1.2: Government activity to, for and with the public

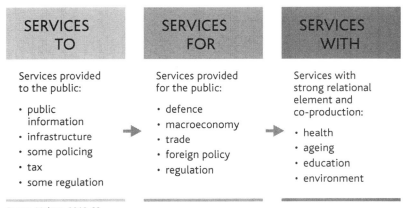

Source: Mulgan, 2012, 23.

Reflecting this argument, survey evidence suggests that the English population are prepared to tolerate different degrees of localism in service provision. As indicated in Figure 1.3, the Future of England survey asked residents about their preferred level of consistency of provision across the country and there was greater openness to diversity in relation to refuse collection and housing than in some of the more 'relational services', such as schools and social services. The latter are exactly the kind of services that can never be standardised, as they depend so much upon the quality of human relationships between staff and service users, yet these are the areas where the public are most concerned about the social and spatial justice of the provision. As such, this evidence exposes some of the challenges to be faced in localist policy making. There is a need to free up front-line service workers while also ensuring good quality service provision (see also Lowndes and Sullivan, 2008). Centralism focused on the latter part of this equation and localism is, in theory at least, about the front end of the argument. However, it is not yet clear how open the public, nor their elected politicians, are to taking the risks associated with the more radical decentralisation of these core tasks of government and service provision.

Figure 1.3: Preferred level of consistency across England

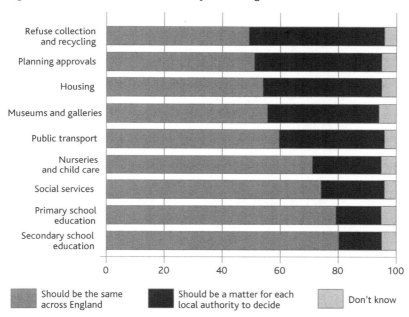

Source: Cox and Jeffrey, 2014, 12. Future of England survey data, 2012, N=3,600.

Conservative forms of localist thinking

From the point of the view of the Conservative Party, arguments for localism pay more attention to reducing the size and changing the role of the state. In this regard, advocates draw on long-established ideas about the importance of what Edmund Burke (1968 [1790]) referred to as the 'little platoons' that make up civil society. Given that Conservatives believe that a strong state has come to replace self-organised community groups and local civic capacity, their vision of localism has been about resisting the over-centralised and powerful state in favour of greater liberty and a stronger local civil society (what is now sometimes called the Big Society) (Clark and Mather, 2003; Barrow et al, 2010; Blond 2010; Norman, 2010; Dorey and Garnett, 2012).

From this perspective, it is striking how un-conservative Mrs Thatcher was in relation to her approach to the state. Her vision of public sector reform and the desire to introduce market discipline required extraordinary centralisation. Thatcher's governments (1979–90) were about a strong state imposing a new vision of political economy and culture on the nation at large. Driven from the cabinet, the transformation of the country required a strong police force to put down resistance and ensure that compliant public institutions (particularly local government councillors and officers in 'looney Left' councils) did what was being demanded. As Simon Jenkins (2004, 41) describes it, 'Local Government in Britain ... was treated as if it were part of a colonial empire.' As outlined in more detail in the following chapter, there was little space for local democracy in Thatcher's regime.

As a reaction against this, a new generation of Conservative politicians have sought to revisit their approach to the state (Dorey and Garnett, 2012). Politicians such as Jesse Norman (2010; Glasman and Norman, 2012) and commentators such as Philip Blond (2010) have focused on the importance of developing a facilitative state that prioritises the role of civil society in order to effect social change. This is underpinned by a broader argument that state intervention often serves to replace the local solidarities and self-help on which communities have historically depended and which would grow again, however unevenly, in the absence of state-funded work (Oakeshott, 1962 [1947]; Nisbet, 1962 [1953]; Scott, 1998; Tilly, 1999). In this context, Nisbet argues that people have a 'quest for community' in order to provide a sense of belonging, purpose and solidarity. As he puts it, 'The administration of charity, hospitalization, unemployment assistance, like the administration of the huge manufacturing corporation, may be more efficient and less given to material inequities, but the possible gains in technical efficiency do not minimize their underlying impersonality in the life of the individual' (Nisbet, 1962 [1953], 72). These pundits argue that well-intentioned service providers unwittingly undermine the activity of self-organisation and community building that would otherwise exist (and did exist, however imperfectly, in earlier times).

In this regard, it is striking that the Conservative political philosopher Michael Oakeshott anticipated many of the contemporary arguments for localism by 70 years. Writing in 1947 during the formation of the National Health Service, Oakeshott (1962 [1947], 6) sounded an alarm over what he identified as 'rationalism in politics' such that politicians felt able to try to bring order across the diversity of the country's communities. As he put it, 'If the rational solution for one of the problems of a society has been determined, to permit any relevant part of the society to escape from the solution is, *ex hypotheri*, to countenance irrationality ... Political activity is recognized as the imposition of a uniform condition of perfection upon human conduct.'Oakeshott argued that, in taking this rationalist approach, a new generation of politicians – on the right as well as the left – were overlooking the importance of what he referred to as 'practical knowledge', whereby people were able to use their skills to act in context without following a formula laid down by the expert. Rather than having confidence in the 'habits of behaviour' that had grown up over time, politicians sought to find the technical solution to a series of problems, imposing new policy ideas on local professionals and communities. Rather than recognising the impossibility of their mission, and the alternative solution to be found in local traditions of problem solving through the practice of politics in civil society, Oakeshott argued, politicians would move from one proposed enterprise to another, responding to failure with another idea. While some commentators now suggest that localism is a return towards the prioritisation of local practice and civil society, and away from the imposition of national goals, targets and blueprints from central government, it is also part of a wider argument about the end of expert rule and the need to recognise the power of socially and spatially uneven patterns of local tradition (Scott, 1998; Tilly, 1999; Leighninger, 2006; Norman, 2010; Finlayson, 2012; Glasman and Norman, 2012).

Following the general election in 2010, a number of prominent localist Conservatives took up important positions in government and they were then able to agitate and legislate for localism. Nick Hurd, Eric Pickles and Greg Clark took up new roles at the Department for Communities and Local Government (DCLG) and the Cabinet Office (CO). These individuals were well positioned and ready to make the case for localism once in office and, as outlined in the final part of this chapter, it was their departments that led the localism agenda in government, although the publication of Lord Heseltine's (2012) report on economic growth prompted a late upsurge of support from the Treasury and the Department of Business, Innovation and Skills (BIS). Following the 2015 general election, and the establishment of a wholly Conservative government, these trends are set to continue, not least because Greg Clark has taken over at DCLG.

This section has demonstrated that, from left and right, there is now an emerging 'common sense' that the British state has become too centralised and that localism is a way to unlock the wider potential of the nation and its people in relation to economic growth, public sector innovation, greater efficiency and effectiveness, civic initiative and creative experiment. Localism has become something of a policy 'silver bullet' that now has cross-party support as a means to save the nation's economy as well as its democracy. The Right have adopted it as a retreat from Thatcherite centralism and as a boost to more traditional themes such as liberty and civic action; the Left have adopted it in recognition of the limits of using the central state to control local outcomes and the need for popular engagement in social reform. As such, localism is argued to be key to creating a better society – or, in the words, of Prime Minister David Cameron, a less broken 'bigger' society – as well as a more innovative, successful and spatially balanced economy (Cameron, 2009; Heseltine, 2012; RSA, 2014).

Although it is less prominent in the policy debates than it is in academic critiques, localism has also been associated with austerity and the need to reduce levels of national spending on welfare. While this fits snugly with Conservative justifications for localism in their pursuit of a much smaller state, it has prompted some on the left to adopt localism as a more pragmatic response to financial constraints. As outlined in relation to local government in Chapter Four, dramatic cuts in state spending mean that service providers are having to rethink the work that they do, and localism provides a potential policy solution to getting things done on a much smaller budget (Lowndes and Pratchett, 2012). While this context has prompted many academic critics to associate localism with business-as-usual neoliberalism, dismissing it as a veneer for cuts in services and further privatisation, this is an over-simplification of the emerging localism agenda in England (Hickson, 2013). As outlined in the following two chapters, there is a much longer pedigree and a more sophisticated case for localism than these critics suggest, and charges of neoliberalism do nothing to explain the longer history of its development or its implications for the state and the people (and for a flavour of these academic critiques of localism see, Featherstone et al, 2012; Allmendinger and Haughton, 2013; Davoudi and Madanipour, 2013; Deas, 2013; Bulley and Sokhi-Bulley, 2014).

Localism and reform since 2010

Following their election in May 2010, the Conservative–Liberal Democrat Coalition made an agreement for government that opened with a strong emphasis on the shared intent to decentralise political authority and power in the UK. Prime Minister David Cameron and his deputy, the Liberal Democrat leader, Nick Clegg (2010, 7), declared that they 'share the conviction that the days of big Government are over; that centralization and top-down control have proved a failure'. They pitched localism as a way to reverse 'successive waves of centralisation [that] have pushed Westminster politics and Whitehall bureaucracy into aspects of public life that once belonged to local people and communities' (HM Government 2010, 4). As outlined above, they made an argument that the British state is too centralised and that there is insufficient space for citizens to do things for themselves (in what would be a Big Society) and that localism is needed to decentralise power and (re)engage citizens and communities in political life. As such, the decentralisation of political power – and the opportunity for citizens and their communities to engage in decision making – was supposed to be central to all that the new government would do. Indeed, the government sought to create 'a turning point in the relationship between government and people – and the beginning of a new chapter in our democratic history' (HM Government 2010, 4).

To this end, the government produced a major statement of its vision for decentralisation alongside plans for the Localism Act that was given royal assent in 2011 (HM Government, 2010). In the introduction to the 'essential guide' that accompanied the Act, Greg Clark MP argued that there were 'six concrete actions … [to] be taken by every department and every level of Government to return power to the people to whom it belongs'. These six actions were to: lift the burden of bureaucracy; empower communities to do things their way; increase local control of public finances; diversify the supply of public services; open up government to public scrutiny; and strengthen accountability to local people (HM Government 2010, 3). In combination, and as shown in Figure 1.4, these measures were envisaged as taking the country from the Big State to the Big Society. As Minister for Decentralisation, Greg Clark MP, later told the House of Commons Select Committee on Communities and Local Government 'Localism is the ethos; decentralisation is the process and the outcome is the Big Society' (House of Commons Select Committee on Communities and Local Government, 2011, 13). In this endeavour, all levels of government were urged to develop a more reciprocal relationship with citizens and their communities. As stated in the 'essential guide', 'Government must commit to the active empowerment of local communities' reflecting a new 'freedom of local communities to run their own affairs' (HM Government 2010, 7).

In developing this new civic offer to the people, the government hoped to mobilise a range a different actors: the state, interest groups, citizen and civil society groups. Indeed, from the top down, localism envisaged a new role for national civil servants to act as the champions of localism and local civic capacity. Rather than being the bureaucrats who develop and manage policy on behalf of the government, civil servants were re-imagined as the people who can help the public to

Figure 1.4: From the Big State to the Big Society

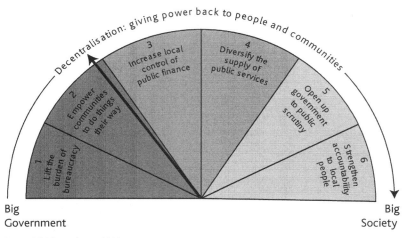

Source: HM Government, 2010

get things done. The then Secretary of State for Communities and Local Government, Eric Pickles, was a particularly vocal advocate of this scale jumping, such that the local would-be activist could secure support from the centre to challenge the small-mindedness of various obstructive local officials. As such, he envisaged a new vision of the civil service in which 'civil servants act as "bureaucracy busters" for community projects, providing local people with the back-up they need to unblock obstacles and achieve their goals. Placing civil servants at the service of civil society may be a revolutionary concept, but by turning government upside down our aim is to make Whitehall the ally and not the antagonist of local control' (HM Government 2010, 7).

Over its time in office, the Coalition government developed a more ambitious vision for local authorities, agreeing a number of City Deals whereby some of the largest cities were granted greater fiscal freedom along with control over a wider range of activities. Manchester led the way in this regard by becoming the first Combined Authority, incorporating 10 different local authorities into the Greater Manchester Combined Authority with an agreement to take over transport infrastructure, economic development, housing, skills and health from Westminster and Whitehall in 2015 (Greater Manchester Combined Authority, no date; Leese, 2014; O'Brien and Pike, 2015). Following the Heseltine report (2012) into economic growth, the government promised to extend these City Deals to a wider range of cities and, from April 2015, a Single Local Growth Fund included money set aside for housing, transport and skills to which Local Enterprise Partnerships and local authorities could bid to secure more ambitious planning for growth. Large local authorities were also given access to borrowing via a Public Works Loan Board, such that 'every locality must be able to fulfil its full potential by taking responsibility for decisions and resources that affect their local economies' (HM Government, 2013, 12). In its Commission to explore the potential for greater political autonomy for the 15 largest city-regions of the UK, the Royal Society of Arts (RSA) welcomed these new opportunities, calling for greater fiscal powers to be granted where appropriate in future (RSA, 2014; see also Blond and Morrin, 2015; Figure 1.5). In the wake of reform, leading politicians in the largest city-regions organised themselves to secure greater political jurisdiction over the development of life in their cities, but at the time of writing it is not yet clear how they will include local citizens in the work that they do (NALC, 2015).

In addition to such political devolution, the Coalition introduced a range of measures to foster greater localism. As characterised in Table 1.6, policy has ranged from efforts to change the way in which public services are organised, to the creation of new elected positions to try to increase public engagement, new rights to set up free schools and engage in neighbourhood planning, and a national programme of citizenship training for all 16- and 17-year-olds who want to take part. These measures have, in turn, had a 'shadow effect' across the voluntary and charitable sector, such that a number of important localist initiatives have been launched by the Lottery, the Joseph Rowntree Foundation (JRF) and the RSA.

One of the most significant reforms has been to grant new rights of neighbourhood planning, and this is explored in more detail in Chapter Five. Through neighbourhood planning, established by the Localism Act (2011), local people can now develop a plan for their community while also securing some of the revenue that comes from the new developments that take place (via the Community Infrastructure Levy). These neighbourhood plans can be developed by parish councils, but in urban areas any group of people can constitute themselves as a neighbourhood forum (of at least 21 people), delimit a clear geographical area around which they have consulted, and seek designation by the local authority. Once properly constituted, these forums can then work to develop a neighbourhood plan. Although any plan has to be in line with existing planning guidelines and is subject to independent scrutiny, there are few official controls over what has to go in to the plan. The latest figures indicate that more than 1,500 local plans are being developed as part of this process; hundreds of urban forums have been formally designated by their local authorities;

Figure 1.5: The city-regions targeted for greater devolution in the RSA's commission

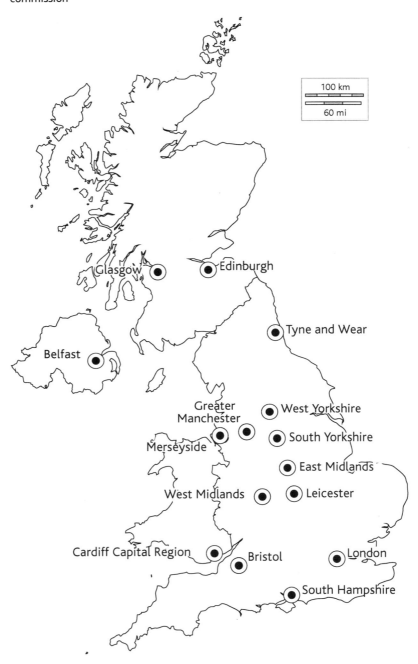

Source: The City Growth Commission, 2014, 4.

Table 1.6: The emerging policy and practice of English localism

Activity	How is it localist?	Examples
Restructuring state-funded services	Taking decision making closer to people via devolution to new and existing structures.	City Deals; Local Economic Partnerships (replacing regional policy bodies and targets); Clinical Commissioning Groups in the NHS (replacing Primary Care Trusts).
Changing the culture of existing state-funded services	Working together across services in place, and engaging service users in co-production.	Neighbourhood Community Budgets; the Our Place programme. Local government given the 'general power of competence'. Culture-change programmes such as Lambeth's Co-operative Council.
Creating new elected posts and structures	Identifying responsible local people who can be held accountable.	Elected Police Commissioners.[4] Support for elected local Mayors.
Granting new rights	Facilitating local activity and devolving control.	Free schools; Neighbourhood Planning; Community Right to Buy; Community Right to Bid; Community Right to Build.
Fostering active citizenship among particular groups	Training citizens to engage and to act at a local level.	The National Citizen Service; Locality's Community Organisers programme.
Generating a 'shadow effect' among other service providers and 'think and do' tanks	Funding local projects that engage citizens in their local community.	The Lottery's Big Local; The Big Lunch; My Square Mile; the RSA's Citizen Power in Peterborough; JRF's Working in Neighbourhoods project in Bradford; National Endowment for Science, Technology and the Arts' (NESTA's) mass localism work.

and increasing numbers have completed a referendum that provides a mandate for their neighbourhood plan (Figure 1.6; see also Chapter Five).

Related developments have been implemented in education, with new rights for groups of local people to establish free schools. By early 2016 as many as 304 free schools had been established, some of them linked to existing chains of education providers, but others being managed by local people and their advisors.[5] Although it was not part of the research reported in the rest of this book, there is a growing debate about the extent to which free schools are contributing to the Big Society and localism (Hatcher, 2011; Leeder and Mabbett, 2011). On the one hand, free schools and academies are accountable to Whitehall rather than to local politicians and this is a form of centralisation, but, on the other hand, free schools also have the potential to allow local people greater control over what is provided.

Figure 1.6: Map of neighbourhood planning areas, England, 2014

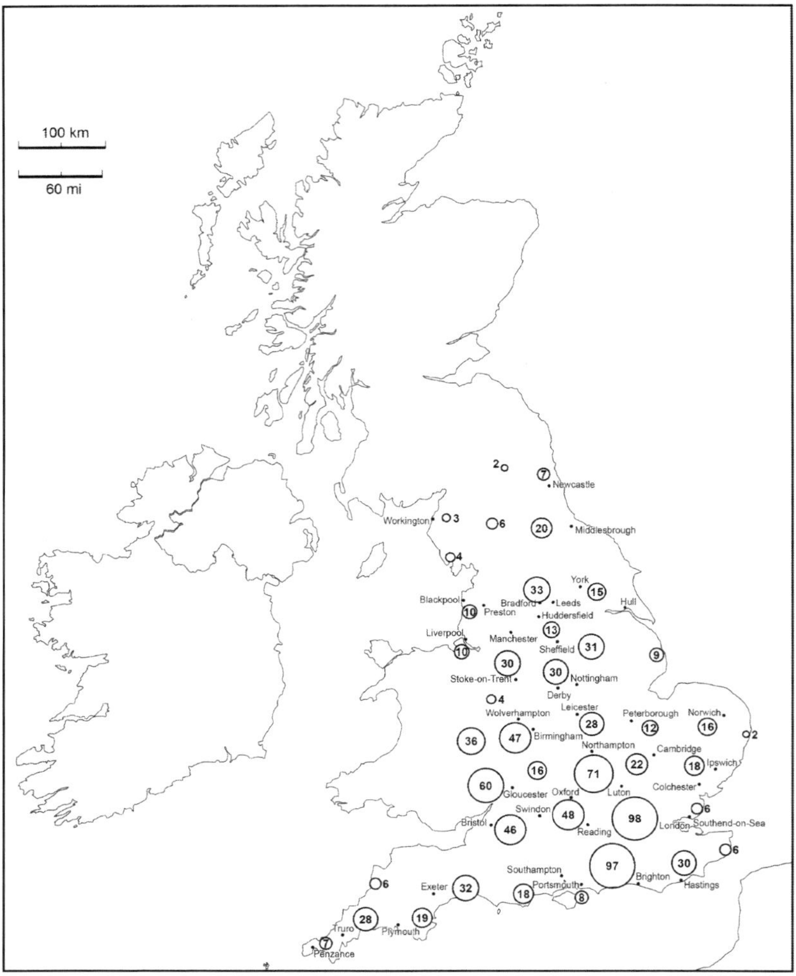

Source: www.ourneighbourhoodplanning.org.uk/ (this is an interactive map that is regularly updated)

In relation to the development of local civic capacity, the strongest intervention – albeit very limited in scope – has been support for community organising, a model of politics and civic activity that is further explored in Chapter Six. In early 2011 the government commissioned the charity Locality to train 500 community organisers and to build a wider network of up to 4,500 volunteers who had the skills to help identify problems and facilitate local people to act. These organisers were placed with a variety of host organisations for a year in the first instance, with the potential to raise matched funding from the government to extend their work for an extra year. Funded by the

Office for Civil Society (within the Cabinet Office), this programme reflected the history and experience of community organising in the US, where this form of local civic agency is much more firmly established (Wills, 2012; Bretherton, 2015). Establishing it more firmly in England would require much greater investment, more widespread adoption of the methods involved and greater cultural acceptance of non-partisan approaches to getting things done.

Relatedly, however, the National Lottery has also funded as many as 150 Big Local projects across England, each with £1 million to spend on activities that work with local people to effect local change.[6] Although these are much more autonomous than Locality's work, in some cases the funds have similarly been used to develop local civic capacity around shared interests and social action. The People's Empowerment Alliance for Custom House (PEACH) in East London is an example of this kind of project. Rather than having changes imposed on them – often involving the relocation of people outside the area – PEACH was created to organise around an alternative agenda to keep the community together and negotiate with Newham Council on its own terms (and for this and other examples of community organising to resist housing regeneration schemes, see the London Tenants Federation et al, 2014).

The final area of localist activity led by the government was the creation of a new National Citizen Service through which all 16- and 17-year-olds had access to training in order to learn the skills needed to foster stronger civic capacity and social action. This incorporated a residential placement with a new group of peers, incorporating team building and social skills as well as locally oriented volunteering activities and the development of a social action project. Up to 150,000 places were available for young people during 2015. Although the scheme is voluntary, the idea was to establish the habit of citizenship in young people at a formative time of their life, and evaluations indicate that the scheme has been popular with those taking part (NatCen Social Research, 2013). The Conservative government announced a continuation of this programme in 2015.

Of course, talking about localism and making it happen are two very different things. Changing the deeply rooted culture of government and the expectations of the population will be very hard to achieve. The short-term electoral cycle and the need to demonstrate results in order to win the next election also make it particularly difficult to focus on securing long-term cultural change. Reflecting on what he called the 'skin-deep localism' of the Coalition government, Ferdinand Mount argued that 'All political parties are decentralizers in opposition and centralizers in government. Once you have power it is very hard to give it up, especially if you find that you are still held responsible for the decisions made by people to whom you have passed them' (Mount, 2012, 247–8). Indeed, Bogdanor (2009) argues that politicians will recognise the perils of centralisation in general but find the levers of government irresistible when in office and under pressure to act (see also Parker, 2015).

In a government review of localism in 2012, Greg Clark MP (2012) looked at the progress being made by 12 different government departments, scoring their contribution to the emerging agenda of decentralisation. None was making 'optimum' progress, but DCLG and the Department of Education (DoE) were in the lead with four stars each, and this implied that they were both perceived to be 'well on the way'. Making changes at the top is relatively simple, of course, and the extent to which such changes filter down to shape the day-to-day operations and culture of organisations – and the practice of citizenship – is much more complicated (and for a wider argument to this effect, see Bevir and Rhodes, 2006). However, even if progress is slow, there is widespread support for localism from the major political parties in England and it remains a core part of the Conservative Party's agenda for government after 2015. Exploring the history, potential and pitfalls of localism and the wider implications it has for English government, politics, society and culture is the focus of the rest of this book.

Notes

[1]   MORI data collected in 2003 and used to conduct cluster analysis to explore political behaviour similarly found that just 6% of the population were what the researchers called 'enthusiasts'. As they put it, these people were 'probably the initiators and main driving force behind almost all political activity in Britain' (MORI, 2004, 5).

[2]   It is worth noting that this poll was conducted to coincide with the 2010 General Election when the Conservatives made invited the people of the United Kingdom to join them in Government and create the Big Society. A year later, in 2011, a COMRES poll found that as many as 41% of the public thought that the Big Society was 'merely a cover for spending cuts' and in 2012 a YouGov poll found that only 9% of the public thought that policies to create the Big Society would work (Dorey and Garnett, 2012, 408, 409).

[3]   Rao (2000, 134) points out that as early as 1997 there was some official party support for more localism. The manifesto for the general election in 1997 declared that the party would aim to take decisions 'as near to local communities as possible'. However, once New Labour was in office, this got rather lost in the focus on targets.

[4]   The hope was that these elected positions would increase political interest and accountability in public services but the turnout in the first round of the Police

and Crime Commissioner elections in November 2012 was extraordinarily low, averaging just 15% across the 41 areas where voting took place.

5   The latest figures for the number of free schools opened are available from the Department of Education website: https://www.gov.uk/government/policies/increasing-the-number-of-academies-and-free-schools-to-create-a-better-and-more-diverse-school-system (accessed on 17.3.16).

6   More information is available here: www.localtrust.org.uk/

TWO

The geo-constitution and the long history of localism

As outlined in the previous chapter, advocates of localism see it as a way to respond to a perceived over-centralised state that is argued to have prevented the local state and local communities from taking their own decisions and determining their own destiny. They argue that during the 20th century an expanding national government took over the work that was traditionally done by local government, communities and charities, and this had negative consequences for local democracy, the efficiency and efficaciousness of the services provided, civic engagement and capacity. The reforms and measures associated with localism are thus designed to re-engage people in local decision making through a 'double-shift'; impacting on the way that politicians and the state work, thereby remaking the civic offer, as well as changing the way that citizens think and act, thereby generating civic capacity.

This chapter provides important historical contextualisation to this debate by exploring the development of the English state and its geography over the last 500 years. This history highlights the way in which local government emerged as part of a centralising state in the years after the Norman Conquest in the 11th century. In a process that is now characterised as a battle between the 'Norman Yoke' and an older Anglo-Saxon 'Gothic culture' that had already established the rights of the 'free-born Englishman', exemplified by the signing of Magna Carta in 1215, England's constitution emerged as a way for the crown to work in tandem with representatives of the people (Loughlin, 2013). In this period, England was unified as a space for government, but in a way in which the crown was accountable – however remotely – to the people via recognition of the rule of law. English common law provided the foundation through which the 'crown-in-parliament' was able to govern, using a network of county-level legal representatives to oversee the practices of political administration. Despite being unable to exercise direct control except in exceptional circumstances, the crown used these local representatives to appoint lay justices who oversaw both law and administration across the country. As such, the emerging geo-constitution protected the liberties of local people while also bringing them into a national framework of administrative government.

After the Reformation (from 1529) the 'crown-in-parliament' was further able to co-opt the infrastructure of the Church of England to administer the local provision of services and the protection of public goods.1 The county justices provided oversight and used the institutional infrastructure laid down by the courts, as well as the Anglican Church, to foster the self-administration of important tasks such as support for the poor, maintenance of highways and managing common resources. This juridical and ecclesiastical regime was part of an emerging constitutional settlement in which the map of local government was uneven, reflecting different circumstances, custom and practice (Bagehot, 1867; Dicey, 1885; Scruton, 2006 [2000]).

As urbanisation, industrialisation and demographic growth occurred during the 19th and 20th centuries, this system of amateur government and administration was increasingly strained. People were more mobile and there was greater awareness of and concern about the plight of the poor, the need for improved public health and the provision of welfare. In part, this consciousness was a product of a growing national middle class who were attracted to new religious and political ideas that prompted some form of collective response. This emerging social group took up the cudgels of administration to govern their localities and, in tandem with parliamentary reform, a new spirit of government emerged. National and local politicians, and particularly those associated with non-conformism and utilitarianism, sought to intervene directly and indirectly (through permissive legislation) in the provision of local administration and services.[2]

Whereas local government had its birth as part of the crown's legal system, with a focus on local law, order and administration, it thus had a rebirth as part of a system of political administration, directed by Parliament. This national oversight proved to be a mixed blessing for the autonomy of local government and, over time, the desire for national standardisation in both political systems and administrative outcomes increased. As such, local government was subject to ever-greater central intervention in the pursuit of national standards and outcomes. This desire for standardisation was at its peak during the 20th century and was most clearly demonstrated in the legislative reforms made by national governments in 1945–51 (Labour), 1979–97 (Conservative) and 1997–2010 (New Labour). As might be expected as a result, the English electorate came to expect national standards of service delivery and, reinforced by the dominance of national political parties in the operation of local government, have tended to vote locally on the basis of national partisan affiliations (Copus, 2004; Bogdanor, 2009; Loughlin, 2013). Despite the façade of democracy, local government was largely reduced to being part of the national administrative state, managed by politicians who reflected the views of their national political parties and paymasters, and it largely lost political credibility as a result.

Thus, while contemporary politicians may declare their ambitions to localise power, the historical legacy means that they face two key challenges in achieving their ends. First, there is only weak governmental practice of localism and very little popular experience of local political capacity. Second, the electorate have been encouraged to expect standardised services across the country as promised to them by national political parties. As such, there is an entrenched centralisation in the English geo-constitution, its political practices, culture and the production of citizenship. Added to this, national politicians are all too eager to wade in to micro-manage the affairs of local government, and the people expect them to do so. As Parker (2015, 20) explains: 'When things go wrong with our local services, the public and the media demand that ministers take action. The problem is that most of the tools at the government's disposal involve taking more central control of public services.' Thus, although increasing numbers of people now recognise the limits of centralisation and the need for greater local democracy, autonomy and civic engagement, overcoming these historically and experientially entrenched hurdles will be very hard to do.

History tells us that it is not impossible to develop a system that incorporates a multi-scalar framework of government in which local democratic government is a functioning part of a national system of government. Indeed, it is striking that in their efforts to advocate a new ontology that can underpin a more distributed model of political power and its geography, as outlined in the Introduction to this book, Frug (1999) and Magnusson (2005b) highlight the charters and freedoms granted to many municipalities in the evolution of government in England. However, at present there is a question about the extent to which local government has the space and capacity to do more than administer and deliver nationally determined objectives and practice. Historically, local government had much greater political freedom and local autonomy in decision making. Shifting back in this direction would necessarily generate geographical diversity, but it would also signal much greater confidence in a system of multi-tiered democracy (Maas, 1959). It is somewhat ironic that during the 20th century, as the English constitution took on the universal franchise and the extension of democracy to all adult residents, it was accompanied by increased centralisation – enacted in the name of the people – that reduced the space for those citizens to engage. This chapter sets out this history, with a view to clearer thinking about the challenges and possibilities of localism in England today.

Crown, church and local government

England's local government emerged from the mosaic of legal systems operated by the manorial courts (courts Baron and Leet), the municipal corporations, boroughs and liberties that had been granted freedom by the monarch, as well the county-level justices who were appointed to uphold the law in the name of the king.[3] The Domesday Book (1086) described 32 shires in England (later augmented by a number of northern counties and Rutland to produce 42, Figure 2.1) and these each had a Sheriff and a county court that upheld criminal and civil justice on behalf of the crown. As these judicial and administrative systems developed, the role of Sheriff was augmented by the appointment of a Lord-Lieutenant (from 1549) who oversaw the formation of the county regiments and the appointment of lay justices of the peace, who were able to service the courts, as well as the Custos Rotulorum, who kept county records. The county justices were notable local men who were ultimately accountable to the King's Council and the King's Bench, but who upheld the law of the land via their various courts, enlisting juries when required in criminal trials. These men were responsible for overseeing the appointment of lay parochial officers to look after the basic requirements of day-to-day administration such as maintenance of the highways and common resources and looking after the needs of the poor.[4] As such, civic administration was accountable to the king, yet also close to the people and organised at the scale of the parish. The lay parochial officers were well-known local residents and all those who paid rates were liable to be called to such office themselves. The most important of these local lay officers were the overseer of the poor, the constable, who controlled behaviour, and the surveyor of the highways. In addition, the churchwarden straddled the boundaries of civic and ecclesiastical service, looking after the needs of the church as well as any parochial resources that needed attention during the year.

These institutions of county and church administration depended on volunteer labour and an obligation to serve. The posts were filled in rotation or by nomination, and occasionally through open election, generally being filled for a year at a time. In addition, all parishioners were expected to give up to six days' labour a year to maintain the local highways, generally under direction from the lay highways surveyor

(Webb and Webb, 1924 [1907]). Each parish had its own resources and facilities that needed to be maintained and managed by the local priest, a churchwarden and the local rate-payers of the parish. Such resources included the 'churches, burial grounds, parish cottages, workhouses, common land, endowed charities, market-crosses, pumps, pounds, whipping-posts, stocks, cages, watch-houses, weights and scales, clocks and fire engines' (Webb and Webb, 1924 [1907], 4). The parish system touched almost everyone in the land and it facilitated the development of civic duties alongside the practice of faith (and contemporary resonances remain in this respect in regard to the work of community organising, as outlined further in Chapter Six of this book).

Figure 2.1: The historic shires of England

Indeed, the existing infrastructure of the church provided a means to collect the rates and organise the labour of the parish. Meetings and appointments were generally held in the church and the parochial boundaries, established over centuries and developed around church buildings and ministry, were co-opted to provide the geographical unit for the administration of basic services for local people.

As the Webbs (Webb and Webb, 1924 [1907], 5) suggest, this ancient parochial geography was established over 'time out of mind' and it represented an 'ancient tradition, handed down from generation to generation, seldom embodied in any document, and ... differing from place to place according to local usages, of which no-one outside the localities concerned had any exact knowledge'. While the church hierarchy and/or the county justices and/or Parliament could call on this parochial infrastructure to fulfil their requirements, most obviously in relation to the Poor Law and the maintenance of the highways, they had little capacity or aspiration to exert firm control over the way things were done. Sidney and Beatrice Webb (1963 [1922], 63) tell us that this 'meant that from one end of England to the other, each of the local Authorities enjoyed, in practice, an almost unchecked autonomy, unless and until any of its actions or decisions happened to be brought into a court of law'. While the parish administrators were accountable to the county justices, the officials running the manors, boroughs and counties could be questioned only by Westminster, and even then any dispute would be tested by law.

By necessity, this parochial or vestry government comprised local people serving their community to provide basic services and manage shared resources in trust for the group. Although some of their tax-raising powers and rates would need to be sanctioned by the county justices in the court of Quarter Sessions, parish officers were able to set and collect a church rate to look after the needs of the church, a poor rate to manage the needs of the destitute of the parish, a constable's tax, as well as a road tax. In addition, the local leadership of the parish had the jurisdiction to collect money from absent fathers and to fine those who refused their duty or their rates. The constable had a particular role in managing the Vagrancy Acts and what we would today describe as anti-social behaviour.

Such local administration varied a great deal across the country; it reflected local custom, the wealth and character of the parish, the people who lived there and those who took office. In many rural areas a 'parish oligarchy' of local families had tight control, and in some cases this extended to wining and dining on the parish account, or even naked corruption. In others, more democratic associations of rate-payers slowly developed, particularly in some of the fastest-growing towns of the North, where a new cadre of middle-class business people took a growing interest in municipal life. The Webbs (1924 [1907]) cite the example of Leeds, where a local elite of evangelical nonconformists with Whiggish and scholarly inclinations dominated the political life of the borough by the early 1700s, raising funds to build new churches, schools, markets and a workhouse (and this legacy was exposed in a part of the city called Holbeck as part of its neighbourhood plan, as is explored more fully in Chapter Five of this book) . In Liverpool too, the Webbs identified an 'organised democracy' that emerged after 1775 whereby an annual assembly of rate-payers elected a smaller executive committee to run the city during the year. This executive would poll rate-payers on important issues and it published annual accounts. This body also established sub-committees to enact important business as determined by the community during the year.

While the national Parliament was benignly present during this period of relative autonomy for local administration, its members generally acted largely only when asked. Members of Parliament had the power to pass Public General Acts that applied to the whole of one or more of England and Wales, Scotland and Ireland, and notable examples included the statutes covering highways in 1535 and 1562, and the Poor Law Act passed in 1601 (Smellie, 1946; Prest, 1990). However, such legislation was rare and, in contrast, Parliament passed many more Local or Private Acts that were stimulated following a petition from a local body, company or person. As local problems and administrative ambitions grew, Parliament spent increasing amounts of time on these Acts covering issues such as paving, lighting and policing in particular towns (Prest, 1990). As such, the initiative for reform was left to the local level, and as people innovated in the development of new services, so Parliament was called upon to ratify their ambitions. This was a form of ad hoc localism, such that places with civic capacity were able to call upon the centre to support whatever they wanted to do.

Despite this local freedom, however, the population growth and mobility associated with the rapid industrialisation underway by the 19th century brought great strain to this regime. Urban areas in particular faced increased demands from pauperisation, challenges in collecting the rates and a reduced sense of obligation to fulfil local political service.[5] In addition, the governing classes were being swelled by a growing middle class, many of whom were attracted to new ideas about the arts of government – often couched in the language of faith. By 1800, for example, a city like Manchester had a population of 60,000 people and divisions between local elites had hampered the establishment of the kind of good government that had earlier been evident in Leeds and Liverpool (Webb and Webb, 1924 [1907]). In such areas, the stable relationships that had underpinned the obligation to serve were eroded and revenues were insufficient to provide the services needed.

Reflecting their concerns about the moral standards of some public officials, the Webbs' powerful documentary about the evolution of local government includes a number of high-profile cases of corruption from this time. With contemporary to today – situation in Tower Hamlets parallels, they bemoaned the way that Joseph Merceron was able to secure a stranglehold of the London parish of Bethnal Green for as long as 50 years. From 1787, Merceron, a man of Huguenot heritage, built up a local power base to secure his political control, while he also developed a large property empire and a string of bars and beer shops over which he had administrative control. Described by the Webbs (1924 [1907], 82) as 'an almost irresistible dictator', he controlled the rates, the Poor Law and local justice. He and his son held control until a court case, jail and parliamentary intervention put an end to their regime in 1823. The Webbs (1924 [1907], 321) report similar challenges in recruiting high-calibre county justices in some parts of the country where, in the absence of suitable candidates, 'basket' or 'trading' justices were known to administer the law for a fee. As they remark, 'When either the work to be done was onerous and disagreeable, or the place in which it had to be done was lacking in amenity, it was impossible to rely on obtaining a sufficient number of residents of leisure, competence, and public spirit to render so large an amount of unpaid service to the county as had become necessary' (Webb and Webb, 1924 [1907], 585).[6]

In this context, and given the growing purchase of religious nonconformity and utilitarian ideas among the rising middle classes, Parliament was under increasing pressure to intervene in questions of local government. Rather than just continue to pass Local Acts when requested, Parliament developed permissive legislation in order to allow local organisations to act without being required to bring a petition to Parliament. This innovation meant that local organisations could take civic initiative in particular areas that were laid down centrally, without tight controls over the way in which changes were made. Permissive legislation made it much easier to make local improvements without the time and cost of legislation in Westminster. Gilbert's Act, passed in 1782, was an early example this kind of permissive legislation, allowing local parishes to secure the support of two justices in order to form a union to build a workhouse without going to Parliament first. As a 'rate-payers' do-it-yourself kit' (Prest, 1990, 7) this permissive legislation was widely used during the 19th century and Gilbert's Law was followed by similar statutes that facilitated rules concerning the local franchise from which civic leaders could legitimately start to develop services in areas such as lighting and watching. As Prest (1990, 13) remarks, 'The initiatives were to come from citizens, the decisions were to be taken at public meetings, and the Acts were to be carried out by *ad hoc* bodies.' Permissive legislation allowed groups of local representatives to judge and act upon their own perceived interests, taking up the opportunity for reform without feeling any compulsion to do so.

The jewel in the crown of this form of legislative development was the permissive Municipal Corporations Reform Act of 1835, which encouraged each of the incorporated municipal corporations and boroughs to introduce a democratic franchise of local ratepayers (and each ratepayer was to have one vote) to elect a local council that could then take over a wider range of functions, including paving, cleansing, watching, regulating and water supply (Prest, 1990). The Act potentially extended the jurisdiction of local government, allowing municipal councils to consolidate their own existing Local Acts where these had been secured in the past and to develop new powers, some of them taken from the work already being done by county-level administration. The Act further required councils to appoint a salaried town clerk and a treasurer and to publish accounts that were potentially subject to audit. The Act excluded the City of London but allowed other cities to petition for incorporation, bringing large cities like Birmingham and Manchester under its brief. As many as 178 boroughs came into line with these rules and the scope of these bodies was further extended to cover museums in 1845, bath houses and warehouses in 1846 and, via additional clauses to the original Act, water and gas, policing, lighting, markets and fairs, cemeteries, harbours, docks and piers in 1847. Similar permissive legislation was enacted throughout the 1860s, allowing local bodies to take up the provision of ambulances (the Nuisances Removal Act 1860), playgrounds (the Public Improvement Act 1860), control over licensing laws (the Public House Closing Act 1864) and the cleansing of houses, bedding and the provision of mortuaries (the Sanitary Act 1866).

Through such permissive legislation, national governments were able to protect some of the autonomy of the counties and boroughs while also improving provision. As Prest (1990, 187) remarks, 'in the new era of permissive legislation the townships could forge ahead on their own, and the great parliament of the nation seemed to have smiled on the little parliaments of the localities.' This situation led to a flourishing of local government, particularly in the big cities. Through the provision of 'gas and water socialism' or, more accurately, 'municipal capitalism', dynamic local governments were able to raise income above the rates and spend on local improvements (Hunt, 2004). This enterprise was found in great cities like Birmingham, Glasgow and London, such that by 1905 local authorities were responsible for half of all national government spending (Hunt, 2004, 267).[7]

Yet, just at the peak of this form of municipal government, pressure was building for more direct control and associated reform. National government started to remove some of the functions that had hitherto been controlled by the counties and parishes (including the Poor Law, highways and the registration of births, deaths and marriages) and, in an important marker of this shift in thinking, from 1888 (in the Local Government Act) the county justices were restricted to a judicial role, while elected local government was developed across the counties to match that already in place in the cities and towns. While this reflected the precedent set by the Municipal Corporations Act, it was not permissive, and the 1888 Act was imposed on the historic counties of England.

The 1888 Act established new bodies of government in each county (called county councils) but Yorkshire was divided into two (West and East Riding) and Lincolnshire into three (Holland, Kesteven and Lindsey), and for the first time London was to have its own county-type administration (the London County Council). In addition, ten cities were granted county status: Bradford, Bristol, Birmingham, Kingston-on-Hull, Leeds, Liverpool, Manchester, Newcastle, Nottingham and Sheffield. Below the counties, the land was divided into urban and rural districts, based on prior legislation that had already established sanitary districts (in 1872). These new bodies were to be led by a mixture of elected and selected councillors, and while parishes remained, they lost almost all their prior role (and particularly so after a further Local Government Act in 1894, Poole and Keith-Lucas, 1994). The functions that had been done in the past by the parishes were passed to either district, urban or county council government to be overseen by elected officials and enacted by paid employees.

This imposition of a new order of government reflected the growing importance of local government to the national interest, as well as the challenges faced by the population and its politicians. That said, however, there were significant divisions between Whig reformers, who were ambitious about developing the new arts of government, and the Tories, who generally sought to protect local custom and practice. The Whiggish drive for efficiency and a new rationality ran counter to the slower evolution of government through tradition, consent and established practice that was later celebrated by Oakeshott (1962). Zealous reformers found it hard to resist the charms of a muscular national Parliament that had the power to impose a new order of government on the localities. This sometimes took the form of permissive legislation, as outlined above, but it also increasingly occurred through more direct intervention and prescription about what would and could be done. Utilitarian thinkers such as Jeremy Bentham and J.S. Mill had little time for sentiment about established custom and practice and they were interested in efficiency and the good government of experts. The influence of such thinkers was profound, encouraging some national politicians to impose a new vision on those who were not inclined to do the 'right thing'. As John Dewey (2000 [1935], 28–9) notes in regard to the influence of Bentham, 'the principle of the greater good to the greatest number tended to establish in Great Britain the supremacy of national over local interests'. In contrast, the United States retained a more Lockean form of liberalism that treated the state with suspicion, retaining a greater role for a plurality of local and regional interests and powers.

Rather than the 'constitutional anarchy' (Webb and Webb, 1924 [1907], 152) of permissive localism, the more radical reformers increasingly wanted constitutional order and what they perceived to be good government. As outlined in the following section, this desire for a brave new world shifted the power geometry towards the centre and away from the localities. The diversity of local governments that had developed across the English localities were increasingly directed by and/or replaced by parliamentarians in Westminster and the growing civil service in Whitehall.

The drive for standardisation via centralisation

The trend towards greater intervention by the national Parliament in local government was evident in a number of the key interventions made during the 19th century, and certainly in those made during the 20th century. New laws were passed to control the way that local government was conducted, setting national standards and firmer expectations for local practice. Most significantly, in some cases, new organisations were introduced to take over some of the activities that had previously been performed by local government and charities, such as the Poor Law and public health. New, centralised departments of state were established with local operational capacity – often with new boundaries of jurisdiction rather than adopting the political cartography used in the past. In addition, national government increasingly took greater control of the money being raised and spent by local government bodies.

These developments reflected a greater concern for public welfare and, in this respect, the central state was seen as a guardian of the interests of local people. Rather than leaving local services to the serendipity of local government, or the arbitrary decisions of local charities, this new brand of politician and zealous reformer sought to ensure that national standards were upheld in the interests of all citizens, regardless of place. As Sharpe (1970, 157) rightly remarks, this meant that in England 'it is central government that is cast in the role of softening arbitrariness ... [acting as] the guardian of the rights of individuals and of groups against the possible depredations of local authorities'. This concern to reduce the influence of local circumstances and differentiated political desire and civic capacity on service delivery and social outcomes has fuelled Parliament's increased intervention in local government over the past 200 years. It also helps to explain the widespread concern about the potentially negative implications of localism today.

The desire for standardisation – removing what we now call the 'postcode lottery' associated with locally determined service provision – has created an ongoing tension over the extent to which local government should be seen as purely administrative or whether it should retain the spirit of the 1835 Municipal Corporations Act and provide a space for local democracy. Over time, there has been less importance attached to the role of local government in representing the interests and desires of local people than to the desire for national standards in policy and practice (Bogdanor, 2009). Local government has primarily been seen as a means of delivering services rather than of ensuring the democratic representation of the local community. In part, this may be because local government had *always* been associated with local administration, even in its more autonomous phase.

However, the journey towards standardisation and centralisation was manifest as early as 1818–19 in the passage of the Sturges Bourne Acts, followed by the Hobhouse Act (1831), which sought to impose order on the way in which parishes were being run.[8] For the first time, local government was subject to standardisation. By 1828, as many as 2,868 parishes had enacted the new rules concerning voting rights, local leadership and procedure, declaring themselves in the lexicon of the Acts to be 'Select Vestries' (Webb and Webb, 1924 [1907], 157).

This strain of thinking was further manifest in the Poor Law Amendment Act (1834), which removed control of the Poor Law from parishes and local overseers altogether, creating instead a new national organisation with central oversight comprising three national Poor Law Commissioners and new local boards, each having their own newly defined geographical area, with the job of implementing rules laid down by the centre. From 1836, these boards took over the additional duties of registering births, deaths and marriages, thus removing this work from the parish officials and the justices who had been doing it for hundreds of years. From 1871, Parliament combined the role of the Poor Law guardians with the work of local public health boards to form Local Government Boards, and from 1919 these became part of the national Ministry of Health (Webb and Webb, 1963 [1922]). As such, the Poor Law acted as a Trojan horse for increased centralisation, setting a trend that only accelerated over subsequent years.

It is significant that the Poor Law Amendment Act (1834) was passed following the advice of a parliamentary Poor Law Commission, administered by Edwin Chadwick, who later took his reforming zeal into the area of public health, again looking to set up a wholly new administrative system, with new geographical boundaries, to administer the desired improvements (Prest, 1990).[9] As such, the reforms to the Poor Law established a new pattern of working whereby a parliamentary commission would investigate a social problem, conduct a number of inspections, write a report and advocate for the legislation that followed (Smellie, 1946, 26). Following reforms in relation to the Poor Law, public health and sanitation, as well as education (1870), new centralised and standardised systems were more widely experienced and accepted (Smellie, 1946, 37). This gave Parliament increased confidence in its ability to exercise local control and, as the Webbs (1963 [1922], 112) suggest, by the end of the 19th century 'the supervising, inspecting and sanctioning authority vested in central government departments … [created] the beginnings of a new kind of national executive control of local affairs'. Even in the areas that were not directly controlled by a new national body, Parliament got a taste for scrutinising local activity that was to pervade the future scalar politics of central–local government relations.

Support for the poor featured again in the drive for service standardisation during the 20th century. Between 1905 and 1909 the Royal Commission on the Poor Laws and Relief of Distress met to review the future of this service. Its 20 commissioners, who included civil servants and representatives of charities and clergy, visited 200 poor unions and 400 other institutions, heard from 400 witnesses and read 900 statements in order to produce two reports (one comprising the views of the majority and the other with a minority view) (Rose, 1986, 42). While the majority report argued that poverty was primarily a matter of morality and behaviour, advocating a continued role for charitable organisations as the first line of response, the minority report argued that structural forces were to blame for the problem, advocating greater state intervention to ensure fair entitlement to assistance without the judgement of the charity sector.[10]

For those on the left, the position of the minority report concerning structural injustice and the need for a more adequate response augmented arguments for a national system of entitlement to the provision of services such that citizens would no longer be subject to the condescension of the rich and the judgements of the philanthropist. As the Labour MP Richard Crossland put it in 1973 when reflecting back on the 1930s, 'We all disliked the do-good volunteer and wanted to see him replaced by professionals and trained administrators in the socialist welfare state of which we all dreamed. Philanthropy to us was an odious expression of social oligarchy and churchy bourgeois attitudes' (in Finlayson, 1994, 250). Crossland and his generation of politicians and publics rejected the serendipity and paternalism associated with local government and charity, in favour of the equality and justice they associated with nationally coordinated state-funded and delivered entitlements and services. While local government was increasingly directed from the centre, so too the patchwork of self-help and charitable organisations that had developed across the country was gradually incorporated into the state. As Finlayson (1994, 176) explains of this period, 'responsibility for welfare had become more a matter for an "active state" which bestowed entitlements on its citizens, and less a matter for "active citizens" contributing, by voluntaristic methods, to their own welfare outside the state'.

This was particularly evident in the work of Aneurin Bevan, MP, who was Labour's first Minister of Health from 1945 (Finlayson, 1994). Against the wishes of some in his Party who wanted to retain a more distributed structure of organisation (most notably Herbert Morrison, MP), Bevan established the National Health Service (NHS) by incorporating 1,334 voluntary and 1,771 municipal hospitals and 340,000 workers into one national system (Bevan, 1952, 82; Foot, 1973, 218; White, 2005). For Bevan, securing control of the national government provided the means to build a new world, on new principles, and the sentiment of the past was to be replaced by a new rational order. He declared that he 'would rather be kept alive in the efficient if cold altruism of a large hospital than expire in a gush of warm sympathy in a small one' (in Foot, 1973, 132). Big was better and central control was essential. Speaking in March 1947, he declared with relish that 'Every time a maid kicks over a bucket of slops in a ward, an agonised wail will go through Whitehall' (in Foot, 1973, 195).

Thus, in building a brave a new world for a very brave generation, Parliament was more open to arguments about the capacity and necessity of the central state to direct local activity with a strong belief in the spatial uniformity of provision and practice (Stewart, 1985). In the period between 1930 and 1950, a wide range of activities were removed from local government control, including: trunk roads, civil airfields, hospitals, public assistance (for the unemployed and pensioners), road transport, electricity and gas supply, as well as the process of valuation for the rates to be charged (Robson, 1954 [1931]). Later described as a move from 'gas and water socialism' to the 'cradle and grave welfare state' (Jackman, 1985, 150–3), these reforms removed many public goods from the jurisdiction of local government, leaving councillors to focus on the redistributive functions determined (and paid for) by the central government for particular identified groups. As such, local government increasingly became an administrative arm of a national welfare state, catering for a minority of local citizens. As Jackman (1985, 157) explains, 'While in the 1930s its activities were largely collective, providing services for all its citizens for which all would pay, they are now more redistributive. Often those for whom most services are provided pay little or nothing in rates, while those bearing the heaviest rate burdens often receive virtually no benefit from local government services.'

The first national grants for local government services were provided by Parliament as early as 1835, but this trend increased only very slowly at first. As late as 1868 as much as 67% of local expenditure came from local taxes and 29% came from user charges (such as for gas and electricity), meaning that almost *all* local government spending was raised within the boundaries of the local state. However, by 2001 only 40% of local spending was raised locally (Travers, 1989; Travers and Esposito, 2003; also Figure 2.2) and, in addition, the scope for setting the local rates and borrowing money was severely curtailed. While local government's budgets increased in size dramatically during the first part of the 20th century, with the numbers of staff tripling between 1935 and 1985, the money for this came from the national Treasury with strings attached (Jackman, 1985; Loughlin et al, 1985, xvi). Once an increasing share of local expenditure came from the centre, the balance of power shifted away from the local arena (Robson, 1954 [1931]). In addition, dependence on the centre meant that local government took its lead from the centre rather than from the needs of the locality, such that 'The grant system has led to local councils seeking guidance, and taking their lead, from central government when providing local services, rather than responding directly to local needs and wants' (Travers and Esposito, 2003, 11).

Figure 2.2: The balance of funding in local government finance, 1800–2001

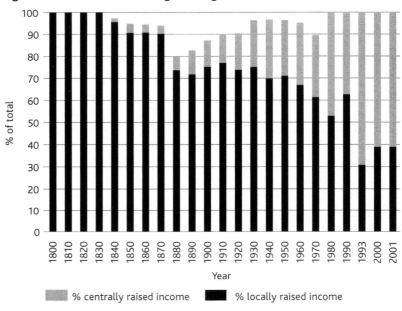

Source: Travers and Esposito (2003, 29).

The 1980s were particularly important in reinforcing this situation. Following the election of left-wing councillors who used local government as a way to challenge the national Conservative government, Parliament legislated to further denude English local government of its power (Crouch and Marquand, 1989; Loughlin et al, 1985; Travers, 1989). In order to limit the capacity of radical councillors to raise income and provide additional services in cities like Liverpool, London and Sheffield, Mrs Thatcher's governments passed a series of local government Acts. The 1984 Rate Capping Act was particularly important in this respect, as it reduced the freedom of local councillors to raise money locally and it gave the Secretary of State for Environment the power to set a limit on the local rates charged (Goldsmith and Page, 1987; Travers and Esposito, 2003). As Howard Davies put it in his role as Controller of the newly established

Audit Commission (a role he filled between 1987 and 1992), the control of budgets demonstrated 'that Parliament is sovereign, that local authorities perform functions delegated to them by Parliament, and that those functions may just as easily be taken away as granted' (Davies, 1990, 204). Once local branches of the Labour Party started to use local government to raise political issues and challenge the centre, a hostile Conservative government in Westminster simply used its power against them. As Davies (1990, 206) put it, 'local politicians trespassed on central politics, [and] now central government is trespassing on their patch [too]'.

Thus the Thatcher governments set the seal on the long decline of local government during the 20th century (Griffith, 1966; Rhodes, 1988; Loughlin et al, 1985, Loughlin, 1996). They used the central state to ensure that local government posed a diminishing challenge to the centre, and at its most extreme this involved abolishing the Greater London Council via the Local Government Act in 1985. As Norman Tebbit, MP bluntly explained, this was because it was 'left-wing, high-spending and at odds with the government's view of the world' (in Jenkins, 2004, 42).

Furthermore, these Conservative governments changed the things that local government was able to do. They used new legislation to enforce the competitive tendering of core services, opening things up to the market regardless of local desires. Local government became more about commissioning (or, in the language of the time, 'enabling') than directly providing services (Ridley, 1988; Bennett, 1990) and these measures reduced the size of local government's pool of employees, fragmented service provision and made it harder to identify lines of accountability back to the political system. The local state was constrained in order to make space for the agendas of national politicians, and in this case they extended the power of the market as well as the centralised state (Crouch and Marquand, 1989).

In addition to this increased control over finance and services, many national governments have also implemented changes in the geographical areas covered by local government and this also fostered greater centralisation. The geography of English local government has been altered to increase the size of political jurisdictions and try to rationalise the work that is done. As we have seen, the way in which piecemeal legislation stretching back over hundreds of years created a palimpsest of local areas with boundaries and jurisdictions going back 'time out of mind' posed a particular problem for reformers in the 19th and 20th centuries who wanted much greater order and rationality in government. In 1894, Mr Henry Fowler, MP for

Wolverhampton and the President of the Local Government Board, introduced a new Local Government Act, complaining that there were '62 counties, 302 Municipal Boroughs, 31 Improvement Act Districts, 688 Local Government Districts, 574 Rural Sanitary Districts, 58 Port Sanitary Districts, 2,302 School Board Districts, 362 Highway Districts (comprising about 8,000 Highway Parishes), 6,477 Highway Parishes (not included in Urban or Highway Districts), 1,052 Burial Board Districts, 648 Poor Law Unions, 13,775 Ecclesiastical Parishes, and nearly 15,000 Civil Parishes'. For Fowler, this 'multiplicity of authority and this confusion of rating power' were in dire need of rationalisation and, following on from the 1888 Local Government Act, he advocated the establishment of elected rural and urban district and parish councils to operate under the counties (Hansard, 1894; Poole and Keith-Lucas, 1994).

More than 60 years later, Parliament was still grappling with a similar set of issues, trying to decide how best to manage local government alongside changes in the economy and society, as well as shifting expectations about standards of government. In 1966, Parliament established a Royal Commission on Local Government to explore the existing framework for local government and to advocate for possible boundary reform.[11] At the time, there were 1,200 different local government organisations, including first-tier counties and county boroughs and second-tier urban and rural districts, as well as rural parish councils (Royal Commission on Local Government in England, 1969, 21). Chaired by Lord Redcliffe-Maud and meeting between 1966 and 1969, the Commission had four things to consider in relation to possible reform: (1) the efficient provision of tasks; (2) the need to 'attract and hold the interests of its citizens'; (3) the importance of developing partnerships with national authorities; and (4) adapting to changing circumstances. As many as 2,156 witnesses gave and/or submitted evidence to the Commission, which then produced proposals for redrawing the map of English local government.

The final report was eventually published in 1969, together with a memorandum of dissent written by one commissioner, Mr Derek Senior, who rather presciently, given the current state of debate (RSA, 2014), advocated a different set of boundaries based on 35 city-regions. The work of the Commission was only ever partially incorporated into subsequent legislation by the Conservative government in 1972, and its legislation reduced the number of county councils, established seven metropolitan county councils (Greater Manchester, Merseyside, Tyne and Wear, South Yorkshire, West Yorkshire and West Midlands, together with Greater London) and brought in second-tier boroughs or districts below this, leaving the thousands of parishes in rural areas largely untouched (Table 2.1).[12]

Table 2.1: English local government bodies after 1972

Type	Number	Smallest population	Largest population
Counties	39	337,000	1,396,000
Metropolitan counties	7	425,000	1,142,000
Shire districts	296	24,000	425,000
London boroughs	32	134,000	318,000
Metropolitan boroughs	36	174,000	1,096,000

Source: Rao, 2000, 44

What became known as the Redcliffe-Maud Commission faced an impossible challenge. Charged with advancing technocratic reform on the basis of efficiency, it also had to try to preserve the role of local government in the democratic life of the country. The commissioners grappled with arguments about the size of a population sufficient to provide efficient services, arriving at a minimum of 250,000, which was larger than 9 of the existing 45 counties, 65 of the 79 county boroughs and all the other districts (Royal Commission on Local Government in England, 1969, 28). Yet, at the same time, they also recognised the democratic imperative that citizens should be able to identify with the political bodies by which they were governed. Faced with a task that was characterised by a tension between efficiency and sentiment, or, we could say, standardisation and democracy, the commissioners had to try to identify boundaries that made practical and administrative sense that were also meaningful to the people who voted.

At the time, and in a re-run of arguments between Edwin Chadwick and Joshua Toulmin-Smith a hundred years earlier (Poole and Keith-Lucas, 1994), the dominant pressure was for larger units and economies of scale, and there were more politicians, civil servants and academics advocating efficiency than those who wanted to respect the old boundaries and traditions of government from earlier times. Exemplified in Thomas Walter Freeman's book (1968) *Geography and regional administration*, a new cadre of technocrats were confident in asserting the power of planning over sentiment, and order over tradition (see also Savage, 2010). As Freeman (1968, 9) put it early on in his book, rational planning had been 'hampered by the survival of boundaries, especially of counties, established as much as a thousand years ago'.

The Royal Commission did acknowledge the more democratic – and emotional – side of these arguments, stating that local government is important because 'it is the means by which people can … take an active and constructive part in the business of government; and can decide for themselves, within the limits of what national politics and local resources allow, what kind of services they want and what kind of environment they prefer' (Royal Commission on Local Government in England, 1969, 10). Going on, it argued that 'Local Government is the only representative political institution in the country outside Parliament; and being, by its nature, in closer touch than Parliament or Ministers can be with local conditions, local needs, local opinions, it is an essential part of the fabric of democratic government' (Royal Commission on Local Government in England, 1969, 11). However, by the time it was meeting (1966–69), local government only inadequately represented local interests and it hardly provided the space for people to make decisions about their own government. Local government was already dominated by the national political parties and it was more dependent on national finance and decision making than on local resources and ideas for reform (Bulpitt, 1989; Copus, 2004; Bogdanor, 2009).

In its heyday, as we have seen, local government had necessarily involved at least some local people in their own government – often as amateurs and lay representatives – and while it had always been focused on administration, the payment of rates had ensured local interest and the need for accountability over what was being done. Although the almost full integration of local government into national government and party politics, as well as its dependence on national funding decisions and statutes, has squeezed the democratic space to breaking point, contemporary demands for greater localism partly reflect this longer history of local government as a site – however limited – for democratic engagement and perhaps represent a desire for greater local democracy than has ever been practised before.

Small steps in the development of localism

In the small print of its report, the Royal Commission on Local Government in England (1969) reported on some original research that it had conducted into the potential for creating new community councils. These would mirror parish councils and be established in urban areas in order to better reflect the geographical imaginations and capacity of citizens to engage in public life.[13] In a community attitudes survey, researchers found that three-quarters of respondents could identify a 'home area' that was especially strong if they had lived there a long time and had family and friends who also lived there (Royal Commission on Local Government in England, 1969, 62).

Picking up on this work, a small group of activists led by Michael Young set up the Association for Neighbourhood Councils to 'press for the establishment of neighbourhood or urban parish councils as part of the reformed local government' (Baker and Young, 1971, inside front cover; and in so doing, developed an idea raised earlier by the socialist G.D.H. Cole (1947) although always disputed by others (Dennis, 1958)). Challenging the way in which Parliament was advocating ever larger units for political administration that were increasingly remote from the people, the Association wanted to create new councils as 'champions of general community interests on a geographical basis' (Baker and Young, 1971, 1). The Association conducted its own research, commissioning a poll to ask 789 people 'Do you think it would be a good idea or a bad idea to have a number of local neighbourhood councils under your current local councils to help with such things as local schools, housing etc?' Just over half (53%) gave positive answers and as many as 27% said they didn't know, with the strongest endorsement coming from London, where 63% of respondents affirmed their support (Baker and Young, 1971, 5).

This work was extended with a series of case studies in Hornsey, North London picking up from work done for the Hornsey plan (Baker and Young, 1971), as well as taking place in Worcester, Reading, Newcastle and the three towns of Maidstone, Medway and Gillingham in Kent. This later research similarly exposed some scope for civic engagement, asking: 'Do you think that ordinary people should help with local problems or do you think it should be left to the people who are running things?' Affirmative responses ranged from a high of 68% in Newcastle to a low of 53% in Hornsey (Baker and Young, 1971, 8). The Association promoted the idea of community councils to foster local representation and consultation and provide the institutional infrastructure for innovation. They were to be funded from some sort of precept on local government rates (Baker and Young, 1971).

Such demands attracted little attention. They were included in evidence presented to the Royal Commission, and featured in the subsequent parliamentary debate in February 1970 (Rose, 1971), but they were not picked up at that time.[14] However, the desire for greater democracy was a growing feature of popular political life in the 1970s. In 1971, a group of community activists formed their own neighbourhood council in the ward of Golborne, in the Royal Borough of Kensington and Chelsea, acting without any legal jurisdiction to do so. Initiating action after local riots in 1958, up to 120 local people, including local clergy and community workers, secured funding from the Joseph Rowntree Social Service Trust to appoint a neighbourhood worker who organised the constitution and a local election. In April 1971, 1,415 local people (28% of the local electorate) voted for some of the 38 candidates who were contesting 26 places representing seven different parts of the ward. As a participant reported at the time, the council was 'operating under the principle that a People's Council must initiate a People's Plan: it will call upon all the relevant professionals, authorities and developers to help the people of the area formulate and finance a community plan, a development corporation and a housing association' (Blair, 1971). While Golborne was described as having the potential to start a 'revolution in local government, not only in London, but throughout the UK' (Blair, 1971), many of the innovations from this period are only now resurfacing, more than 40 years on.

In the 1970s, and as discussed further in the following chapter, local government was increasingly under pressure to reform from demands being made from below. Led by a new generation of activists often associated with the New Left, people started to organise in inner-city communities around perceived local interests and the demand for wider reform. This activity started to shape the culture of the Labour Party and the development of local government in the areas affected (Baine, 1975; Gyford, 1976; Loney, 1983; Hoggett and Hambleton, 1987; Cochrane, 1993; Atkinson, 2004; Newman, 2012; Rowbothom et al, 2012 [1979]). As an example, a group of activists started to organise for greater neighbourhood engagement in one part of the city of Walsall in the West Midlands during the 1970s. They formed the Caldmore Residents' group and set up a new a Housing Association and an Advice Centre. One of these activists, Dave Church, later became a Labour councillor and from there he drew on his own community experience to develop an agenda for more radical decentralisation. In 1980, he and a group of Labour activists launched a manifesto called *Haul for Democracy* incorporating a plan to set up neighbourhood offices across the council area (Seabrook, 1984). The 33 (and later 35) neighbourhood offices that were opened provided space for staff to manage housing and repairs and give advice to tenants and residents (Whitehead, 2003).[15]

Similar experiments influenced local government in the London borough of Islington, where a range of different groups saw the people, rather than the Labour Party, as the solution to local concerns (Baine, 1975). In organising around shared local interests, and taking collective action, these groups were trying both to develop their own solutions and to challenge the local authority over issues like housing. As Baine (1975) points out, these groups incorporated middle-class residents organising over their own interests (in relation to the preservation and renovation of existing buildings, for example), those campaigning for others (in relation to homelessness, housing or poverty, for example), broader coalitions focused on particular services (the Barnsbury Action Group or the Holloway Housing Aid Centre) and housing tenants and residents (self-organising over their own housing concerns). As in Golborne, these activists were able to secure charitable funding to support their community work – in this case from Christian Aid, Rowntree, Shelter and Urban Aid – and they established a new playground, a Housing Aid Centre, a tenants' cooperative and a housing rights project. This activity impacted on local government decisions and influenced a new generation of activists, some of whom later went on to high office (Baine, 1975; Hain, 1980; Hodge, 1987).

In this environment, more mainstream commentators became increasingly mindful of the dangers of local government being remote from the people, and this promoted renewed debates about how to enliven the work of the state. Drawing on Department of Environment research into local government in Oldham, Rotherham and Sunderland, for example, journalist Chris Crossey (1974, 13) called on councils to act as 'social entrepreneurs' to 'seek out unidentified needs and then marshal local resources – individuals, organisations, funds – to meet them'. Local authorities were urged to find new ways of engaging local people through neighbourhood forums, newsletters and communications, and a number experimented with decentralisation. In 1969 the Home Office also launched a national Community Development Project that was based in 12 neighbourhoods and was designed to focus on local civic capacity building around identified local interests (this is further explored in the following chapter; but see also Loney, 1983; Newman, 2014).

Echoing wider international trends at this time (Yates, 1973; Sharpe, 1976; Page and Goldsmith, 1987; De Vries, 2000), up to 40 English local authorities explored decentralisation as a way to get closer to their residents and increase their effectiveness in service provision (Hoggett and Hambleton, 1987). However, while citizens might get a better service from a local office, this was not necessarily true and decentralisation did nothing to shift the prevailing balance of power. From their research, Hambleton and Hoggett (1987) reported that some local authorities – and they looked at experiments in Birmingham and Newcastle – sought to combine decentralisation with democratisation by setting up new ward or neighbourhood committees or forums, some of which included councillors with newly elected and/or nominated representatives and a chance for public engagement. These tended to remain council-led, with a limited role for the public, illustrating the extent to which decentralisation does not necessarily increase democratisation (Fesler, 1965; Conyers, 1984; Purcell, 2006).[16]

Thus, while some parts of local government experimented with decentralisation during the 1970s and 1980s, this took place alongside a growth in more grassroots neighbourhood organisations and campaigns in the UK, as well as in Europe and further afield (Alinsky, 1946, 1970; Morris and Hess, 1975; Castells, 1983; Fisher, 1994). These groups tended to be more successful in developing local voice and local political leadership than in democratising the state. Indeed, their very success depended on having a critical distance from the arms of the state, and in instances where the state initiated or funded any such activities this tended to reduce their community strength (Yates, 1973, 24). In some cases, however, these movements challenged and/or influenced the policies and practices of local government and, in England, they were critical precursors to the way in which local government became a vehicle to challenge the national government during the political battles of the 1980s as outlined in the previous section (Boddy and Fudge, 1984; Gyford, 1985; Cochrane, 1993). A new generation of political activists came to see extra-parliamentary community campaigns *and* local government as arenas for struggles around race, gender and community and this then inflected local Labour Party policy and practice (Newman, 2012). The political battles of the 1980s were critically important in pitting some local communities and local governments against the national government, although, perhaps predictably, the centralised state was the victor.

By the time the Labour Party secured national office in 1997, debate about community engagement and local government was much less radical. In office, the Party developed a battery of new performance targets to ensure that local bodies met the goals set out at the centre. Rather than freeing up local government to innovate on its own terms, New Labour implemented tighter controls over its work, while at the same time encouraging contracting with the private sector and charitable organisations and setting up wholly new structures for the delivery of some strategic ideas. Using a combination of new organisations (as in regional government), new partnerships (such as those used in fostering and adoption) and new arm's-length structures (such as housing associations and new tenant-management bodies), New Labour sought to govern via centralised targets and audit while incorporating partnerships and relationships with a wide range of organisations (Lodge and Muir, 2011). At the same time, however, the Party did focus on increasing levels of public engagement in the work of local authorities, and this experience is outlined more fully in the following chapter. While increasing numbers of people were consulted about council decisions and services, through a new diversity of techniques, prevailing power structures remained largely unchanged (Wilson, 1999; Rao, 2000; Lowndes et al, 2001; Amin, 2005; Dinham, 2005; Barnes et al, 2007; Copus, 2010; Copus and Sweeting, 2012).

New Labour's focus on community consultation reflected a wider explosion of similar experiments across the globe, promoted by governments within Europe (Guarneros-Meza and Geddes, 2010; Silver et al, 2010), and also by bodies like the World Bank (Mohan and Stokke, 2000; Kothari and Cooke, 2001; Cornwall and Coelho, 2007). In the main, these initiatives were tightly controlled: people were invited to sit on the boards of new organisations, to take part in consultation exercises and to join local forums, but the rules of engagement were already agreed. As is outlined more fully in the following chapter, government encouraged the people only so far, consulting them over decisions that had already been made or with marginal room for manoeuvre (Imrie and Raco, 2003; Somerville and Haines, 2008).

As suggested in the previous chapter, New Labour's approach did start to change towards the end of its period in office. Some ministers acknowledged the limits of their approach in relation both to national targets and to the roles proffered to citizens and communities (Stoker, 2004) and, in the spirit of a 'new localism', Ministers of State for Communities and Local Government (Ruth Kelly, MP and Hazel Blears, MP) published two White Papers that promised greater local freedoms for local authorities as well as to citizens and communities (*Strong and Prosperous Communities*: DCLG, 2006; *Communities in Control*: DCLG, 2008; see also Stoker, 2004). The second White Paper argued that the modern state should be 'devolved, decentralised, with power diffused throughout society [and] that people should have the maximum influence, control and ownership over the decisions, forces and agencies which shape their lives and environments' (DCLG, 2008, iii).

The New Labour government also charged Sir Michael Lyons to lead an inquiry into local government funding, and he called for a change in the balance of power between the centre and local authorities (Lyons Inquiry into Local Government, 2007). As such, Lyons recognised that this would require greater acceptance of local differences in the policy and practice of different local authorities. Rather than bemoaning the 'postcode lottery' associated with the lexicon of the past, he argued for greater acceptance of 'managed difference' as people came to recognise 'the right and the ability of local communities to make their own choices, confident in their own competence, and in the knowledge of their own preferences' (2007, iii).

Lyons (2007) advocated the re-banding and revaluation of council tax and rebates and, in the longer term, a chance to consider raising local income taxes and tourist taxes and the use of local supplements to business rates in order to support particular projects. He also advocated a stronger role for local authorities in 'place-shaping' through building stronger local alliances and much deeper public engagement. As he put it in the final report, 'If local government is to act in the interests of its community, influence its partners and ensure it tailors its work to the most important local priorities, it needs to make a step-change in the quality of its engagement work' (Lyons, 2007, 19). This agenda is picked up in more detail in the following chapter and, in relation to Lambeth Council, in Chapter Four.

The political and cultural legacy and its challenge to localism

As we have seen, the early history of English local government reflected the established constitutional balance between the authority of the crown and local liberties, enshrined in common law. This started to change during the 19th and 20th centuries, such that the central state extended its power over local government (Loughlin, 2013). Following a brief flowering of local democracy (albeit that the franchise was not universal), with greater freedom and responsibility for a wider range of functions, local government was increasingly seen as a means to administer services that were funded and directed from the centre in order to serve national goals. More than ever before, local government became part of the armoury of a national welfare state, redistributing resources to those who needed them most on the basis of national concerns. From this point of view, citizenship entitled people to a certain level of service wherever they lived, and as such, the potential of local government to act as an organ of democratic government was a political impediment. The national political parties had no interest in granting greater political freedom and autonomy to local government and when any such independence was manifest (as during the rate-capping disputes of the 1980s), the centre simply legislated to reduce the room for manoeuvre. Given that the national political parties continue to dominate local government, and the national Parliament allocates almost all of the budget, the centre has ready mechanisms for enforcing local control.

Over time, as local government has had less autonomy and less capacity for innovation, people have been understandably less willing to engage with it. As the practice of our constitution – the 'set of rules' concerning government that 'evolves through usage' (Loughlin, 2013, 8) – has been associated with ever-greater centralisation of the state, the local state has less credibility in the eyes of the public as well as politicians. As Ashford (1989, 92) puts it, without 'limit to national demands then local discretion and eventually self-respect wither. Worse perhaps, local government cannot experiment to solve new problems, to diffuse social crises or to mobilise public support.' There is a 'vicious cycle of centralism' that is becoming reinforced over time and through practice (Lodge and Muir, 2011, S105).

For Bulpitt (1983), this situation reflects a long-established 'dual polity' whereby local politics is represented by politicians in Westminster who represent their constituencies (in what he calls 'high politics') while local politicians remain constrained to the tasks of local administration (or 'low politics'). As such, the local state is seen as being inherently inferior to the national domain. Funding has reinforced this centralisation and, rather than face the wrath of their local citizens by putting up the rates, it has been easier for local councillors to rely on money that comes from the centre. Commenting on this shifting balance of power more than 80 years ago, Robson (1954 [1931], 42) noted that 'Local authorities are themselves largely responsible for this state of affairs. They have for many years, through their associations, demanded more money from the central government regardless of the consequences to their own dignity and freedom.' In addition, however, the people have been promised a uniform entitlement and delivery of services across the country. They have voted on the basis of national political party programmes for these services to be delivered – often by representatives of the same national parties who serve as councillors in local government – without any expectation that they might have to engage in local deliberations or lobby to get the services they need and desire (Game and Leach, 1996). There is little popular experience of a genuinely open form of local government to which citizens can make the case for their needs to be met. Since the era of the mass franchise, the autonomy of local government has been in decline and, as Ashford (1989, 79) remarks, 'history never presented the British people with a situation where its value as a reservoir of democratic faith might be demonstrated'. Without this, there is little chance that the citizens will rush to its defence and, as such, the restoration of more meaningful forms of local government will also prove difficult. As Bogdanor (2009, 259) suggests, 'Any attempt to revive local democracy must tackle the root cause of its decline, which lies in the replacement of local democracy by a very rigid form of local party government, the replacement of local authorities which represented local communities by larger and unwieldy units, and the concomitant rise of a professional political class in local government, a class apart.' The citizens are largely disinterested in local government and it will be very difficult to reverse this state of affairs without an increase in the level of non-partisan politics conducted in the local arena.

This chapter has highlighted the history of local government and its role in the public realm in organising things like street paving, lighting, water, electricity and transport. These interventions transformed our settlements, and in the early days this was done through the leadership of self-appointed guardians of the local civic sphere with support from Parliament when required. Permissive legislation allowed local people to take up new possibilities without being forced to do so. However, in the paradox of English local government, greater democratisation was associated with ever-greater centralisation. While more people had the potential to engage in local government they were also promised a brave new future that would come from decisions taken in Westminster and Whitehall rather than in the local town hall. Citizenship became associated with a national set of entitlements that did not depend upon geographical residence or public engagement. Indeed, geographical difference – the 'postcode lottery' – was seen as a problem to be overcome. Even though many services are necessarily differentiated through the serendipity of personal relationships (between a social worker and their client, a teacher and their pupil, a nurse and their patient) as well as the professionalism of the staff, there has been a tendency to try to standardise such relationships through statutes, targets and audit (and for the pernicious effect on professional autonomy see Marquand, 2004).

If localism is to have a future it will require a reversal in this state of affairs such that local people have a different view of the local state, the entitlements of citizenship and the benefits of local organisation. Local government will have to be opened up such that people come to see it as an arena through which they can raise local concerns and negotiate for change. If they experienced success, citizens will come to see the entitlements of their citizenship as partly produced by their own actions in the local arena rather than being handed down from on high. Thus, while localism requires much greater autonomy for local government, greater control over finances and decision making, it also requires much less control by national political parties, freeing up councillors to represent local concerns and innovate on the basis of their own situation (Copus, 2004; Bogdanor, 2009). This freedom at the local level would have to be mirrored by greater restraint on the part of national politicians. Rather than being quick to denounce local failings and assert their control, national MPs would have to allow local government representatives the space to sort out their problems. In their recent deliberations on localism, the parliamentary Select Committees scrutinising local government and the constitution have each advocated some sort of statutory codification of the relationship between central and local government such that the rights of local government are much better respected and national politicians are more firmly restrained (House of Commons Select Committee on Political and Constitutional Reform, 2011; House of Commons Select Committee on Communities and Local Government, 2009).

Of course, the call for a more vibrant local democratic state and active citizenship is nothing new. More than 50 years ago William Robson (1954 [1931], 310) concluded his book on the history of English local government by arguing that 'The greatest need in English local government today is a recapture of the kind of civic sense which invested some of the older cities with a special glory in the Tudor age … Our aim should be to combine the efficiency and scope of twentieth century municipal government, with its free universal education, increased public safety, improved health, ease of communication, higher standard of living and other advantages, with the civic spirit of the fifteenth and sixteenth and seventeenth centuries, shorn of its narrow exclusiveness and undemocratic basis of representation.' This call for greater local democracy is explored further in the following chapter.

Taking the long view of localism

This chapter has explicated the way that English local government shifted from a juridical regime embedded in the legal and ecclesiastical infrastructure provided by the crown and the church, towards one more focused on the power of national Parliament. As outlined in Table 2.2, over time, the state became less focused on the old job of securing the sovereign peace and more exercised about the nature and conduct of the population at large. In his analysis of similar developments across Europe, Michel Foucault (1991 [1978], 100) characterised this period as one in which political power became increasingly 'governmentalized'. By this he meant that the state was increasingly focused on 'the welfare of the population, the improvement of its condition, the increase of its wealth, longevity, health' (Foucault, 1991 [1978], 100; Elden, 2007).[17] National parliaments began to deploy an armoury of statistics to understand their people and to pass laws in order to manage their populations. In the UK, the 19th century was associated with a strengthening of the central state, which was then able to act to increase the size and role of the local state to provide things like paving, lighting, policing, sanitation and public health. During this period a burgeoning urban middle class took a greater role in the government of their cities while working-class communities were organising an ever-greater array of new forms of collective self-provisioning as manifested in burial societies, friendly societies (covering sickness and pensions), housing associations, trade unions and educational institutes (Green, 1996). This was the period associated with a 'golden age' of municipal government and institution building in the UK (Finlayson, 1994; Hunt, 2004) and, although it was facilitated by the national Parliament, it was

Table 2.2: The shifting governmental regimes and spatial orders of English statecraft, from the 17th century

Time	Regime	The major political tradition	The institutional infrastructure of the state	The geography of power relations	The 'civic offer' to citizens
C17th–C18th	Juridical	Conservative	Crown, parish, borough	Semi-autonomous localism	To be self-appointed and anointed guardians of order; to serve
C19th	Governmental	Liberal	Parliament, local authorities (county, city, borough, district)	Central oversight of local expansion	For some: to vote, join a party, stand for office
C20th	Welfarist	Social democratic	Government, Parliament, civil service, local authorities	Centralisation	Universal: to vote, join a party, stand for office, join a movement
C21st	Localist	Liberal-republican/ institutional	Government, Parliament, civil service, local authorities, state-funded bodies, civic organisations	Towards subsidiarity, dispersed away from the centre	Universal: to vote, join a party, stand for office, organise, negotiate, co-produce

largely realised by local people who organised their own responses to their own sets of problems.

This regime of government changed again during the 20th century when the combined effects of war, the mass franchise, growing social democratic parties and the development of a national welfare system led to changed expectations of the role of the state. As exemplified by the Labour government of 1945, government was increasingly focused on securing standardised welfare provision across space, incorporating the local state more firmly into national objectives. Citizens were granted entitlements to a range of standard services regardless of their own actions or their place of residence, or the judgement of others, and, as outlined above in this chapter, this involved the significant centralisation of political power, authority and responsibility. In a zero-sum game, the local state and the local charity sector lost power as the centre took over. During the 20th century this model of government came to be widely accepted but, as the Conservative politician Sir Lord Keith Joseph put it in a defence of a more republican model of political power in which authority is distributed across multiple sites, 'The unbridled supremacy of Parliament is quite recent, historically speaking. Parliamentarians of the past believed that Parliament though first among equals among the powers of the state, should respect the independence of other institutions. They saw the liberties of Englishmen, as actually enjoyed, as the great barrier to despotism. Parliament was respected precisely because it rested on a great base of independent and private institutions' (in Poole and Keith-Lucas, 1994, 254).

As outlined in the previous chapter, localism potentially represents a shift back to this more republican model of government in which political power is distributed across a wider range of institutions that are not necessarily understood in a hierarchy of 'high' and 'low' power. If it comes to fruition, localism will require a wide range of actors to enter the field of government (and for the example of the way in which Scottish devolution allowed the increased engagement of the business community in public life, see Raco, 2003). Rather than being about the exercise of control *over* population, this form of government is supposed to be about the freedom of a range of actors operating in a diversity of spaces to engage in public life, politics and government. As part of this effort, many of the aspects of government that concern the management of population (such as health, social services and justice) are being re-imagined as part of a more relational state (on the left) or a Big Society (on the right) in which people work *with* providers to determine and meet their own needs. In theory at least, 'power-over' is to be replaced by the 'power-to' act (Mulgan, 2012). Furthermore, in some accounts, there is a sense in which localism is partly about governing 'via the withdrawal of the state' (Rose, 2014, 215). Rather than prioritising the role of the political party to secure the state to act as a Leviathan protecting the community, debates about localism are reflecting a new argument: that the party needs to liberate the people from the delusion of being 'saved' by the state (and, as we saw in the previous chapter, there is a long tradition of this kind of thinking about the importance of self-organisation to resist the power of the state as well as the market, see Oakeshott, 1962 [1947]; Nisbet, 1962 [1953]; Scott, 1998; Tilly, 1999).

As such, there are indications that a new regime of statecraft is emerging. Just as a regime of juridical government gave way to one more associated with governmentality during the 19th century, and one focused on welfarism in 20th century, the embryo of something new may now be emerging through arguments and experiments for localism. Each regime of government implies a different geographical balance of power, a different understanding of democracy and the prioritisation of a different set of organisations and agents (as summarised in Table 2.2). The implications of localism for the policy and practice of statecraft and citizenship are explicated in the rest of this book.

Notes

[1]   The Church of England retained the parish structure from the Roman Catholic Church and both traditions still organise themselves around the parish today (see Coriden, 1996).

[2]   It is significant that this middle-class and professional engagement with local government was still evident in the early 20th century; a good example is Ernest Simon, who was elected to Manchester City Council as a Liberal between 1912 and 1925, before becoming MP for Manchester Withington in 1923–24 and 1929–31, and becoming a Labour Peer in 1947. He donated land to the city for housing.

[3]   In 1689 there were as many as 200 municipal boroughs in England, each with legal freedoms to establish its own government, sometimes with differentiated boundaries depending upon the matter to be governed (Webb and Webb, 1924 [1907], 288). Most had governing councils with different rules about service and franchises for particular voters. An ancient body like the Liberty of the Cinque Ports comprised 39 boroughs and villages that were outside the control of the counties of Kent, Sussex and Essex, forming their own body with their own courts that could stretch as far as the management of the Yarmouth Fair in Norfolk. Following the custom of local fishermen using land at the mouth of the River Yare for a Michaelmas Fair, the Cinque Ports extended their jurisdiction to Norfolk for 400 years (Webb and Webb, 1924 [1907], 376).

[4]   It is important to note that some parts of the country fell outside parochial control, either because the king had granted privileges to some monasteries, colleges,

cathedrals, places and castles, or because some areas were newly inhabited and/or outside church control. In their remarkable overview of this period, the Webbs (1924 [1907], 10) tell us that the latter included Canvey Island and 'a fringe of land on the coast of Essex which was common land between several villages'. In addition, it is important to note that in some parts of the country the work of administration associated with the overseer, constable and surveyor of highways fell under the jurisdiction of various manors and/or boroughs within or without the parish.

5   It is well known that Daniel Defoe paid £10 to be excused from serving the parish in Stoke Newington in 1721. Others were reported to buy a 'Tyburn ticket' whereby those who helped apprehend a felon were granted a 'ticket' that excused them from public service. These sold for a high price on a secondary market (Webb and Webb, 1924 [1907], 63).

6   Of course, the Webbs wrote this once they were already fully committed to the idea of state socialism, whereby the idiosyncrasies of humanity could be ironed out by the efficient workings of good government. They probably over-egged the failings of the old system because they had a new one in mind. However, with hindsight, it is significant that parochial *and* state-led government are vulnerable to ossification, the operation of self-interest and service failings. At the time of writing, during a slew of very public failures in relation to child protection in Rotherham and Oxford, and in many NHS establishments in relation to the abuse perpetrated by Jimmy Savile, it is clear that the Webbs' faith in the state was highly misguided.

7   The most celebrated example of civic leadership is usually thought to be Joseph Chamberlain, who played a key role in the improvements made in Birmingham during this time. Chamberlain was born to a family of non-conformist industrialists and educated at University College School in London, where he was exposed to the rising ideas of utilitarianism. Following the radical spirit of his time, he saw civic engagement as a Christian duty and a virtue and he campaigned first for elementary schooling and later for good civic government. He stood for election to Birmingham Council in 1869, later winning control and becoming Mayor in 1873 (Hunt, 2004). He later went on to play a key role in Parliament as a Conservative MP.

8   The Right Honourable William Sturges Bourne MP (1769–1845) chaired a House of Commons committee looking at the management of the Poor Law, while also being a member of the parish government of St George's, Hanover Square in London. Drawing on his experience of the latter in order to reduce the costs of the former, he proposed two new Bills to lay down firmer rules for parish government, including the operation of relief to the poor. Sturges Bourne proposed excluding those who didn't pay rates from meetings, but including newcomers and joint stock company representatives. He proposed a voting scale depending on wealth, up to a maximum of six votes for the richest, seeking to ensure that the interests of those who paid the most in rates were more closely protected. Administratively, he advocated having a parish committee that was elected every year, with the compulsory keeping of minutes and the publication of financial accounts. In relation to the management of the Poor Law, he advocated that an overseer should be appointed to do the work on an ongoing basis, rather than as a lay appointee as had been the case in the past.

9   As Sharpe (1970, 159) describes it, Chadwick established a new approach towards local government that is about 'a series of agencies for providing national services

as efficiently as possible to national minimum standards'. Over time, and in tandem with the rise of utilitarianism, Chadwickian local government gathered momentum.

10   The Webbs were strongly associated with the minority report and public support for state intervention, but it is important to note that they often advocated the role of the local rather than the national state. As Robson (1954 [1931]) notes, they advocated municipalisation rather than the nationalisation that became increasingly popular after the Second World War (see Webb and Webb, 1920).

11   This Commission was working alongside a number of other related inquiries such as the reviews led by Mallaby (1967), Skeffington (1969), the Study Group on Local Authorities (1972) (the Bains report) and Layfield (1976) on the finance, management and culture of local authorities and planning.

12   For Roger Scruton (1980, 184) this was the final phase in the erosion of the older political geography of England, such that 'The names of the shires were eventually scrubbed from the map, England was carved up for the convenience of bureaucrats and local administration became just another form of government from elsewhere – the elsewhere often bearing the name of a river ("Avonside", "Thameside", "Humberside") in order to emphasise that the old ties to the land had now been flushed away into the ocean.'

13   At the time, 95% of those living in rural areas had a parish council, involving some 57,000 councillors, but these were not present in urban areas, where government was much more remote (Baker and Young, 1971, 4).

14   The right to set up a parish council in an urban area in London was actually later granted by the New Labour government via the Local Government and Public Involvement in Health Act (2007) and it is perhaps not surprising to find that a community near to Golborne – in Queen's Park, West London – is one of the few urban communities to have subsequently taken this up (Pike, 2006; Jones, 2007; Bailey and Pill, 2015). More broadly, however, the new neighbourhood forums that are being established as part of the new right to develop a neighbourhood plan under the Localism Act (2011) are filling a similar political and community space (on which much more is said in Chapter Five).

15   When a more radical proposal was developed during the mid-1990s, the national Labour Party intervened and expelled the councillors involved (Whitehead, 2003).

16   It is interesting that Heller's (2001) research into these issues in very different contexts (in Brazil, Kerala India and South Africa) found that decentralisation led to increased democratisation only when there was a strong national state able to ensure coordination between scales of government, a well-developed local civil society with the ability to challenge the national authority, as well as strong social movements committed to defending decentralisation. When these factors were in place, the decentralisation of political power could involve greater numbers of people addressing a wider number of issues: extending citizen engagement and the reach of democratic decision making (see also Fung and Wright, 2003). None of these factors has characterised English local government and its hinterland over the past 200 years.

17   In this book, I am using Foucault's term 'governmentality' to capture a historical period in which the focus of political administration shifted towards a concern with the government of population. This is the way in which Foucault (1991 [1978]) himself presented the term in its first articulations. However, it is not the way in which most scholars have subsequently adopted the term. In academic circles, 'governmentality' has generated its own sub-field, coming to mean the way in which governmental discourse facilitates government at a distance, shaping the 'conduct of

conduct' (Rose, 1999). I am wary of this latter approach and am not using the term in this way (see also Barnett, 2005). For many academic commentators, however, governmentality has provided a way to understand localism and the Big Society as manifestations of the ways in which politicians use the state to recalibrate local behaviour, subjectivity and identity (Davoudi and Madanipour, 2013; Bulley and Sokhi-Bulley, 2014). These discourses are understood as a veil behind which the powerful aim to foster greater self-reliance, responsibility and resilience among the poor and those who cost the state money. There is a related argument about planning that provides another footnote to the text in Chapter Five.

THREE

The place of the people

The history of the development of the British state has understandably left its mark on forms of citizenship and our expectations about democratic engagement (Almond and Verba, 1963; Whiteley, 2012). As outlined in the previous chapter, the legacy of centralisation has reduced the salience of local government and limited the incentive for popular engagement at the local scale. Centralisation has also meant that government can seem very remote: not only are local authority areas often very large, with key decisions being taken a long way away in the county or metropolitan centre, but the most important decisions are taken even further away, in the Parliament in Westminster. Although citizens are represented by local councillors and Members of Parliament, personal interaction is only likely in order to ask for help, to protest about something or to secure votes in the run-up to an election; there is little call to contribute on a more ongoing and positive basis.

This chapter further explores the implications of the prevailing geographical division of political power in England, and it moves on to look at questions of political practice. As suggested in Chapter One, localism is, in part, a 'top-down' response to a variety of concerns including the need to save money, a desire for more appropriate decision making and a perceived gap between the political elite and the people (Flinders, 2012; Mair, 2013; Chwalisz, 2015; Parker, 2015). In this regard, it is a contemporary manifestation of long-standing efforts to foster active citizenship, and there are important questions about the extent to which this will be a success.

As outlined in the previous chapter, the administration of local and national government always depended on an active minority taking up the cudgels of government in a voluntary role. Before the advent of the mass franchise, this expectation was placed upon the wealthier members of society who could afford to adopt the sentiment of noblesse oblige that was associated with the duties of wealth (Dorey and Garnett, 2012). In the era of the mass franchise, however, this tradition of political service was slowly reformed.[1] The old formulation that political representation and activity were associated with status and wealth was re-imagined through the twin processes of democratisation and professionalisation. After 1911, Members of Parliament were paid and the job was increasingly seen as full time (Pelling, 1967).[2] In this regard, the Labour Party was also particularly important in providing a route for more working-class people to take up political work that provided an income. The Party grew very rapidly, winning seats in local and national government such that it was able to challenge the Conservatives and Liberals for parliamentary power after the First and Second World Wars (Pelling, 1967; Savage, 2009).

During the 20th century politics became more professionalised and the national parties became ever more important in coordinating election manifestos, providing publicity, selecting candidates and generating support. This became true for local as well as national elections, eroding the sense of politics as an amateur sport. By the middle years of the century, the Labour and Conservative parties dominated national politics and secured almost all of the votes. The population became used to voting for one or other party and there was little experience or expectation of getting more involved at either local or national scales (Ashford, 1989; Katz and Mair, 1995; Mair, 2013).

Triggered by demands for greater democratisation that were set in train by the social movements of the 1960s, however, there has been a slow erosion of this model of representative democracy over the past 50 years. On the one hand, there is a sense that the mainstream political parties no longer represent the people and that the political class are no longer serving the public. Indeed, a visceral current of anti-politics is now widely expressed and if people do vote, they are more likely to choose populist options than ever before. On the other hand, however, there is also a popular feeling, at least among some groups of people, that they would like to get more involved in representing themselves (Smith, 2009; Chwalisz, 2015; Clarke, 2015).

It is in this context that localism has come to the fore. Capturing the desire for more meaningful forms of political representation as well as the potential for more direct engagement, localism potentially provides a stimulus for a new round of efforts – and institutional innovation – to engage the people in political life. Moreover, if it is to be successful, it will involve innovations in representative democracy as well as more direct engagement. In relation to the latter, localism builds on long-standing calls for what Conservative MP Douglas Hurd (1989) called 'active citizenship', but it also highlights the weaknesses in our existing political infrastructure and culture at the neighbourhood scale. It is not enough to call for greater engagement without thinking about why people might decide to engage, and the institutional arrangements that facilitate the kind of engagement that is productive for them. All too often, calls for public engagement are made on the terms laid down by the central state, and they produce very mediocre effects. Going beyond tokenism will require much greater effort to think about the creation of new neighbourhood-level structures and systems for representation that can operate on non-partisan lines.

This chapter draws upon a range of published research to explore how and why people might chose to engage in civic and political life, and the institutional mechanisms required to do so. While many state-funded organisations such as local authorities now regularly invite representatives from the local community to sit on local forums and user groups, these are often compromised by the power relations involved. It is very difficult for local people and even their community groups to effect major change when working as part of government-led initiatives. If, however, community groups retain their independence, they are better able to establish their own agenda, but they then need to develop the capacity to effect local change. Such capacity depends on the creation of non-partisan relationships across the diversity of residents living in an area such that they develop the ability to organise around a locally determined agenda and then secure the power to create local change. While some areas already have the residents who are able and willing to do this, the material presented in this chapter queries the extent to which it will prove possible in every location, suggesting that localism may further extend the uneven distribution of civic capacity in England today.

As such, it is particularly important to explore the potential for establishing new local institutions with the capacity to bridge the gap between the state and its citizens. As outlined in the previous chapter, parish government was closer to the people and, where they still exist, parishes could be better integrated into the wider processes of government. However, in addition, the new rights to neighbourhood planning established by the Localism Act (2011) have, perhaps inadvertently, created new lay representative bodies in hundreds of urban communities. Neighbourhood forums are developing in urban areas and, once planning is done, a number of these bodies are going on to explore a wider agenda (see also Chapter Five). With parallels to the 'permissive legislation' outlined in the previous chapter, the Localism Act (2011) has enabled local people who want to act over planning to take the initiative. Although they are still in their infancy, there is scope for thinking about these neighbourhood forums in terms of their wider potential contribution to community, civil society and democracy. Indeed, a flurry of interest in forming community councils in urban areas like Queen's Park in West London, as well as efforts to reinvigorate existing local councils, speaks to the growing importance of this level of government across England today (MacFadyen, 2014; NALC, 2015; see also Chapter Seven).

Towards the end of this chapter, I introduce a case study of one form of localist statecraft that clearly exposes the limits of our existing civic infrastructure in urban areas in England. Research into a Neighbourhood Community Budget that operated in East London between 2011 and 2013 exposed the extent to which the state-funded organisations in charge of the project lacked any means to engage with the local population beyond another round of consultation that had no effect on the decisions they made. Without an independent organisational structure that could facilitate its political voice and capacity, the local community had no place at the table to negotiate over the changes being made. As such, the example highlights the need to think about the creation of new institutional mechanisms and associated processes to enable the representation of the people at the neighbourhood scale. It also exposes the challenges of trying to realise localist statecraft by relying on state-funded organisations to lead the reform. As outlined in Chapter One, localism implies a new civic offer as well as having the civic capacity required to mount a response. In this example, the state-funded organisations tried to work in new ways but they had no community partner to help with this work. The project exposed the lack of community organisation and the absence of local representative structures and processes to bring local people to the table of government and political decision making on their own terms.

Public engagement in political life

Debates about the need to engage the citizenry in democracy have a very long pedigree going back to the experience of the Athenian polis (Dahl, 1989). However, whereas the polis relied on the direct engagement of all citizens, larger political communities have come to deploy various forms of representation in order to act for the people. As outlined above, the size of the political units, the calibre of the representatives and the culture of their parties, as well as popular faith in the electoral and representative process, will play a major part in determining the success of this system. In addition, however, going back to arguments first conducted between Aristotle and Plato more than 2,000 years ago, there is an ongoing normative argument about the proper place of the people in this form of representative democracy. For some, the place of the people is to choose the professional elite required to rule (Lippmann, 1925; Schattsneider, 1975 [1960]; Schumpeter, 1976 [1942]), while for others, democracy requires higher levels of popular engagement in order to secure better outcomes for all those involved (Dewey, 1954 [1927]; Pateman, 1970; Mansbridge, 1995). While the latter camp argue that democratic engagement provides the opportunity to learn civic skills as well as deepening the arts of good government, there are some who go as far as to suggest that democracy is incompatible with any form of representation. The self-organisation and self-government embodied in the democracy of the Athenian polis remains a beacon for this tradition of radical thought (Purcell, 2013).

In this regard, it is significant that the current focus on more participatory models of democracy actually emerged from outside the state, as a radical movement *against* mainstream politics during the 1960 and 1970s. As we saw in the last chapter, localist political experiments developed as a new generation of political activists grew increasingly frustrated with electoral democracy and began to argue that politics was about more than voting, paying your taxes and leaving decisions to an old-fashioned elite. In the spirit of the rising social movements that reflected a shifting consciousness among young people and women, as well as those marginalised on the basis of their race and/or sexuality, politics was recast as something open to all (Pateman, 1970; Mansbridge, 1983). These activists created new spaces (or what Evans and Boyte 1992 [1986] called 'free spaces') from which they created new sets of political demands, new organisational tactics and new cultures of political action. Self-help groups, workplace cooperatives and new social movements were all important during this period. Faced with the failures of mainstream democracy, a new generation demanded a more engaged form of democracy to be practised in a wider range of locations.

Over time, these ideas about the power of self-organisation and the potential of radical democratic politics found their way into more mainstream manifestations of political life and they started to shape government policy. As Boltanski and Chiapello (2007) suggest in relation to changing forms of economy, this was partly about a generation of political activists coming of age. The young people who cut their political teeth in the new grassroots organisations of the 1960s and 1970s subsequently took up positions in government during the 1980s and 1990s. The development of state-led race equality and feminist mainstreaming was particularly prominent in this regard, but these political experiences also provided a wider 'structure of feeling' that shaped the debate about democracy for a new generation. People were less deferential and more willing to challenge the establishment, and state-funded bodies had to respond (Finlayson, 2012; Newman, 2012; Flinders, 2012). In this context, politicians have tried to bridge the gap between the state and its citizens, seeking to find new ways of fostering increased rates of public participation in civic and political life. The challenge, however, is to find the ways in which such participation can be fostered to greatest effect for the *demos* as well as the *kratos*.

As early as 1969, Harold Wilson's Labour government agreed to adopt an experiment in community development that focused attention on 12 poor neighbourhoods in order to improve cooperation between service agencies, build local community and involve local people so as to bolster 'mutual help amongst the individuals, families and social groups in the neighbourhood' (Loney, 1983, 3). In what became the Community Development Programme, community development workers and action researchers were recruited to work in relatively poor areas, map out the physical and social resources of the area, open an office in order to reach local people and develop links with local organisations. Over time, they began to organise around issues of local concern, and, in a list that would be little different today, these included housing, employment and better service coordination around the needs of the people. In many areas, these emerging campaigns involved challenging the local authority and, in some areas, conflict increased. Weak central government management meant that the projects were largely autonomous and, in the spirit of the time, some of the community workers and researchers began to develop a more radical analysis of the problems facing these and other communities and to agitate for more radical change. Although these projects were passed to the control of local authorities during the mid-1970s, and many of them were subsequently shut down, the programme raised many of the issues revisited later during the New Labour years (1997–2010).

Indeed, 30 years later much of this policy programme was re-articulated in New Labour's efforts to engage citizens in community life. In contrast to the individualism associated with free-market Thatcherism and the sense of entitlement associated with social democracy and the welfare state, these governments argued for a new 'Third Way' (Giddens, 1994, 2001). Echoing the republican and communitarian arguments that were introduced in Chapter One, government sought to encourage citizens to develop a stronger sense of moral responsibility for the wider society. This was to involve active citizenship (voting, taking up public office, standing up to anti-social behaviour) as well as volunteering to support civil society organisations and charities. Alongside a new policy to teach citizenship in schools (Crick, 1998), policy attention focused on the work of local authorities. The White Paper *Modern Local Government: In touch with the people* (Department for Environment, Transport and Regions, 1998) set out an ambitious programme for local renewal that put a major focus on efforts to foster democratic renewal and increased levels of public participation in civic and political life (Jochum, no date; Rao, 2000; Stewart, 2000; Lowndes et al, 2001; Wilks-Heeg, 2009; Andrews et al, 2011). As the government put it, it wanted to see 'consultation and participation embedded in to the culture of all councils … and undertaken across a wide range of councils' responsibilities' (in Lowndes et al, 2001, 205). Local authorities were encouraged to experiment with a range of new tools to engage residents and service users, including citizens' juries, focus groups, neighbourhood committees and referenda (Pacione, 1988; Wilson, 1999; Barnes et al, 2003; Barnes et al, 2007; Copus, 2010; Copus and Sweeting, 2012). The idea was to encourage local authorities to provide new experiences to citizens and to foster a 'habit of citizenship' (Pratchett and Wilson, 1996, 241). In addition, the government channelled money and authority directly to community groups in order to further activate local capacity and foster an appetite for local engagement.

The government's Community Empowerment Programme that accompanied the National Strategy for Neighbourhood Renewal launched in 2001 was particularly important in this regard. Part of the programme of work, developed by the Social Exclusion Unit, was to use local regeneration activity as a means to develop the leadership of local people and strengthen local community groups. Each of the 39 regeneration areas had to establish a community empowerment network – led by the voluntary and community sector – that was government funded to provide grants to assist local groups (Houghton and Blume, 2011). Overall, the regeneration programme involved nearly £2 billion of expenditure in 39 areas between 1999 and 2008 and there was great potential to bolster local civil society (Coats et al, 2012, 64). However, over time, and just as had happened in relation to the Community Development Programme in the 1970s, the national government started to rely more heavily on local authorities to manage this work. The tensions between participatory and representative democracy became increasingly evident and, whereas the community representatives could claim to represent local people through the strength of their relationships (even if they didn't live in the area themselves), local authorities were able to use the mantle of electoral legitimacy to assert political control (and for earlier arguments that anticipated this tension, see Gyford, 1976). Decision making tended to rest with the local authorities, and the community-level investment and independent organisation were insufficient to reconfigure the local balance of power (Wright et al, 2006; Barnes et al, 2007).

McKenna (2011) points out that local authorities – backed by national governments – have advocated greater public participation and civic engagement for at least 40 years, but there is little sign that it has fostered major behaviour change or increased rates of engagement (see also Wilson, 1999; Rao, 2000). Local authorities may have a better idea about the concerns of local people and even make better decisions as a result (Lowndes et al, 2006), but it is still the councillors who make decisions on behalf of the people (Copus, 2010; Copus and Sweeting, 2012). Political power is not necessarily shared. Indeed, civic culture and democracy are more likely to be strengthened by the development of independent organisations as well as oppositional political parties and social movements that can challenge the council's decisions. If the local civic and political culture were more adversarial, such that the community had a chance to challenge the council, this would have the potential to secure greater change while also providing opportunities for people to learn from experience, increasing the store of civic capacity within the locale.

In their overview of 17 different examples of participation projects in the public sector in two English cities, Barnes and her co-authors (2007) found that, all too often, public sector bodies paid lip-service to participation and complied because they had to. At best, they used the new forums and initiatives as a space to talk and share information rather than as a platform for significant change. As the researchers suggest, 'initiatives that start out with good intentions – the "empowerment" of new social actors, the inclusion of new voices in the shaping of policy, or a shift in power relationships between public bodies and the public they serve – often end up as a process in which participants become captured in governmental fields of power' (Barnes et al, 2007, 185). While the civic offer being made to citizens and the degree to which the community was already organised and able to respond did vary between these projects, the research highlighted a strong institutional resistance to radical change. When the partner group was independent, autonomous and created through a challenge to the status quo that meant they 'had their roots in social movements, community activism and service user struggles' (Barnes et al, 2007, 204), these encounters were much more productive for the community, albeit that these were exceptional cases. In the main, the research highlighted the paradox of government efforts to foster increased rates of participation: the state recognised the need to strengthen social capital and foster civic engagement but remained hostile to the social movements, political activity and independence on which such outcomes depend.

As such, this research exposed the inevitable limits to these state-led efforts at increasing participation and boosting civic life. Without the independent organisation needed to develop a collective voice, agenda and capacity, political power relations tend to be skewed against civil society. While local authorities have involved the public in their communication strategies, these efforts generally do not shift the wider civic culture and patterns of citizenship as much as is desired. Indeed, in the terms of Sheryl Arnstein's (1969) well-known 'ladder of civic participation', New Labour's policy interventions moved the state from very little engagement towards the middle of the ladder as organisations extended an invitation to some community representatives to participate in various boards and forums, but there was little willingness to enact the shift in power relations that is required to reach the top of the steps with what she refers to as 'citizen power'.

The state-led participation efforts that were developed during the New Labour years even had costs for the communities that tried to engage. In her research on similar developments in Australia, Eversole (2011) found that engagement was always on the government's terms and the community's existing work was ignored; that it cost the community in terms of volunteer and staff time and energy; and it even increased social disadvantage, as those easiest to engage tended to be put to the front of the queue. Echoing Scott's (1998) arguments about the dangers of a well-intentioned state, she argues that 'government's well-meaning efforts at engaging communities may threaten existing local community systems by replacing often functional community forms of governance with less functional or more costly bureaucratic ones' (Eversole, 2011, 64; see also Adamson and Bromiley, 2013).[3]

Data collected during the New Labour years actually indicates something of a decline in rates of civic participation, despite government efforts to get us engaged. As indicated in Figure 3.1, data from the Citizenship Survey collected between 2001 and 2009–10 shows a slight decline in the percentage of respondents who took part in civic engagement of various kinds. Moreover, although as many as a third of respondents took part in consultation activities, this rate fell to 1 in 10 of respondents when it came to taking up some sort of official position (as a magistrate or school governor).

More generally, data about political participation at the national scale shows a decline in almost all forms of political and civic activity, including voting, contacting a politician or public official and signing a petition (Whiteley, 2012, 39; and for data collected between 1984 and

Figure 3.1: Participation in civic engagement activities, 2001–2009/10

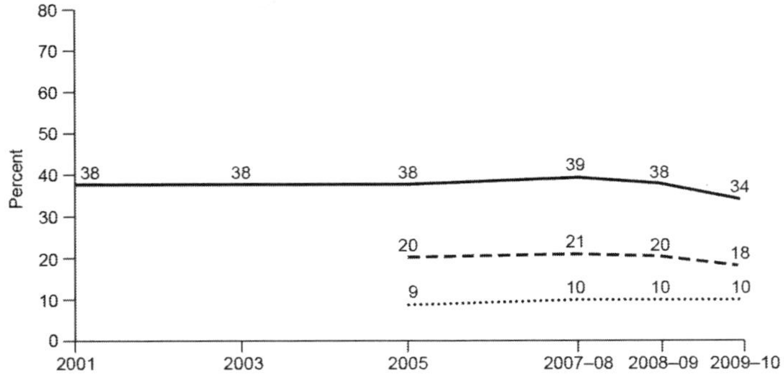

Base: Core sample in England, (2001: 9,430, 2003: 8,920, 2005: 9,195, 2007–08: 8,804, 2008–09: 8,768, 2009–10: 8,712)

············ **Civic Activism**
This includes involvement in decision-making about local services or in the provision of these services (for example, being a school governor or a magistrate).

– – – – **Civic Participation**
This includes engagement in democratic processes, such as contacting an elected representative or attending a public demonstration.

───── **Civic Consultation**
This includes taking part in consultations about local services such as completing questionnaires, attending public meetings or being involved in discussion groups.

Source: Rutherfoord (2011, 26 and 25)

2002, see Figure 3.2).[4] Rates of engagement fell in all categories except more market-oriented pursuits such as boycotting goods and spending money for ethical ends. This rise of market-oriented activism has been documented in more detail in other accounts and it chimes with the increased consumer orientation of everyday life, but it is generally not well connected to more traditional forms of citizenship and civic organisation (Norris, 2002; Barnett et al, 2010; Michelletti, 2010).

In addition, data that explicitly explores feelings about civic engagement shows significant declines in both perceived influence and aspirations to shape local political life (Figures 3.3 and 3.4). Indeed, despite the priority afforded to the decentralisation of political power as outlined in the Coalition government agreement in 2010, introduced in Chapter One, just 20% of respondents perceived themselves to have some influence over local decision making in 2015 (a fall from 25% in the last days of the New Labour government in 2009). Although these

Figure 3.2: Changes in political activity, 1984–2002

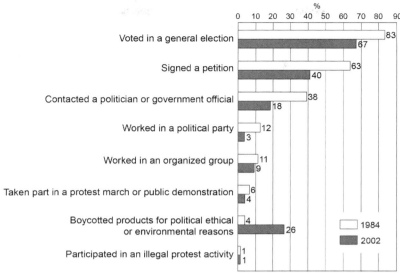

Source: Whitely (2012, 39)

surveys do indicate a significant latent desire to engage that reached almost half the population in 2009, this rate had also fallen from 48% to 38% by 2015.

In this regard, it is useful to explore what we know about the people who *do* engage in civic and political activities. In their research into levels of civic engagement, John Mohan and his colleagues in the Third Sector Research Centre have used the idea of a 'civic core' to map the proportion of citizens involved in different types of activity and the hours that individuals contribute to the work that is done. Using data from the Citizenship Survey they focused on the hours of unpaid help given to organisations, the donations given to charity in the previous four weeks and the number of civil society organisations to which people belonged (Mohan, 2011; 2012). While only 15% of the population were found to do nothing, they also found that 30% of the population provided 90% of the hours, 80% of the money and 70% of the participation involved (Mohan, 2012, 1123).

As might be expected, this group was not typical of the population as a whole. They were more likely to be older, wealthier, better-educated, longer-term residents with religious beliefs (Mohan, 2011, 9). Echoing the history outlined in the previous chapter, civic life has often depended upon exactly these kinds of people. Those with higher levels of income and greater security, and those who have experience of membership in civil society organisations, are more likely to have

Figure 3.3: Perceived influence over decision making, 2009 and 2015

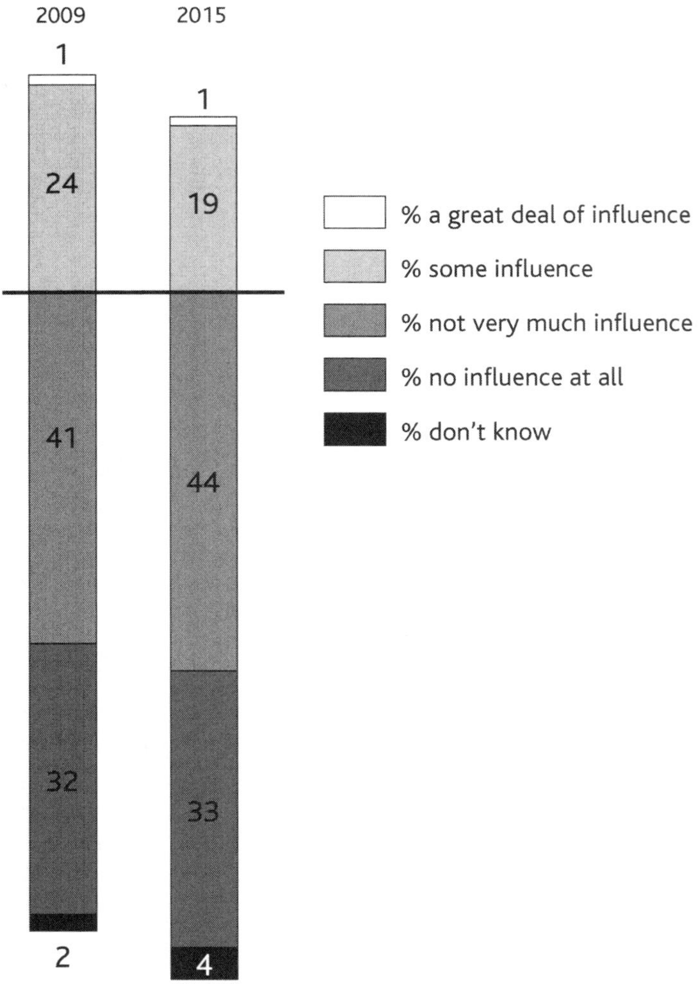

2009   2015

1

24

1

19

41

44

32

33

2   4

☐ % a great deal of influence

▢ % some influence

▢ % not very much influence

▢ % no influence at all

■ % don't know

Source: Audit of Political Engagement (2009; 2015); *Hansard*, Audit 12 (2015, Figure 36, p 36)

the skills and interests needed to readily engage in civic and political life. Such people are unevenly distributed across the country and these patterns are further reinforced by the distribution of local organisations. In his analysis of the distribution of organisations working at the scale of the neighbourhood, Clifford (2012) found an inverse relationship between the number of organisations, their financial independence from the state and the socioeconomic status of the area. As illustrated in

Figure 3.4: Desire for engagement locally, 2009 and 2015

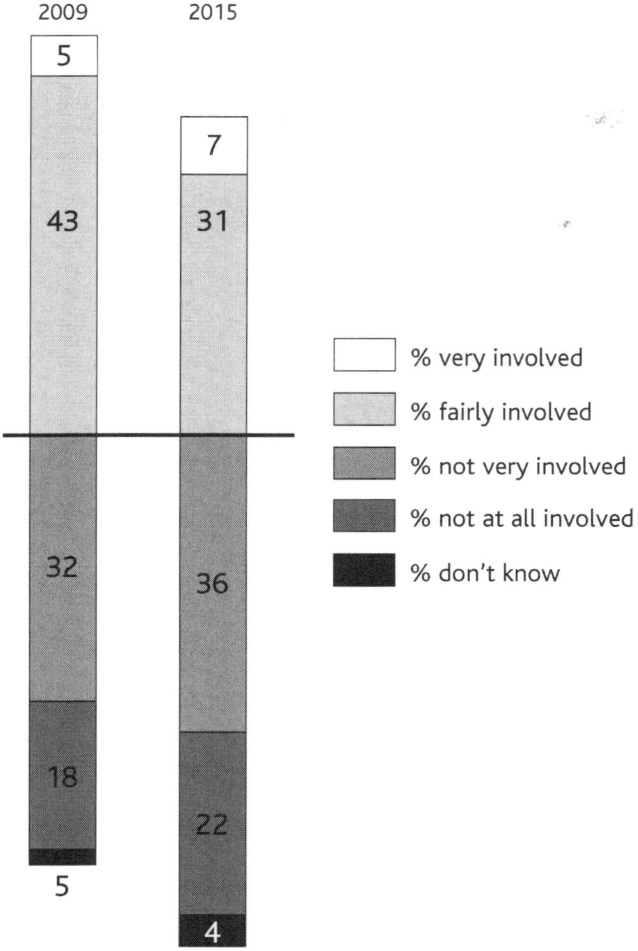

2009   2015

5

7

43   31

% very involved

% fairly involved

% not very involved

% not at all involved

% don't know

32   36

18

22

5

4

Source: Audit of Political Engagement (2009; 2015); *Hansard*, Audit 12 (2015, Figure 40, p 48)

Figure 3.5, there were fewer organisations focusing on local activities in poorer areas than in richer ones, and the former were more dependent than the latter upon public funds for their work. As he suggests, such patterns of civic and organisational activity reflect processes of demographic sorting associated with housing markets and the related distribution of amenities. While there is evidence of high rates of informal social interaction in poorer areas (Williams, 2003),[5] this is not likely to be sufficient to develop the civic capacity to engage in localist statecraft and citizenship (Hays, 2015). Indeed, history would suggest that it will require the creation of new institutions and greater efforts to organise people in order to foster higher levels of civic engagement in poorer parts of the country (and for international arguments to this effect, see also Jun and Musso, 2013).

Figure 3.5: The number of community and voluntary sector organisations working at the neighbourhood scale, by the socio-economic deprivation of the area and funding sources

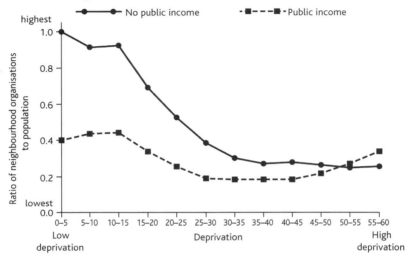

Note: The vertical axis shows the ratio of charitable organisations operating at the neighbourhood scale in relation to population, standardised to 1 for the highest ratio. This ratio is mapped in relation to the Index of Multiple Deprivation (IMD) for the area on the horizontal axis.

Source: Mohan (2011, 7)

In this regard, it is highly significant that membership of political parties, trade unions and religious organisations has fallen very sharply in recent years (see Tables 3.1 and 3.2). These organisations often provided a direct route for less advantaged people to engage in self-organisation, to develop leadership and organisational skills, and to enter political life (Oldfield, 1990; Parry et al, 1992). Although there is some dispute about the extent of decline in social capital, and the degree to which ongoing changes simply reflect the shifting education and class structure of the wider society (Hall, 1999), there is no doubt about the decline of faith and labour organisations, and the impact this has on the opportunities for civic engagement.

The civil society organisations that used to be particularly important in connecting working-class people to political life have suffered dramatic decline, and localism raises the question of intervening in order to strengthen the capacity that exists on the ground. While permissive legislation has opened up a space for those who are able and willing to act, the data presented in this chapter raises the question about what is to be done where existing organisation and capacity remains too weak to respond in a significant way. This is particularly important when the very rationale for localism is based on improving the quality of decision making and service delivery, as well as increasing democratic engagement. Without intervention, the areas that most need improvements and political voice are least likely to be able to mount a response.

Table 3.1: Membership of civil society organisations, as a proportion of the people living in Britain, 1981–99

	1981 (%)	1990 (%)	1999 (%)
Welfare service for the elderly	8.6	7.1	6.8
Religious organisation	21	16.6	4.8
Arts, music, cultural organisation	8	9.3	10.4
Trade union	19.9	14.4	7.3
Political party	4.7	4.9	2.6
Human rights group	1.5	2	2.6
Youth work organisation	7.6	4.6	5.5
Local political action group	-	2.7	3.5
Conservation, environmental group	-	5	1.5
Sports or recreation group	-	16.9	3
Women's group	-	4.8	1.5
Peace movement	-	1.1	0.5
Health organisation	-	3.5	3.3

Source: Whiteley (2012, 84) (using World Values Surveys data (www.worldvaluessurvey.org/)

Table 3.2: Membership of the Labour and Conservative parties 1964–2010

	1964	1997	2010	Change over 36 years
Conservative	2,150,000	400,000	177,000	Decline 1,973,000
Labour	830,000	400,000	193,961	Decline 636,039

Source: Whiteley (2012, 63), and published records for 2010

Localist institution building for political voice and civic engagement

As intimated above, the existing evidence about efforts to foster greater civic and political engagement is not wholly positive for the future of localism. While governments have sought to encourage greater levels of civic engagement, rates of engagement have actually dropped and there can be little certainty that efforts to support localism will fare any better. Indeed, as Rowson and colleagues (2012, 9) suggest, 'the idea that the population has what it takes to participate in the requisite ways is based largely on wishful thinking rather than evidence'. In their analysis of the challenges in creating the Big Society, Rowson and colleagues argue that widespread civic engagement would require as-yet unwitnessed levels of autonomy, responsibility and solidarity in the population at large. Drawing on the literature about human development, they argue that the 'hidden curriculum' of the Big Society demands relatively 'high-level' psychological characteristics in relatively large numbers of people: 'The behavioural injunctions of the Big Society agenda: "do it yourself", "cooperate", "participate", "take responsibility for society bigger than yourself" do not sound unreasonable, but they ask a lot of our ability to distance ourselves from our social conditioning and our emotional reactions' (Rowson et al, 2012, 32). While the desire to create the Big Society as part of a localist policy agenda might provide the impetus to provide a project of adult education in order to foster these skills, it is not clear how this might happen in practice.

One obvious solution to this conundrum is for politicians to moderate their expectations: they should expect less of the citizenry (just as the citizenry need to expect less of them, see Flinders, 2012). One option is to re-embrace the idea that politics is necessarily a professional activity and a minority interest, and to recognise that effort is better spent on improving the way that the elite do their business. Indeed, liberalism developed as a political platform to liberate citizens from the duties and obligations of community duty and service and, as outlined in relation to the published research, there is little sign of a majority desire to engage (Oldfield, 1990). Moreover, while citizens are disillusioned with their politicians, they are probably more likely to look for an alternative group to support – such as the United Kingdom Independence Party (UKIP), for example – than they are to want to engage directly themselves. In this regard, energy can be usefully spent in developing democratic innovations to improve the functioning of more traditional forms of representation as well as trying to foster more active forms of citizenship and political engagement on a much wider scale. Possible ideas include Fishkin's (1991) support for the deliberative opinion poll, Susstein's (2001) suggestions regarding new technology and Goodin's (2003) advocacy of reflective deliberation (and for a wider range of innovations see Smith, 2009 and Chwalisz, 2015).

However, political philosophers and scientists have long considered how to engage the citizenry in larger-scale, necessarily representative, forms of democracy and the idea of protecting smaller units for local representation has always formed part of the suggested solutions (Mill, 1890 [1861]). In their overview of the debate over the scalar architecture of democratic institution building, Dahl and Tufte (1974, 135) echoed the arguments made by J.S. Mill more than a hundred years earlier, to suggest that 'very small unions seem to us necessary to provide a place where ordinary people can acquire the sense and reality of moral responsibility and political effectiveness in a universe where remote galaxies of leaders spin on in courses mysterious and unfathomable to the ordinary citizen' (Dahl and Tufte, 1974, 140). Such arguments are even more pertinent today and yet, as we have seen in relation to civil society organisations and forms of political participation, it appears that fewer people may be engaging at the local scale than was the case in the past.

In this regard, a new generation of civil republican and communitarian thinkers have advocated support for the creation of new neighbourhood-based institutions and practices that can support the kind of everyday citizenship that provides opportunities for learning new skills (Barber, 2003 [1984]; Sandel, 1996; Sirianni and Friedland, 2001; Boyte, 2004; Saegert, 2006). Such institution building might include explicitly political institutions that are designed to connect citizens to the democratic process – what Barber (2003 [1984] refers to as the infrastructure for 'strong democracy' – as well as the broader range of civil society organisations that facilitate the creation of the social capital that, in turn, promotes the social values and practices upon which democracy has come to depend (Sampson, 2012). Indeed, as Robert Putnam (2000, 401; see also Putnam et al, 2003) puts it at the end of his influential book *Bowling Alone*, 'My message is that we desperately need an era of civic inventiveness to create a renewed set of institutions and channels for a reinvigorated civic life that will fit the way we have come to live. Our challenge now is to reinvent the twenty first century equivalents of the Boy Scouts or the settlement house of the playground or the Hadassah or the United Mine Workers or the National Association for the Advancement for Colored People (NAACP).' Such civic inventiveness will necessarily come from the grassroots, but it is argued that government can help to create the environment in which such experimentation is encouraged and nurtured, and it can facilitate an opening up of the local state to improve the civic offer that it makes to the people.

Putnam's arguments highlight the role to be played by civil society organisations in strengthening the foundations for democracy, even if they ostensibly have very little to do with political life. In his research in Italy, he pointed to the importance of local organisations' fostering of the skills, social relationships and civic culture that then underpinned the development of a successful political infrastructure at a regional scale (Putnam, 1993).[6] This analysis is further endorsed by research in Chicago, where Sampson (2012) has found similar relationships operating at a much smaller scale. He argues that the 'mundane' everyday activity organised by local organisations such as tenants' groups, afterschool clubs, neighbourhood watch groups and community forums shapes the dynamic of local community life and contributes to lasting differences in neighbourhood character and collective efficacy. By shaping social expectations about behaviour, creating a sense of social control and raising levels of trust and social cohesion, local activity can impact on civic behaviour. As Sampson (2012, 358) explains, the differential distribution of organisations and their civic effects means that 'neighbourhood contexts are socially productive – important determinants of the quality and quantity of human behaviour in their own right' (Sampson, 2012, 358). Indeed, his data to map the density of neighbourhood organisations and the incidence of collective civic activity highlights a clear, and path-dependent, relationship between organisations and action (Figure 3.6). This body of research demonstrates that geography shapes opportunities for civic engagement because the number and activity of local organisations vary significantly between areas and, over time, this has path-dependent effects on informal networks, attitudes and capacity (see also Hays, 2015). For Sampson, these neighbourhood effects are actually more important than individual-level characteristics (such as ethnicity, class, gender or age) in determining civic activity rates.

While these scholars advocate the creation of civil society organisations that can underpin the development of local democracy, there are others who advocate the creation of a new layer of explicitly political institutions in order to foster higher levels of civic engagement. As outlined in the previous chapter, a group of activists used the opportunity posed by the Redcliffe-Maud Royal Commission on Local Government, held between 1966 and 1969, to advocate the creation of community councils in urban areas in England (Baker and

Young, 1971; and similar bodies already exist in Scotland, see Raco and Flint, 2001). In similar vein, Benjamin Barber's (2003 [1984]) call for the creation of 'strong democracy' would involve the creation of a range of new political institutions, prime among which was to be the 'neighbourhood assembly'. Barber envisaged this as a new representative body that would cover up to 5,000 people and facilitate deliberation in open meetings as well as ensuring the accountability of elected representatives, much as has been practised in some states in the north-east of the US for hundreds of years (Macpherson, 1977; Mansbridge, 1983). Other ideas included national citizen service, additional civic education, the use of referenda, the deployment of new technology and increased amateur involvement in political life. While this programme is

Figure 3.6: Organisational density and civic activity in Chicago's neighbourhoods, 1990–2000

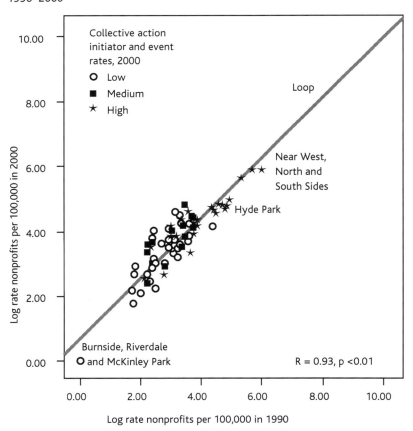

Source: Sampson (2012, 197). This graph shows the long-term geographical stability of non-profit organisations (from 1990–2000) by density of organisations and collective civic engagement.

much more ambitious than that being advanced as part of the localism agenda, it raises important issues about the importance of creating local political institutions through which people can engage in decision making to effect major change.

In this regard, efforts to develop localism in England now need to focus more attention on the work of the neighbourhood-level organisations and capacity that are so important in shaping opportunities and capacities for local engagement (Ware, 2012). In his overview of 'the next form of democracy', in which 'expert rule' is replaced by 'shared governance' in the US, Leighninger (2006) found that temporary pan-community organising efforts and more permanent neighbourhood structures were the most effective way to secure non-partisan community engagement and develop sustainable relationships allowing 'public officials [to] bring politics to the people, … and people [to] take active roles in problem-solving' (Leighninger, 2006, 22). Left to their own devices, local people will generally mobilise against change when their existing interests are threatened, and only a very small minority will be willing to take part in the more proactive structures set up by the state. Thus, without more careful thought about the infrastructure required to support localism, this status quo will prevail. For Leighninger (2006, 47), experience indicates that 'if you want to succeed, you can't just involve citizens in ways that supplement the political process – you have to construct *new avenues* where citizens are at the centre of the system' (emphasis added). This takes us back to the arguments raised by Putnam, Sampson and Barber: local institutions and their cultural effects matter a great deal in shaping civic engagement and the possibilities of localism.

However, the pattern of community and civil society infrastructure – and related neighbourhood effects – is bound to be uneven across any country and within any jurisdiction. This means that the existing – and latent – civic capacity of neighbourhoods will vary greatly from one place to another. In England, the data suggests that there is less organisational infrastructure and capacity in poorer areas, and that what there is depends more heavily on the state. However, while 'liberal localism' is bound to reveal such geographical variations, because those who are more able and willing will be the first to seize new opportunities, it also raises new questions about the lack of civic capacity in some parts of the country. To be effective, localism will demand investment in efforts to identify talent, develop leadership and organise civic capacity in those places where it is not yet possible to organise a response.

Experience during the New Labour years points to the dangers of relying on the state to lead the work of civic engagement. If people are to engage, they need to have a reason to do so, and a belief that it will have a positive effect. This perceived effectivity is critical in driving any decision to get more involved, and all too often citizens rightly judge that the civic offer being made fails to give them the necessary power to effect any change. As Arnstein (1969, 216) suggests, 'participation of the governed in government is a cornerstone of democracy ... [but] participation without redistribution of power is an empty and frustrating process'. The people employed by various arms of the state are often reluctant to share power with the people, and the desire for engagement is all too easily reduced to processes of information sharing and consultation, rather than a more radical redistribution of the power to act. In this regard, civic engagement will need to be rooted in bodies that are non-partisan and largely independent of the state, with a genuine capacity for getting things done. This is demonstrated very clearly in the original research findings reported in more detail below and in the rest of this book.

State-led localism and the missing community

In this final part of the chapter I highlight the importance of local organisation and civic capacity through a case study of one of the first initiatives developed in the arsenal of localist statecraft: the Neighbourhood Community Budget (NCB). In brief, the NCB involves efforts to pool funding from different organisations working within a locality in order to develop improved working relationships between agencies, generate better service outcomes for local people and find more efficient ways of delivering services. The idea is that joined-up working across public services can be more effective and efficient by providing a closer focus on the needs, interests and ideas of particular communities. Rather than engaging clients or customers in relation to their separate concerns as tenants, patients, students or residents, or via different 'siloed' government agencies (such as housing, health, education and the job centre), the idea is to approach the community as a whole. In so doing, in the spirit of localism, state-funded organisations are charged to work more closely with the local community in identifying shared problems and creative solutions that can be realised through working together. This is about the national government making a civic offer to the local state to take a different approach by working together and including local citizens in the work that is done.

The initiative has strong resonances with the Community Development Projects that were launched in 1970 but, in this instalment, the programme was first launched as Whole Place by the New Labour administration in 2009. At that time, the projects were exclusively focused on local authorities, encouraging them to bring together some of the different organisations working in their geographical area in order to focus on particular community problems. The initiative was subsequently re-branded and re-launched as a pilot programme by the Coalition government in 2011 and what were known as NCBs were then further developed and rolled out as a national programme called Our Place! (from 2013). This initiative was primarily targeted at state-funded organisations and, although it is 'permissive' in the sense that organisations have to bid for funding to create them, the NCB pilots were shaped by the DCLG with a clear set of expected outcomes that they were designed to achieve.

This rest of this chapter looks at one NCB pilot in Poplar, East London that ran between 2011 and 2013 and although this pilot failed to satisfy the goals it was expected to meet, it highlighted some very important lessons about localism. First, it exposed the extent to which the local community lacked the civic infrastructure to provide the means to engage in any meaningful way. Second, and relatedly, it exposed the extent to which the state-funded organisations retreated to the use of basic community consultation activity in the absence of a strong community voice. Indeed, without any local pan-community organisation to represent them, local people had no means to shape the agenda and the state-funded partners had no imperative to do anything other than what they were already planning to do. In the absence of the organised community, the partners paid lip-service to the requirement for consultation and then pursed projects that they already planned to achieve. The case highlights the extent to which the money (some £100,000) would have been better spent on developing the neighbourhood-level organisation that could have facilitated local people having a seat at the table of decision making in this and future endeavours.

While Poplar has a range of local civil society organisations that could have been brought together to form an alliance, these groups could have also included local residents who had an interest in getting involved, and this emerging body could have then developed an agenda for change in the area. The Poplar case exposes the danger that 'working with the community' is interpreted to mean another round of consultation, led by professionals and their existing priorities, despite the fact that many communities are already over-consulted without having the power to act. The example helps to put the issue of community organisation and local civic infrastructure at the centre of the challenge of localism and I go on to explore different models of community-level infrastructure in the rest of this book.

Whole Place, Neighbourhood Community Budgets and Our Place!

In the prospectus calling for the development of Whole Place and Neighbourhood Community Budgets in October 2011, the Secretary of State for Communities, Eric Pickles MP, argued that NCBs provide the means to promote the decentralisation of service provision and planning, saying: 'Control from Whitehall has created uncoordinated, inefficient and unnecessarily expensive public service silos, with professionals constrained in how they deliver better services for their communities' (DCLG, 2011b, 4). The prospectus signalled that NCBs were to champion new ways of planning and delivering public services to be more responsive to the needs and ideas of service providers, their clients and the local community:

> At the heart of a Community Budget is a new freedom: freedom for all public service providers to come together to design solutions; freedom for local partners to tell Government how things can be done differently with a presumption that Government will listen and then respond positively when it can; freedom to use resources flexibly to support service redesign; and, freedom to give communities and people influence and control over services. A successful CB replaces complexity, duplication, waste and gaps in service provision with demonstrably effective interventions, coordinated service provision which prevents as much as it tackles problems, a more efficient use of resources and increased influence and control for people. (DCLG, 2011b, 10)

In response, as many as 46 expressions of interest were submitted to DCLG in December 2011 and 12 were selected – and funded – for further development. Those selected ranged in population size from 6,849 to 25,000 residents and were spread across England, often in rather 'unexpected' locations such as Haverhill in Suffolk, Sherwood in Tunbridge Wells and Ilfracombe in Devon (Figure 3.7). The funding ranged from £30,200 to £122,000. Half were led by local authorities, two by town or parish councils and the remainder by third sector organisations (Rutherfoord et al, 2013).

Figure 3.7: The pilot Neighbourhood Community Budget areas

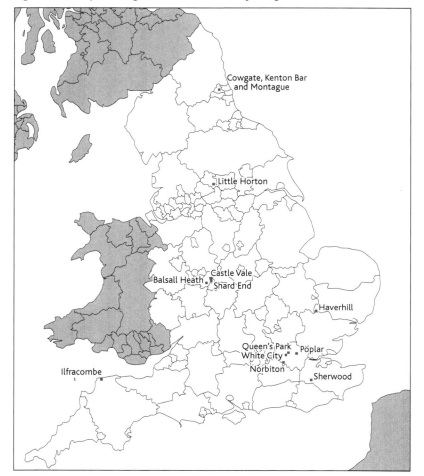

In accordance with the time frame set out by DCLG, the 12 NCB pilot areas were launched in December 2011 and they had to produce a draft plan by March 2012, being ready to submit and implement a final Operational Plan by April 2013. The final Operational Plan had to detail the NCB (pooled) budget, the potential outcomes to be delivered through the NCB, and any fiscal benefits (that is, overall savings compared to government expenditure), economic benefits (increases in income through direct gains or savings to individuals and companies) and non-economic benefits (any social benefits to individuals and society, perhaps in terms of health, community cohesion or other social gains) of the NCB.

These pilots were to test two primary government objectives: (1) How control of services and the budgets to run them can be pushed down below the statutory sector level to communities and neighbourhoods; and (2) How an NCB comprising all spending on local public services might be developed and implemented (DCLG, 2011a, 11). Importantly, the pilots were also designed to find ways to give local public service partners the freedom to work together to redesign, and co-design, services around the needs of the community, hoping to improve outcomes, reduce duplication and waste and, thereby, save significant sums of public money.

As such, the pilot NCBs were tasked with experimenting with deeper forms of community engagement to the point of co-design, co-production, co-commissioning and co-management of services (and for the wider field see Boyle et al, 2010; Durose, 2013) while also pooling existing budgets in order to develop more integrated, streamlined and appropriate services, with the expectation of improving the consumer experience and saving money. Of course, both objectives demanded major changes in public service provision and culture, and required that state-funded organisations should be willing and able to respond as requested, working more closely with the community. Both objectives proved very challenging in the Poplar example, as is outlined further below.

The Poplar NCB

The Poplar NCB pilot covered the wards of Mile End East and Bromley by Bow (previously known as Local Area Partnership 6 (LAP 6)), which in 2010 were the 21st and 9th most deprived of 628 wards in London (Figure 3.8). The area is home to a population of some 25,000, half of whom were younger than 30 years old at the time of the project. The area has the highest proportion of people in social housing and the highest rate of out-of-work benefit claims in Tower Hamlets, a life expectancy for men that is three years less than the national average and a very high proportion of residents of Bengali origin (PNCB, 2011). The bid to be a pilot NCB involved five local partner organisations: Poplar HARCA (the lead accountable body and the largest Housing Association in the area); the Bromley by Bow Centre (a pioneering health and community centre); St Paul's Way Trust School; the GP Network (involving five practices in the area); and Andrew Mawson

Partnerships (a consultancy led by Lord Andrew Mawson, founder of the Bromley by Bow Centre).

These partners had prior relationships and were keen to use the NCB as a way to further strengthen their work. The bid document included a number of potential areas for policy focus, including health, child poverty, domestic violence, debt and social isolation. Once the pilot bid was approved, the lead partner, Poplar HARCA, took the initiative to appoint a consultant, and subsequently a manager, to facilitate relationship building, planning and commissioning. Following the practical formulas laid down by DCLG required that the NCB should

Figure 3.8: The Poplar Neighbourhood Community Budget area

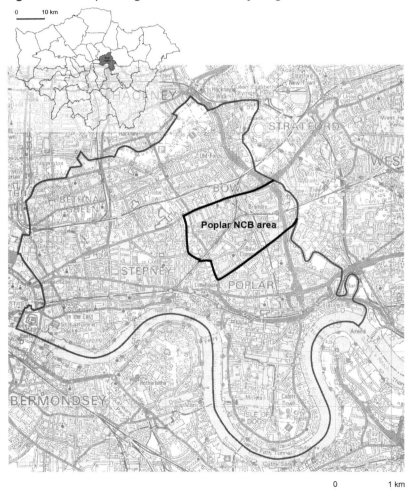

map public spending in the area; develop a plan for further activity, which was subject to a cost-benefit analysis; outline a governance structure for the new project; and ensure ongoing evaluation and measurement of impact.[7] Given the time-scales involved (and the need to develop a final Operational Plan by April 2013), the project consultant and project manager had to spend a considerable amount of time meeting the demands of DCLG and/or commissioning other bodies to deliver parts of the project.

The key milestones of the project are outlined in Table 3.3. These involved early recognition that the project required leadership from a full-time project manager as well as commissioning a consultancy to do the community engagement work, an expert who could map public spending in the area, a legal firm who could advise on governance and an accountant who could conduct a cost-benefit analysis of the proposed new project. The development of the NCB thus required considerable additional resources over and above those normally spent by the partners, and DCLG provided £104,624 for the cost of this work.

Pooling budgets

In the initial stages, PNCB had to map the amount of public spending reaching the 25,000 people living in the two wards. Having found the necessary data hard to access, due to their lack of a local authority partner, the team appointed a specialist analyst who used figures for the average per capita public sector spend in the UK for 2010–11 and applied this to the local population. Given that the two wards actually have a relatively young population, very high levels of worklessness, high housing need and additional health problems, these figures are likely to have been a very conservative under-estimate of the money spent in the area. However, using public spending rates of £10,165.50 per head in the country at large, those living in the PNCB area were estimated to be in receipt of an aggregated amount of at least £245 million in 2010–11.

The idea behind spend-mapping is that a neighbourhood team will better understand the scale of resources coming to an area from a range of sources and then identify ways of better spending the money through pooling resources. However, in Poplar, the housing association, school and GP partners argued that they controlled relatively low amounts of the existing public resources and, given that they were already expected to provide statutory services and meet local demands, it was very difficult to find ways to release additional funds. Furthermore,

Table 3.3: Key milestones in the development of the Poplar NCB

Date	Events
December 2011	Submit the bid and secure funding as one of 12 pilots.
January–March 2012	Preliminary scoping by staff at Poplar HARCA in order to submit a Project Delivery Plan to DCLG.
March–June 2012	Appointment of a project consultant to develop the plan.
April 2012	Appointment of full-time programme manager from within Poplar HARCA's staff. Partners' planning away-day to explore issues; present spend-mapping data.
May 2012	Partners' meeting with consultants to explore community consultation activity.
June–July 2012	Community consultation with 1,170 people.
July 2012	Partners' planning day, report-back from community consultation, debate over budgets and issues.
August 2012	Community consultation consultants present final report.
September 2012	Partner meeting to further develop the plan and develop a focus on health. Draft Operational Plan subsequently submitted to DCLG.
October 2012	Government minister visits PNCB and DCLG provides peer challenge responses.
January 2013	Additional partner meeting to confirm plan for diabetes project and its wider implications, with debate about the scope for community engagement.
March 2013	PNCB holds workshops to explore the 'Healthy Poplar Project' (incorporating the diabetes work) involving 64 people in organised groups.

the absence of high-spending bodies such as the local authority (the London Borough of Tower Hamlets), the Department for Work and Pensions (controlling benefit payments and job centres) and the police made it even more difficult to pool budgets across the 'silos' through which money is spent and decisions are made.

The PNCB thus failed to pool any budgets – even those of the partners themselves. Indeed, both the initial project work and the final project proposal required additional money from DCLG. As one of the respondents from the Bromley by Bow Centre put it succinctly, 'The label on the tin is about trying to get hold of long-term, mainstream, statutory budgets and getting them handed down to local communities for local ownership, control, management, whatever. This pilot budget has singularly failed to achieve that. We haven't got a penny off anybody.'

As might be expected, the PNCB demonstrated that there was no appetite from local publicly funded organisations to relinquish their funds, and the partners had no mandate to make this occur. The project would have required a much more comprehensive engagement from all state-funded organisations in the area, and the leadership of the local authority, to make this more likely to happen. Even then, experience elsewhere is mixed and local councils rarely have the authority they would need to negotiate and secure the pooling of significant streams of resources (Rutherfoord et al, 2013). Beyond this, however, it was also clear that the PNCB actually required *additional* funds for its work. The project partners were all used to bidding for government money and, in this regard, the NCB pilot was seen as simply more of the same. There was a new initiative, a new pot of money, and the project partners decided to bid. While DCLG wanted the team to explore the pooling of budgets, the partners had very little interest in this part of the plan. They did, however, see the NCB project as a way to secure additional funds for their ongoing work.

Working with the community

Early on in the planning and implementation of the pilot, the team appointed a specialist consultancy firm to conduct an ambitious programme of community consultation in order to determine what local people thought about Poplar and their ideas about priority issues for local reform. Between June and July 2012 (and mindful of the start of the Olympics in August 2012) the consultants contacted 1,170 people living and working in the area (a sample that represented about 5% of the population living in the area). The research process included: 795 individual interviews organised around a simple questionnaire; 375 people contacted via group interviews; and five focus groups. A number of key informants from local institutions such as schools, churches and mosques were also contacted and interviewed by phone.

This was an ambitious consultation and respondents were asked about their relationship to the area; about the things they liked about Poplar; their use of local public services; the degree of influence they had over those services; and their views about people getting involved in their neighbourhoods and volunteering. They were also asked about their key priorities for the area and whether they were willing to get involved in developing the PNCB. Regarding these priorities, respondents had been asked to list their top three priorities from a list of agreed categories (including an option called 'other'); in terms of their first-choice priorities, health was first with a combined individual and group score of 25% followed by jobs (22%) and young people (20%). While this highlighted local concerns, it did not very clearly prioritise them – all three attracting support from between a fifth and quarter of those questioned – and the survey failed to further specify the nature of the problems being faced.

Perhaps more helpfully, this consultation clearly demonstrated very high levels of support for community engagement in Poplar. As many as 85% of the individuals and 90% of the group respondents felt that 'people have a responsibility to do their bit to improve their neighbourhoods'. Furthermore, as many as 68% of respondents (and 59% of those questioned in groups) expressed an interest in getting involved. Importantly for the project, the consultants collected the contact details of 621 of these people, 113 of whom expressed an interest in being involved in the strategic decision making involved in the project. A further group who were interested in volunteering were also reported back to the partners.

While there is bound to be a gap between sentiment and action – and this was highlighted in Chapter One in relation to polling about engaging in the Big Society – these respondents could have been followed up to develop a new group who could have then engaged in the neighbourhood project. However, there was no effort to follow up in this way. Indeed, the partners were unsure and rather divided about the role and status of the community in planning the project.

The idea of co-production – as promoted by DCLG – was new to all the partners and they didn't have the experience or the partnerships required to deliver anything that was genuinely community led. Even the project manager only fully appreciated what was being expected of them by the end of the project and, in her reflections on the challenges of the project, she told us that 'we're ... programmed into thinking that *we* are the people that deliver the service on *your* behalf; and you the grateful recipient better receive that service during times that we stipulate. This is about a complete transformation in that relationship. And I do get it now ... this is about co-design and developing a different relationship between service providers and the community.' However, as outlined, there was no prior experience of this way of working, nor was there an established authoritative representative body that could justly claim to represent and negotiate for the diverse local community. Furthermore, even though they had asked people in the local area if they wanted to engage, the project partners didn't follow this up.

To make matters worse, some of the partners were never fully committed to the community-led work expected by DCLG. One respondent told us that government ministers and their civil servants were naïve in assuming that people know what they want and, as he remarked:

> We've been doing community engagement for many, many years. We don't buy the civil service view of the world (or I don't), which says, 'Ask the residents what they want and everything will be wonderful.' Not true! If you asked an east ender who used a mangle, 'What do you want?' they'll say, 'We want a *super* mangle.' If I then say to them, 'Have you ever heard of a spin dryer?' they'll say, 'Oh, of course we want a spin dryer but we'd never heard of one.' This naïve stuff about engaging with communities is rather more complicated than that ... with this programme, we want to challenge what community engagement is about: to really challenge some of those naïve assumptions of the civil service.

For this respondent, the NCB was a means to carry on developing links with other service providers in the area and to continue their ambitious programme of activity, but it was not about the co-design, co-delivery and co-commissioning of services (nor, indeed, the pooling of budgets). Indeed, the NCB was a vehicle for the continuation of business as usual in the context of cuts and it provided a potential way to raise additional funds for the partners to support their work in the future. This respondent had engaged as a means to secure funding to continue working in the old ways rather than doing anything new.

When the then government Minister for Communities, Don Foster MP, visited the PNCB in October 2012, he urged those involved not to scale back their ambition, and to aim 'for as wide-ranging a shift of power and control to local communities as possible'. However, in practice, the need to develop a project in a short time, divisions within the partnership and the lack of a strong community voice advocating its own agenda meant that PNCB ended up adopting a project that was already being developed and led by the GP practice, without the need for the community to get more involved.

As early as July 2012, before the community consultation had even begun, one of the GP partners made the argument that diabetes could be a focus for the PNCB's work. This GP informed the partners that there were 2,000 patients with the condition in the local area and that 70% of these individuals had another health problem, and that improving their well-being could have significant benefits for health outcomes as well as saving money from emergency treatment and hospitalisation. Rather than waiting to hear the priorities for Poplar set out by the local community consultation, or finding community partners to work with, the GPs understandably saw the PNCB as a potential way to make progress on an existing goal of their own. Given that health was clearly a concern for the community, it was very easy to adopt the focus on diabetes without too much debate. As the project manager explained, 'We were being pushed heavily by DCLG to come up with at least one priority, and ... we [already had] a health project to be run by the GP network ... to focus on diabetes prevention.' This project was also attractive because it was seen as being relatively easy to measure any progress being made.

Following more internal debate about the role and purpose of any community engagement in the emerging diabetes project, PNCB held a series of workshops with local groups to explore the ideas being developed, and a range of local community groups were consulted about what became known as the Healthy Poplar project. This was more akin to traditional forms of local service consultation than anything like co-design, and it followed from the ideas laid down by the experts. Moreover, given that the partners had failed to 'top-slice' funds from any statutory health provider and were struggling to gain the full cooperation of any mainstream provider or its agencies, the project was also unlikely to happen without additional funds.

Localism's missing social and civic infrastructure

While PNCB failed to secure its specified goals as laid down by DCLG – to secure pooled budgets from existing organisations in order to provide services more efficaciously and efficiently by working with the local community in conceiving, designing and conducting the plan – the project *did* expose the need for two key players to be at the table if this form of localism was to be a success. These were the local authority and the local community. The local authority was the one body that might have had the jurisdiction and authority to coordinate across the public sector in the area and to advocate for the top-slicing of budgets to work in this way. In addition, the project also exposed a vacuum in community leadership. There was no recognised and authoritative body that could represent the diversity of the local community and its interests in the work of the project and, without these missing partners, there was no way that PNCB could meet its intended goals. Furthermore, although the project partners sought to fill this vacuum with a large-scale consultation exercise, this had no impact on the decisions that were made and the project team failed to follow up with the hundreds of people who had expressed an interest in getting further involved.

As such, the research highlighted a conundrum regarding the institutional infrastructure and agency required to realise localism. If PNCB had been led by Tower Hamlets council, with much greater effort made to marshal some sort of representation of community interests, there might have been a greater chance of success. Of course, creating such a community body is no small undertaking and the lessons from local government in Lambeth, neighbourhood planning and community organising (covered in Chapters Four, Five and Six) indicate that it is best done through self-organisation, outside the arms of the state, and it certainly can't be done in a hurry. However, for now, PNCB suggests that localism demands much greater attention be paid to the craft of building and sustaining some sort of non-partisan neighbourhood forum that is able and willing – and has the authority and credibility – to engage and negotiate with state-funded bodies in relation to place. Once this kind of infrastructure is in place, it would be possible to develop a more sustained engagement over the co-production of services, across local service providers, in projects like neighbourhood budgets and Our Place! Such infrastructure is unlikely to emerge on its own, especially in areas where the local community face a number of challenges as they do in Poplar today, and the lessons of the PNCB suggest that state-funded bodies are ill-placed to lead in this work. In this case, the desire to engage was reduced to a process of consultation that yielded next to nothing for the people consulted. Going forward, the development of localism needs much greater attention to the lessons of Poplar; the success of the policy demands the creation of non-partisan neighbourhood-level structures that are able to operate across the diversity of any local community, develop an independent agenda, negotiate with the key stakeholders involved in shaping that place and mobilise people to act.

Notes

[1] By 1885 the franchise included all adult men who owned property or who were tenants in a separate dwelling for at least a year prior to the election in question. This excluded lodgers, tenants who rented rooms, domestic servants, sons living at home, policemen and soldiers living in barracks (Pelling, 1967). Universal male suffrage was secured only in 1918, when women over 30 were also given the vote. Universal suffrage for women over 21 was not achieved until 1928.

[2] Pelling highlights a number of expenses that used to be associated with standing for office beyond self-sufficiency, including public support for good causes, covering the expenses incurred by the returning officer and the cost of hiring the boxes needed for voting. In this regard he cites the author Rider Haggard, who wrote

about his experiences contesting the seat of Norfolk East for the Conservative and Unionists in 1895: 'From the moment a candidate appears in the field he is fair game, and every man's hand is in his pocket. Demands for your "patronage and support" fall on him, thick as leaves in Vallombrosa. I remember that I was even pestered to supply voters with wooden legs!' (quoted in Pelling, 1967, 11).

[3]   Similar research in the US has highlighted the challenges for community groups that decide to engage with the state. They can risk losing their independence (and funding has been particularly important in silencing potential critics) engagement can also threaten their very legitimacy to speak for the people (Hodgson, 2004; Herbert, 2005; de Filippis et al, 2010; McQuarrie, 2013). As Newman and Lake (2006, 46) boldly suggest, these forms of government meant that 'potentially insurrectionary community-based organisations have been transformed into bureaucratized and acquiescent appendages of the shadow state'.

[4]   Although these data show a decline in the levels of civic engagement, it is important to remember that such activities were always a minority sport. Using data collected during the 1960s and 1970s, for example, Gyford (1976, 99) reported that only one in four residents had met a council officer and only one in five residents had contacted a councillor at some time. He argued that the minority of active citizens were 'trustees of the idea of local democracy in which the majority of their fellow citizens place their faith' (Gyford, 1976, 121; see also Boaden et al, 1982).

[5]   Williams used the 2000 General Household Survey to explore patterns of formal and informal community organisation. While only 13% of respondents had been involved with some responsibility in a local organisation in the past three years, as many as 74–72% had done or received a favour for/from a neighbour in the past six months (Williams, 2003, 535). He further found that, in contrast to patterns of formal engagement with organisations, patterns of informal interaction were not clearly differentiated by the affluence or otherwise of the area concerned.

[6]   It is significant that Putnam echoes the influential arguments developed by Berger and Neuhaus (1985 [1977]), who were themselves building on the legacy left by Burke, de Tocqueville, Nisbet and others, to highlight the way that mediating institutions can play a critical role in shaping democratic engagement and fostering a culture whereby people feel they have the skills and power they need to make change. However, whereas Berger and Neuhaus argued that these mediating institutions included the family, church, neighbourhood organisation and voluntary group, most subsequent interest has focused on the final group of these four, particularly in debates within the UK where family, faith and neighbourhood organisation are much weaker than has been the case in the US.

[7]   The research presented in this section was collated as a result of taking on this work to evaluate the project as is outlined more fully in the appendix at the end of this book.

FOUR

Localist local government

Thus far, this book has highlighted the potential to revisit the history and geography of English government and to explore the creation of neighbourhood-level infrastructure that is able to facilitate the organisation of local communities and foster their engagement in local initiatives. Such innovation will necessarily involve working with existing state forms, and, in this regard, local authorities remain critical in shaping the local political culture and have the greatest potential to create new opportunities for getting people involved (Lowndes et al, 2006). However, whereas previous initiatives have tended to secure the state's control of this process, there is now an opportunity to go beyond full control by the state.

This chapter focuses on the experiences of the London Borough of Lambeth in its quest to become a cooperative council. It outlines the way in which the council has tried to develop a new culture based on a more reciprocal relationship with local people. In its more recent manifestations, this initiative has had a 'localist turn' as the council has grappled with ways to better engage people through their local community groups at the neighbourhood scale. Whereas much of the national debate about localism has been about devolving political power and authority from Westminster and Whitehall to other state-funded organisations, in Lambeth, localism has been about devolution from the town hall to local people and their community groups. As such, Lambeth's experience has resonance across the public sector as organisations like housing associations, the NHS and the police try to better engage local citizens in the work that they do.

Lambeth is a large and diverse London borough comprising some 300,000 people among whom some 142 languages are spoken (London Borough of Lambeth, 2011, 10). Stretching from the river Thames in the north, it includes Brixton in the middle and greener areas such as Thornton Heath in the south (Figure 4.1). Lambeth's boundaries were established in 1964, incorporating the old boroughs of Lambeth, Clapham and Streatham, and it now comprises 21 wards, each with three elected representatives who sit on the council. In the 2014 elections the Labour Party increased its hold of the council, taking 59 of the 63 seats, a historic high, albeit that only a third of the 220,000 residents who were registered to vote turned out on the day (GLA,

2014). This is in line with other local authorities in London and the rest of the country. Despite the important services provided by the council (which include social care, education, re-development, street cleanliness and leisure amenities), most residents do not exercise their right to vote for the people in charge.

Figure 4.1: Map of the London Borough of Lambeth showing the study areas of Tulse Hill and West Norwood

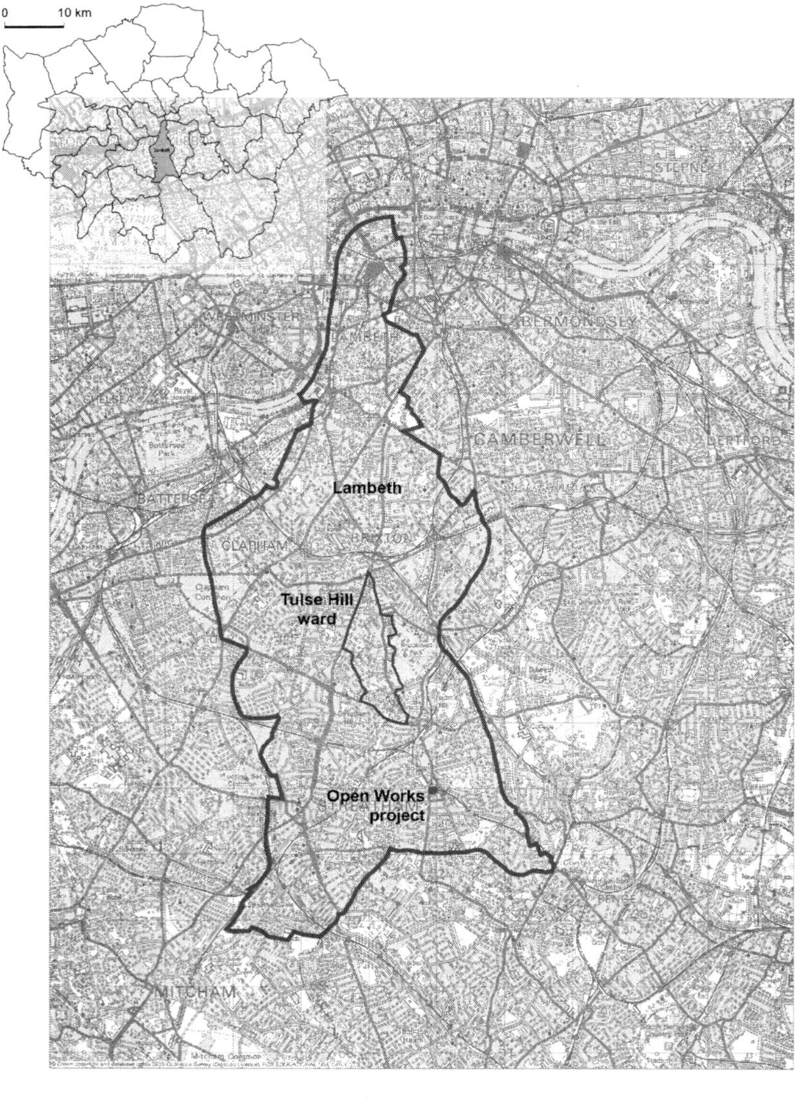

The chapter begins by telling the story of Lambeth's development as a cooperative council. It then focuses on the ways that the council has tried to shift decision making and initiative to the neighbourhood level. In this regard, the chapter looks at two 'localist experiments' in more detail: one where the councillors have worked with local community groups to take new initiatives (called Community Based Commissioning) and the other where the council has funded an outside organisation to develop a new platform to reach local people and engage them in brand new activity, starting from scratch (called Open Works). After capturing this experience, the chapter ends by highlighting the wider implications of these initiatives for other local authorities as well as state-funded bodies that are trying to adopt localism in various ways. Unlike the example of the NCB in Poplar, where there was no organised or institutionalised voice for the local community to have a place at the table of government, Lambeth has developed a network of independent neighbourhood forums that span local interests and provide a mechanism for the community to engage in a more meaningful and sustainable way (and it is interesting that Lambeth has experimented with these in the past, Poole and Keith-Lucas, 1994).

To some extent, these forums fill the same institutional space as the neighbourhood forums that are now being established to take up neighbourhood planning, explored further in the following chapter, but other local government bodies have been doing similar work (for examples see Coaffee and Healey, 2003; Barnes et al, 2007; Murat and Morad, 2008). These neighbourhood-level institutions work by capturing the diversity of the local community and incorporating existing organisations as well as individual residents who want to engage. As such, they provide a credible representative body with authoritative leadership with which state bodies can relate and negotiate over change. Although still in their infancy and largely overlooked, these new neighbourhood-scale organisations represent an emergent civic infrastructure that is starting to underpin localist citizenship and statecraft in Lambeth as well as in other parts of the country.

Adopting a cooperative approach to government in Lambeth

As outlined in Chapter Two, the 1980s were years in which local government was used as a space to conduct a national battle for supremacy by the Left as well as the Right. As Gyford (1976, 146–7) puts it, 'In each case, the rights of local government were accorded second place to other imperatives, respectively those of socialist strategy and the triumph of the market.' Lambeth was at the forefront of these developments and local councillors provided leadership to those on the left who wanted to challenge the rate-capping exercised by Mrs Thatcher's Conservative governments. Caricatured as a 'loony-left' council by those on the right, Lambeth was known for supporting a range of national political battles such the miners' strike, opposition to nuclear weapons and the call for new civil rights.

By the late 1990s, however, the political landscape had changed. A new generation of Labour politicians took control of the council and began to develop very different ideas. In tandem with their own party holding office at the national level, local Labour councillors became more focused on the task of managing and delivering council services. Rather than using the council as an institutional space from which to participate in national (and international) campaigns, the local party repositioned itself as a party of responsible government – in Lambeth town hall – as well as in Westminster (Parker, 2015).

In the council's own public narrative about this period, it shifted from being 'a failing local authority … to become a high performing council with many of its services recognised as being among the best in the country' (London Borough of Lambeth, 2011, 11). The council's political leadership adopted a new mantle of economic competence and, as the leader, Councillor Lib Peck, put it to me during interview, also started to experiment with service provision. A number of the councillors began to realise 'that the [new] projects that really worked were the ones where we were working very genuinely with the community. Those were the ones where we were getting the best extra added social value and we found that despite the improvement in services, we somehow weren't cracking through to what people wanted, and what people needed.' As such, a number of the councillors began to explore new ways of working more cooperatively with local residents and community groups.

Following the economic crash of 2008, the possible benefits to be gained by adopting a more cooperative approach were even more tempting for the political leaders in Lambeth town hall. It was clear that the local authority was facing a major cut in its funding and, in line with many other local authorities, Lambeth had a 50% cut in its budget between 2010 and 2016. Moreover, while cuts in services were inevitable, the Labour leadership saw the development of a more cooperative approach as a way to use the remaining resources more effectively by tapping into the talents and assets of the local population in order to work together in pursuit of shared goals. As the then Chief

Executive explained in a public address, 'we needed to create a new paradigm for Lambeth', and the idea of the cooperative council was born (Anderson, no date).

From 2010, the then leader of the Council, Steve Reed, and the then Chief Executive, Derrick Anderson, championed a vision to become a cooperative council.[1] A White Paper setting out the idea went to full council in May 2010 (just at the time of the general election) and the council subsequently launched a Commission for a Cooperative Council that met, heard and digested evidence in order to explore the idea and determine the best way to proceed (London Borough of Lambeth, 2011). In reflecting back on this period of development, Councillor Lib Peck highlighted the way that the initiative combined important elements of the Labour Party's history and values as well as pragmatism about local government and its role in much straightened times. As she explained, becoming a cooperative council was about 'the values that were [part of the] origins of the Labour Party – a belief in the power of community and wanting to see citizens engage in a political process'. Echoing the arguments set out in Chapter One, the idea of the cooperative council reflected a belief in the power of communities to address their own problems and it was focused on developing a new relationship between the council, local residents and civil society organisations (or making a new civic offer).

In the foreword to the final report produced by the Cooperative Council Citizens' Commission, Steve Reed set out a vision for reshaping 'the settlement between citizens and the state by handing more power to local people so that a real partnership of equals can emerge' (London Borough of Lambeth, 2011, 1). This was about 'finding new ways in which citizens can participate in the decisions that affect their lives', and the council doing 'things *with* its community rather than … *to* the community' (emphasis added). This approach has subsequently been taken up by other Labour-led councils across the UK (Reed and Ussher, 2013; Shafique, 2013).

The Commission for a Cooperative Council invited people to submit written and oral evidence. It held public meetings, conducted consultation and used social media to reach people, and some 3,000 local residents and 130 organisations contributed their views to the group. In digesting the evidence and determining a way forward, the commission agreed five cooperative principles that would shape the work of the council in future (Table 4.1). It also identified changes that would be needed within the council as well as the wider community, and developed a plan for making the change.

Table 4.1: Lambeth's cooperative principles

1	The council as the local democratic leader and civic society partner (in the borough)
2	Public services planned together and delivered through a variety of organisations, which will improve outcomes, empower citizens and users, and strengthen civil society
3	Citizens incentivised to take part in the provision of public services ('the relationship of co-production must be underpinned by reciprocity')
4	Public services enabling residents to engage in civil society through employment opportunities
5	Public services accessible from a variety of locations

Source: London Borough of Lambeth, 2011, 24–5

In the subsequent period the council largely focused on internal reorganisation and the development of a new model of commissioning. In this new model, citizens were envisaged as working alongside councillors and officers to make key decisions about how to achieve the outcomes desired (Figure 4.2). Indeed, as outlined in the Commission for a Cooperative Council's final report, 'council staff and citizens cooperate together ... they work together to identify a problem, design a range of services that will tackle that problem, and then commission the right organisations to provide these services, including the provision of appropriate support to help build community resilience' (London Borough of Lambeth, 2011, 32). Rather than leaving procurement decisions to staff and representatives in the town hall, the idea was to incorporate citizens into every stage of the process. Providing an example of this, Councillor Lib Peck reported doing a review of special educational needs whereby 'for the first time we've gone out and ... done a cooperative initiative with the parents to work out what they need, so it's much more parent led'. She reported similar projects to review the services for children in care and the youth service, whereby the Young Lambeth Cooperative had been given control of the budget (some £3 million) to make decisions about how best to meet local needs. The Commission for a Cooperative Council argued that this 'community-led commissioning' was critical to the 'stated desire to rebalance the power relationship between the citizen and the state in favour of the citizen, recognising that both sides bring particular skills and knowledge to the process' (London Borough of Lambeth, 2011, 33).

Figure 4.2: Lambeth's Cooperative Commissioning Cycle

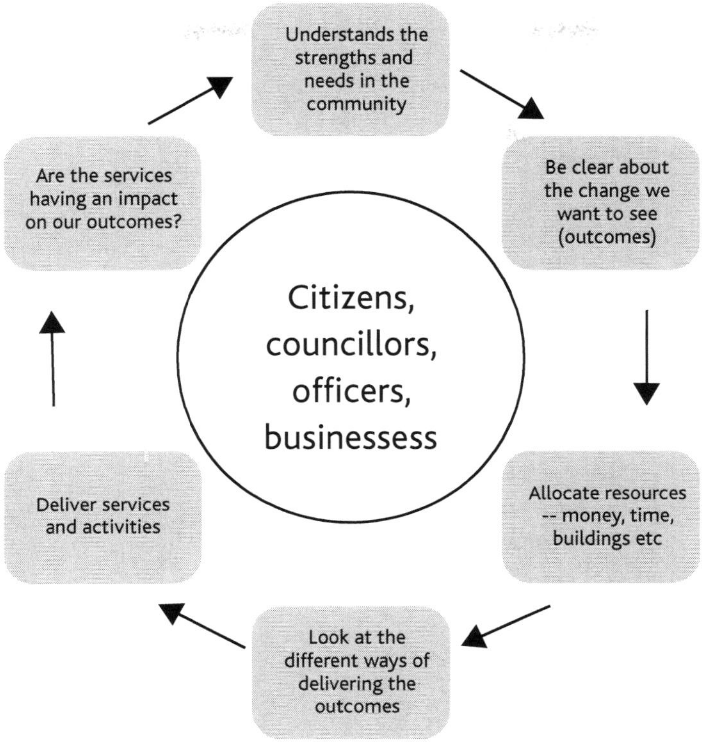

Source: London Borough of Lambeth (no date)

As part of this process the council agreed just three core 'public sector outcomes' for the period between 2013 and 2016. These were: (1) More jobs and sustainable growth; (2) Communities feeling safer and more resilient; and (3) Cleaner, greener streets. Under each heading, a number of further outcomes were highlighted, with an expectation that commissioners would convene teams of officers, councillors and residents to determine the best way of achieving these outcomes, incorporating community ideas and resources along with those of the state (Table 4.2). For Council Leader Lib Peck, this meant 'moving away from a consultation where you determine what's best and invite people to just respond to it, to a situation where you're saying well actually, if you're really honest, this is the scale of the challenge, how are we all going to pitch in and find the solution? ... There's been a very deliberate cultural change going on with councillors, with staff, with community to really try and level-up the decision-making process.' In so doing, the council hoped that outcomes would be better, with the

Table 4.2: Lambeth's commissioning outcomes, 2013–16

(1) More jobs and sustainable growth
Lambeth residents have more opportunities for better quality homes
Lambeth plays a strong role in London's economy
People have the skills to find work
All young people have opportunities to achieve their ambitions
People achieve financial security
(2) Communities feel safer and more resilient
People are healthier for longer
All Lambeth communities feel they are valued and part of their neighbourhoods
Crime reduces
Older, disabled and vulnerable people can live independently and have control over their lives
Vulnerable children and adults get support and protection
(3) Cleaner, greener streets
People lead environmentally sustainable lives
People take greater responsibility for their neighbourhood
People live in, work in and visit our vibrant and creative town centres

Source: London Borough of Lambeth, no date

additional benefits that come from improved working relationships, stronger social capital and increased civic capacity.

After 2010, the council began to move in this direction by developing an 'early adopter scheme' to work with local organisations and residents to pass over the management of some council assets to community groups (Table 4.3). Over the period between 2010 and 2014 the council also launched a number of projects that worked with particular user groups or neighbourhood organisations in order to experiment with new ways of delivering change. In 2015, the bulk of these projects were cursorily evaluated and the key finding was that a culture of collaboration still needed to be more firmly established. While many of the new experiments were on the fringes of council activity, and often represented new areas of work, the core of the council seemed little affected. Furthermore, while the council was developing a better idea of the ways in which it could engage its citizens, it was clear that the council had very little evidence about the impact of this work on the ground.

In what follows, I draw upon evidence from two of the projects developed to better engage at the neighbourhood scale. The first, called Community-Based-Commissioning was about supporting local ward councillors to better engage with the local community around shared concerns; the second, Open Works, involved setting up a new platform to develop relationships with individual residents, explore ideas and set up new projects from scratch. Both involved a closer working relationship between council staff and local community organisations and residents. I was involved in an evaluation of the first of these projects and have had access to the people leading the second,

Table 4.3: Key steps in the development of Lambeth's Cooperative Council approach

Date	Activity/event	Focus of the work
May 2010	White Paper on the Cooperative Council	Set out the rationale and core principles of the Cooperative Council, established the Commission.
May 2010– 2011	The Cooperative Council Commission	Commissioners heard and read evidence about the shift to becoming a Cooperative Council, and published report (London Borough of Lambeth, 2011).
2010 onwards	The early adopter scheme	Focused on a number of projects to change ownership (at a day centre, youth services, the adventure playgrounds and a children's centre).
2012–13	Internal review and restructuring	Reorganised council staff from departments and into functions (commissioning, delivery and enabling); developed a new model of commissioning; embarked on training for culture change.
2012–15	Ongoing experiments with cooperative working	Launched a number of different projects to test the water for cooperative work. These included designing council projects to co-produce new services, a new youth cooperative, the creation of neighbourhood forums, cooperative libraries, green community champions and a project called Freshview. Some involved particular groups and others were focused on neighbourhood working (evaluated internally, with overall assessment in 2015).
2014–2015	Open Works launched in West Norwood	Project based in one neighbourhood. Consultants from Civic Systems Lab worked with the council to make contact with residents and facilitate projects (evaluated in 2015).
October 2014– April 2015	Community Based Commissioning prototype	A project to explore neighbourhood working by supporting councillors to work with local communities (evaluated in 2015).

as well as a copy of their own evaluation report (and for more about the research undertaken see the appendix at the end of this book).

An experiment in neighbourhood work

Since adopting its cooperative approach, Lambeth Council aimed to engage with the community in doing all of its work. However, in line with other local authorities, most of the funding given to Lambeth Council is actually spent on statutory services designed to meet the needs of particular individuals such as those in need of social care, children at risk and those with special educational needs. The budgets for this kind of individualised service provision (accounting for something like 80% of all council spending) are determined in the town hall and then distributed on the basis of individual need, and this has nothing to do with the needs or desires of any local community group. Although cooperative working had meant that some of the major funding decisions were being made in dialogue with community representatives and service users, these budgets could not easily be decentralised or collectivised. As a result, most residents were not engaged in the cooperative commissioning cycle and, although various experiments had indicated the potential to engage people in particular projects – around services (such as youth provision, libraries and parks) or activities (such as environmental improvement) – the council was not really engaging local people on a significant scale.

Lambeth's senior leadership team wanted to explore the ways in which the community could be more deeply involved in ongoing work to improve things in Lambeth, and between 2012 and 2014 there were internal discussions about how to decentralise council decision making in order to reach residents at the neighbourhood scale. Echoing the debates about NCBs introduced in Chapter Three, there was an expectation that funding could be pooled across budgets, with a focus on area-based commissioning. However, while the Poplar NCB sought (unsuccessfully) to pool funding from different statutory services in order to focus on the people of Poplar, Lambeth was considering the extent to which it was possible to pool its internal budgets at the neighbourhood scale. In theory at least, by pooling the budgets and mapping the assets of each local area, it would then be possible to engage local people about what they actually needed and to co-produce the most appropriate services for meeting these needs.

As one respondent suggested during interview, pure cooperative working would mean that the council's funds would follow the needs and desires of the people living in the 'natural areas' or geographic communities of the borough and by 'aggregating the resources within that area that are already been spent on services' as well as the community assets that already exist, you would build from the 'bottom up around outcomes that reflect the assets and the priorities of that local area. And you can then ... jointly begin to determining the best ways of spending that money.' As outlined in relation to the NCB, however, state-funded organisations are required to deliver statutory services and they are understandably reluctant to give up control of their budgets, not least because it means that they can't deliver what the national government – and local people – expects them to do. So too, in the council, many staff are charged to deliver statutory services that are provided to individuals and they can't just stop doing this work.

Thus, while cooperative co-production is an idea that would work if you were starting from scratch to create state-funded services that put communities – and their self-determination – at the centre of service provision, this is not in line with the prevailing distribution of funding, expectations and responsibilities that operate in relation to service provision. Taxpayers' money is actually allocated to individuals – via local service providers – and, as we saw in Chapter Two, the key decisions are often made in Westminster or Whitehall, not the town hall. The unemployed, victims of crime, children at risk, the disabled and infirm, as well as the sick, all have entitlements that are laid down by national government and councils and other agencies are charged to deliver the service. Given this, it is very difficult to pool budgets on the basis of geography in any significant way.

During the development of the cooperative approach to its work, senior managers at Lambeth Council had to grapple with this dilemma and the challenges it posed to connecting the council with the local community. Although they were trying to embed cooperative working practices into the work of the council, they were not able to decentralise control over the way most of the money was spent or to reconfigure the scale at which major decisions were made. While a number of the early experiments in cooperative working explored some forms of local co-production that involved officers and residents working together around shared interests, and periods when officers went out and consulted residents about their hopes and fears for their neighbourhoods, this work was largely funded from soft, time-limited resources, rather than core council budgets.

Despite this, however, a number of senior managers at the council still wanted to explore the ways in which local communities could be more engaged and deeply embedded in the work of the council. As such, they launched an initiative called Community-Based-

Commissioning (CBC) to see if they could replicate the council's cooperative commissioning cycle (see Figure 4.2) on the basis of geography. This new project was charged with exploring whether it was possible to commission services by working with the community around shared interests and desired outcomes. As it evolved, this became more focused on exploring the way that local ward councillors could play a bigger role in mediating relationships between the council and local communities, and finding areas of common concern.

The project was assigned to work on one of the council's 13 core goals – 'to encourage people to take greater responsibility for their neighbourhood' (see Table 4.2) – but this did not necessarily involve any kind of commissioning in the traditional sense of the word. Over a period of six months, the CBC project team of up to 10 officers sought to find a way for the council to better interface with its councillors and for them to have more support in relating to their local community. As such, the project reflected wider debate about new ways of developing state–citizen relationships at the neighbourhood scale (see Cox et al, 2013; also Table 4.4). Rather than providing things *for* people, the council was experimenting to find ways of working *with* people to effect local change. Going back to the arguments about the relational state introduced in Chapter One, this was about the council staff developing new relationships with their councillors as well as both of them better relating to local community groups.

Interestingly, once the council staff began to see and experience what the community were already doing, it became evident that local community groups were already trying to 'take responsibility for their neighbourhood', with very little council support. As such, the CBC project illuminated the extent to which localist local government can work alongside the community, rather than assuming it has to be in control. The project team ended up following the community, rather than the other way around, as outlined further below.

The nuts and bolts of the CBC project

The CBC team met regularly between November 2014 and April 2015 (over a period of 6 months) to pilot this way of working in the ward of Tulse Hill. This area – just south of Brixton (Figure 4.1) – had three elected councillors, all of them Labour, representing approximately 16,000 residents. This area already had a strong neighbourhood forum and a vibrant community centre that provided the civic infrastructure for getting things done. The council had helped to establish the Tulse Hill Forum in 2012, and it was part of a wider network of 10 area-based forums operating with independent leadership across the borough. Membership of the Tulse Hill Forum included a number of Tenants and Residents Associations, the St Matthew's football project and the Hightrees Community Development Trust. The Forum had developed a strong and capable volunteer leadership team, with 11 people on the committee, a mailing list of 600 people and a track record of local activity.

Table 4.4: Old and new ways of neighbourhood working

	Old policy	New policy
Main outcomes	Reducing gaps (in key policy areas) between neighbourhoods	Achieving self-determined goals and changing power relations
Primary focus	Physical renewal	Social innovation and transformation
Theory of change	Needs based approach based on the Index of Multiple Deprivation (IMD)	Asset-based approach
Resources	Large scale national grant programmes	Pooled mainstream budgets (eg the NCB, see chapter 3), some commissioning, grants and voluntary donations/work
Definition of neighbourhood	Clearly bounded neighbourhoods	'Natural areas' based on perceptions and lived experiences with porous borders
Main actors	Councils and other state bodies driven by national policy	Community catalysts including a range of local people and organisations
Decision-making processes and institutions	Formal partnerships and boards focused on delivery targets	Informal collaboration, focused on goals
Role of the state/ public sector	Centrally driven, policy-led activity implemented by statutory bodies	The state being a protagonist and facilitator in a more collaborative, locally-oriented approach
Nature of politics	Characterised by tensions between elected party representatives and other people and organisations	Recognising different forms of power, with official representatives working alongside local people and other actors

Source: Summary from Cox et al (2013, Table 6.1, 62/3)

In addition, the Hightrees Community Development Trust (CDT) had been established on the initiative of local people in an old library building in 1988 and had since expanded to provide training in basic skills and personal development, as well as supporting local people to get back into work. It provided courses in local children's centres and facilitated a network of homework clubs across the borough. As part of the programme of asset transfers from the council that was developed as part of the early adopter scheme (see Table 4.3 above), the centre had taken over the management of the Tulse Hill Adventure Playground and had also taken on three community organisers, initially as part of the government-funded work led by Locality, but subsequently it had put two of them on its books on a permanent basis (see also Chapters One and Six). Margaret Pierre-Jarrett, the director of the centre, reported that it aimed to take a 'holistic approach to community development', meaning that 'if someone comes in to talk about their employment situation then we'll talk to them about their children and then ... after a while they start to open up and we support them as much as we can'. Given its role and philosophy, the centre and its staff encountered hundreds of local people every year and this gave it a deep insight into the dynamics and desires of the local community.

Two of the three ward councillors were already heavily involved in the work of the Forum and the Hightrees CDT. Labour Councillor Marcia Cameron had helped to establish the Forum back in 2012 and Councillor Mary Atkins had been the first secretary of the Forum until her election in a by-election in July 2013. Mary reported that 'it was because of the work with the local community that I decided to stand for election [in 2013]'. Once under way, the CBC project thus had rich ground in which to develop its work: the councillors were already connected to a community that was already organised with the civic infrastructure needed to facilitate local activities and to develop new work. This level of potential capacity was unusual in the borough at large, and it is likely to be unusual in other places as well.

The CBC team started its work by providing background information to the two councillors in Tulse Hill and then working with them to identify potential issues that would be of interest to the community, and around which they could work together in future. These early discussions used census data, previous consultations and personal soundings to identify the potential issues of social isolation and the need to support young people as being especially important to people living in the ward of Tulse Hill. Drawing on their prior knowledge and ongoing relationships with the community forum, Hightrees CDT and local residents, the councillors decided to make the issue of support for young people and families the focus for the CBC work.

Erica Tate, the chair of the Forum, and Margaret Pierre-Jarrett, the director of Hightrees CDT, were then critically important in further exploring ideas. They helped to facilitate an initial community meeting to gather people who were interested in the idea of better supporting parents and children that was held on the Tulse Hill Estate on 24 January 2015. Subsequently, Margaret agreed to allow councillors and council staff to come and consult with people during a community event that was already planned. This was an event celebrating residents who had completed a training course called Community in Action held on 7 March 2015. In addition, Marcia organised a community pampering event held at the Adventure Playground on 28 March in order to get people to come and talk about their ideas for better parental support. The team then organised another, stand-alone event for all those who had expressed an interest in taking forward ideas (held on 6 June 2015).

Interestingly, in the early days of the project, the council staff and the councillors expected the focus to be on parental concern about gangs. As Mary put it in her first interview, 'what I'd like to see is some kind of project where parents who've got their kids out of gangland could run some kind of programme for other parents, because it's kind of a shameful thing if you've been in a gang … and other parents on the estates are really worried that their kids are going to get in gangs, so their kids are practically locked in'. The first meeting raised these kinds of concerns but it was left deliberately open. As Marcia put it, they aimed to talk 'to parents about … how you feel about your children? What would help? Would you be interested in setting up a group where parents would support children? What would that group look like?'

This open approach was followed up at the subsequent events and Marcia described this as being about 'encouraging parents to support each other, rather than [having] officers in the town hall trying to look at the problem and then sending a group to sort out the problem. It's about looking at ways where parents can actually build on something and support each other in terms of the problems that they might be facing with their children.' Marcia argued that if local people created their own projects they 'might last a lot longer', as people would be invested in the work rather than relying on the council to act. In this regard, she echoed the rationale of the cooperative council by saying, 'Historically, we've always tried to resolve our residents' problems or not even problems, but things that aren't working well. We always tried to resolve it in the town hall but if you go to the community, the community knows what will work for them. So the first point of call should be the community because what you find is when you could turn up with something and present it to the community, they're normally like "no, no, no we don't want to do this or why didn't you do it like that?" … So, go to them first, get them to lead on it, and then we support and help formulate whatever they want to do.'

The CBC were caught off-guard by the openness of these discussions. The council officers were expecting to talk about particular interventions and possible models for working together, but the conversations largely focused on building relationships and the need for a stronger local community. As one member of the team put it: 'Pretty much what everyone said was "we want to know each other better and we want events that bring us together, we want to know our neighbours" and that's a very interesting finding. That's very cooperative … there's a community appetite for … networks.' Thus, perhaps unexpectedly for the council staff, the CBC exposed a desire for community; people wanted to be better connected with the other people with whom they shared space.

In this regard, the fact that the CBC team helped to facilitate discussions among parents at the four events in itself helped to build these relationships. As one member of the team explained: 'Those actions have sort of raised parental interest and desire to network … even just by doing those things we have helped to create or sustain an emerging network of parents who are now talking to each other.' By facilitating relationships there was a feeling that the project had created 'some sort of virtuous circle … [even though] nothing's been formally commissioned'.

In many ways the CBC exposed the council staff to work that was already going on in the community, and, to different degrees, this was already being supported by the councillors. The Tulse Hill Forum had already identified the need for parental support and pitched for money to support some training as part of a participatory budgeting event (called Tulse Hill Together) organised by the Forum in 2014. This training was later provided at Hightrees CDT and forum chair Erica Tate reported that parents had wanted to support each other with homework, and to provide emotional support for themselves and their children. In this regard, Margaret and Erica were already talking together about the best way to take things forward. Erica reported making links between a Saturday school based on St Martin's Estate, a summer holiday project based at Holy Trinity Church and the contacts they had made at the four CBC community meetings. Margaret reported that they were hoping to develop a new course for parents supporting parents that could incorporate a popular idea to organise a conference for other local parents as part of the course. If this was successful they would then have the funding to support the idea of 'connecting parents in a bottom up way' with some resources to coordinate a lasting network of parents.

As such, the CBC project highlighted the extent to which the community organisations were already doing important community work. While the council staff and councillors could provide useful assistance, the CBC project exposed officers to the extent of the local community capacity and the involvement of the councillors in the work that was already being done. As outlined below, this has major implications for the way in which other state-funded organisations can better relate to existing community groups and their civic potential. Rather than assuming that they need to be in the driving seat, state-funded organisations can find local people who are already doing things and work together with them. In this regard, and in this example, the existence of the local neighbourhood forum and community centre proved critically important in facilitating the relationships, and the reciprocity, on which such joint working depends. Going back to the example of Poplar raised in the last chapter, Tulse Hill had the independent civic infrastructure that supported non-partisan organisation and action at the neighbourhood scale.

Changing the way that the state sees the people

The CBC project provided an opportunity for council officers to go out and experience the work of local community groups. One person described being 'a bit blown away by the ... stuff that people are already doing. That's really amazing. Some of the women, particularly at the last event ... [are] instinctively ... operating as community connectors, they're operating as community leaders really, they're linking up with services, [and] they're creating networks.' This officer went on to say that she was 'impressed with the existing community infrastructure, the semi-formal community infrastructure that exists in Tulse Hill like the forum ... [there's] a lot of stuff going on, being run by some pretty amazing people.' By encountering the organised community, this council officer had started to develop a better idea of what might be possible from working together. Without seeing what already existed and forming relationships with the key protagonists, council officers had no easy route to finding better ways of working together.

In this regard, another respondent argued that there was enormous scope for widening the opportunities for council staff to engage with the community. Drawing on her own experience with the CBC, she noted that 'I think people feel really empowered once they get out there and they talk to people, and they realise how much resource there is in the community, and how much you *can* let go ... how much people will do for themselves.'

Given the evidence of the capacity of existing community organisations and the strength of the relationships that already existed with the local councillors, the CBC exposed the need to engage the local community alongside the councillors from the start of any new project. Indeed, Margaret Pierre-Jarrett argued that the widespread failure to treat the community as a trusted and equal partner was preventing the council from being truly cooperative in the way that it worked. As she explained, 'if you're talking about co-producing things with the community, then right at the beginning of developing the idea you should have some community sitting with you to talk about how that happens and what it might look like and how it should be implemented, but I don't believe that [has] happened'. Later on, she explicated this argument by saying, 'It's about them [the council] coming alongside and speaking to people who are already on the ground and involving those people in their processes right from the beginning ... so that we can feed into whatever ideas they may be ... you can't say "I've got an idea, let me go and co-produce it with somebody". The idea's got to come from conversations that are had with all the people that need to be in the room as much as possible and that's the way to true co-design isn't it?'

In this regard, Erica Tate, the chair of the Forum, reported being very pleasantly surprised at the way in which the community were being asked to get involved in a project to redesign a local gyratory road system right from the start. She welcomed the way that the particular councillors and officers leading this project were able and willing to include the Forum as respected and equal partners before the consultants had even started their work. At the same time, however, she was concerned that the council 'could pull the plug any minute', and in this regard she was keen on developing a neighbourhood plan that would give the Forum greater statutory power to have its voice heard whether the council liked it or not (an issue that is taken up in the following chapter).

Indeed, during their interviews, the two community representatives both highlighted the challenges they had experienced in trying to work with the council. Erica reported that working with the council seemed to involve a lot of talking and waiting for things to be done. Similarly, Margaret reported that Hightrees CDT had been part of the early adopter programme to take over the adventure playground but she described her experiences as being pretty 'horrific'. She had found that many council officers did not appreciate the role of the community, and there were major delays in getting things done. The council had promised that all the necessary repairs to the Adventure Playground would be done before the agreed handover, but nothing was done for over a year. In addition, even though the council funding would drop to nothing after three years, they were being offered only a seven-year lease, which made it impossible to raise large amounts of additional money. Eventually, the council did come up with the potential solution that groups applying for funding would be given a letter for funders offering a lease extension, should the application be successful, but this had taken a lot of time to negotiate and was still not an ideal solution.

While Margaret praised some members of the council who 'got it' and whom she knew could 'smooth the way in making things happen', she also argued that working with the council had major costs for her small organisation. Echoing the arguments made by Eversole (2011) and raised in the previous chapter, Margaret provided other examples of the difficulties she had experienced in working with Lambeth Council. She had agreed to support a pop-up library that would be based in the centre, but council officers were insisting on volunteers having as much as 28 hours of training 'when they don't want to be librarians, they want to help out the community!' Similarly, Margaret had agreed to help administer a small fund to allow children in care to access small grants, but it had involved a lengthy and difficult meeting with council officers who wanted to run a tendering process that would waste yet more of her time. She found that the council's prevailing bureaucratic culture was ill fitted to the culture of the community organisations that operated on much smaller margins, with a focus on getting things done.

Thus, although the CBC team developed very productive relationships with representatives from the community, the evaluation exposed more general concerns about cooperative (and localist) culture. As one community representative explained, 'officers … need to understand what it means to be a community organisation, they have to have empathy, otherwise they will continue to behave in the way that they do'. She advocated more training and greater community exposure for council staff in order to foster better relations.

As part of this work, there was scope for including a much stronger focus on the role and activities of the network of neighbourhood forums. One member of the CBC team, in particular, reflected on the way that her experience had changed her view of the forums. While in the past she had seen them as 'slightly old style' and hadn't appreciated how important they could be in mediating relationships between the councillors, the council and the community, she told me that the Tulse

Hill Forum was 'really impressive and I wonder whether we could be using those kind of local networks much more'.

While the council provided very limited funding to the 10 area forums (comprising up to £10,000 each in 2015), and even this was allocated competitively by a panel incorporating representatives from the forums as well as the council, two council officers were also employed to help to support their activities. The Tulse Hill contact, Sarah Coyte, proved particularly important in the relationships that underpinned the work of the CBC project. Sarah already knew the key protagonists, she understood the ongoing activities being developed, had a feel for the extent of local support and an understanding of the local capacity that would be key to making things happen. The CBC project thus exposed the importance of supporting the small number of people who were able to facilitate community work in Tulse Hill; the councillors, the council officer who supported the Forum, the chair of the Forum and the director of the community centre. The project exposed the extent to which a small number of people were critical in fostering the connections that allowed the community to organise itself and get things done. While the local authority was an important part of this story, and the councillors and the officer involved were not widely credited for the work they were doing, the civic infrastructure of the neighbourhood Forum and the community centre were even more important in explaining what was done in the local area. By strengthening this infrastructure and communicating its role and importance to the wider council community, cooperative working could have been much more firmly established.[2]

Providing more support for the councillors doing neighbourhood work

The CBC project also highlighted the potential role of the councillors in acting as ambassadors for the council in the community. Highlighting their political credibility, one respondent told us that 'Nobody else has got the mandate that they have, even if it's only 30% turnout and all those other things that kind of cripple local democracy. At the end of the day, their voice is the only legitimate one.' The councillors have to knock on doors to win elections, they attend a range of meetings in their wards and they handle a lot of personal case work. This gives them enormous insight into the dynamics and issues faced by their local communities and, in many ways, the council was very poor at tapping this lay expertise.

Given that the CBC – and cooperative working more generally – was about developing a 'fundamentally different role for councillors' and 'there's varying capabilities as to how well equipped they are to step up and fulfil that role', many of those involved in the CBC project highlighted the gap between previous expectations of councillors and this new CBC role. Whereas in the past they had focused on 'constituency work and advocacy ... [with] occasional meetings of full council', this new role involved 'community leadership.' As another respondent explained, 'the key goal is to explore how we enable the ward councillors to take on this leadership role ... as a community connector ... [a] kind of gatekeeper ... for what the council is doing on an area basis'.[3]

However, even if people opted for the more community-oriented approach, Mary suggested that 'you can't just say to people "now you're leaders in your community!"' Additional support would be needed and this could include rolling out the ward-level information that was given to Mary and Marcia as part of the CBC project. This information included ward-level analysis of large data sets like the census in order to provide more clarity about the characteristics of local residents, areas of need and the assets that could be deployed in finding solutions. Participants also identified scope for providing more careful induction for councillors, possibly in relationship with Lambeth's network of local community forums, as well as offering ongoing support to help them in their role as community leaders. As one respondent suggested: 'I don't see how any of this can be done at any kind of level across the whole authority without there being kind of dedicated resources for ward councillors.'

In addition, even when councillors were able and willing to engage, as they were in Tulse Hill, the CBC pilot exposed the extent to which this raised a host of new issues about the council's relationship with councillors. In particular, council staff needed to develop a better understanding of and more respect for the work councillors were doing. Indeed, at one CBC meeting it transpired that in many cases councillors were not even informed about the council activity going on in their ward – regarding urban redevelopment for example. If councillors were to become community leaders, they would have to be involved in *all* the key decisions that impacted on their ward, however much this might involve a difficult reconfiguration of the relationships between officers and those in elected positions.

Shifting council–community relations of power

The CBC project highlighted the importance of the council more fully understanding the potential of councillors and the existing work of community groups. It provided evidence of the need to provide more support to councillors as well as stronger backing for the neighbourhood forums and community centres that provided the civic infrastructure that was critical to getting things done in the borough. Reflecting her experiences of being on the receiving end of council attitudes towards the community, however, one community representative told me that 'I think the officers have a view of the community which is not helpful ... It doesn't feel like an equal [relationship] ... and it doesn't feel like we're respected for what we're doing ... [They] have got a huge amount of resource and we've got a tiny bit of resource and yet still we get things done ... and then they even obstruct what we're trying to do and take away from the little we've got.' For her, the future of the cooperative council project was now in the balance: 'if it just carries on in the way that it has over the past two or three years then it's just going to fizzle out'. Going forward, she argued, it was imperative for both parties to listen to each other and understand each other's challenges before finding ways of working together.

Moreover, given that the CBC sought to explore the way in which the council and councillors interrelate with the community, it had implications for everything that the council was trying to do. Indeed, for one member of the CBC team the project exposed the 'way we should be working ... [it] is actually what we've said we're going to do as an organisation, so what we've set out to try and do in CBC is really what we should be doing in all our commissioning activity.' She suggested that disseminating the results of the project provided a potential opportunity to 'raise the question: ... as an organisation, are we living the values and ways of working that we've set out, are they still important to us? How do we do it?'

Echoing many of the issues raised in the previous chapter, Lambeth's CBC project exposed the challenges of state-led localism. However, in this case the community was organised, at the initiative, in part, of the council itself. The existence of the Tulse Hill Forum allowed the community to have independent representation in dealing with the council. It also provided the potential capacity to represent the interests of the diverse community in Tulse Hill, as well as sustaining the social network that could facilitate any future activity. While largely overlooked, it was critically important in providing the civic infrastructure that could underpin localism in Lambeth. Indeed, without such organisation, there would be no way for the community to take its place at the table of government, and I return to this issue again in relation to neighbourhood planning in the following chapter.

In addition, however, the role of the forum also raised many of the arguments about the relationship between direct and representative democracy that were raised in the previous chapter. Whereas much commentary highlights the inevitable tension between these two forms of political organisation and the likelihood that elected representatives will 'win out' over local volunteers (Gyford, 1976), the CBC highlighted the necessarily complementarity between the two. The councillors were already working in close relationship with the organised community over mutual concerns.

Before concluding this debate, however, it is important to recognise that Lambeth Council was also experimenting with other ways of neighbourhood work. Whereas the CBC was about relationship building between councillors, council officers and the organised community, the Open Works project in West Norwood provided a different approach. This was about starting from scratch. It started with residents who were not necessarily already connected or organised in any way, as is outlined further below.

Building a network of projects from scratch: Open Works in West Norwood

In 2013, Civic Systems Lab started to explore ideas with Lambeth whereby it would focus on one neighbourhood and establish new projects from scratch.[4] From 2014, it convened a team of people including their own Tessy Britton and Laura Billings, with a number of staff seconded from Lambeth Council, to work on a project called Open Works. They were based in a gallery space that had a shop-front on Knight's Hill in West Norwood that was very close to the station and local bus routes, and they invited people in for a chat. Once in relationship with people, the team explored their ideas, invited them to events and tried to connect them to other people and activities in the area. In the early days, the team were 'looking around at the skills and the resources … in the area … [to] make them visible … and [to] start building networks'. As illustrated in Figure 4.3, the team aimed to establish new activities on the basis of local interests, talents and existing resources (and for Parker, 2015, this kind of work is best described as organising around the commons as a civic concern).

In contrast to other council services where there is a set programme and people are invited to become 'clients' of the service or, at the most active end of the spectrum, to help by fulfilling a particular role as a volunteer or a 'friend' of the library or the park, Open Works took a much less prescriptive approach. As Laura Billings put it, its work was 'much more emergent, making use of underused resources, skills, people, time, ideas and aspirations', and while there were multiple outcomes from the work, there was no set programme for the work to be done.

Figure 4.3: The Open Works model

People   Ideas   Spaces   Projects

Source: www.theopenworks.org/

During the 18 months of the project Open Works engaged with about 1,000 people and helped to support 20 different projects (Table 4.5). To do this people were invited via both face-to-face and email contact to regular potluck suppers at which it was possible to make introductions and identify shared interests. One example included connecting people who were keen gardeners with someone from the bus garage who then provided some ground for planting which was cleared by another group of people with learning difficulties who were supported by a local charity. Other examples concerned the identification of under-used spaces for a range of creative activities such as cooking, gardening, woodwork and craft, and opening these up for local people to use. The vision was to create an alternative ecosystem of spaces and people such that: 'people would be able to have a map and say, I can take part in a repair cafe or a trade school or a cooking project, or I can grow stuff [here] … or I could help with learning a second language over there. [We want] to create a different participatory peer-to-peer network that doesn't exist at the moment'.

Echoing the language of localism and the Big Society, these projects were about 'citizens coming up and making something better, rather than asking someone else to make it better'. And, as such, they were about 'enticing more people into public life' through their own contributions rather than what the state might want them to do. As one participant put it in the project evaluation, 'It hasn't felt like charity, and that's been very important. It's been everybody, there's been real people working together, and on an equal level. People have been sharing their knowledge and ideas and skills − someone putting an

Table 4.5: The Open Works projects, 2014–15

Name	Description
Trade School	Teaching offered by local people in their area of skill, with food and drink served. This involved 42 teachers/classes delivered in 10 different spaces. Skills taught included building websites, beekeeping, guitar, tango, allotment planting, social media skills, photography, preparing sushi and singing.
The Great Cook	People offered a recipe for communal cooking at an under-used local kitchen and took the food home at the end. People registered and agreed to bring one of the ingredients. This involved 53 people in 11 sessions.
Potluck Suppers	People brought food to share in different spaces, with the aim of making new connections and linking projects.
Start Here	An ideas incubator for young people to develop project ideas using local entrepreneurs to mentor start-ups. Six young people were involved, with two projects developed (one in film and one in fashion).
BeamBlock	A yoga teacher offered free classes in local spaces.
Bzz Garage	A project to encourage bee-friendly planting in public spaces that started with space outside a local bus garage but went on to support other spaces. This involved 56 people in clearing the sites, planting, gardening and harvesting.
Library of Things	People donated unwanted things or shared under-used items and skills, hosted by a local library with a website. Sixty-four people gave items and 20 borrowed them.
The Joinery	Links people with skills with local work opportunities.
Festival of Ideas	Publicity for Open Works through a festival day hosted across various different spaces – 270 people attended.
Open Orchard	Encouraged planting fruit trees in public spaces. Eight spaces were identified, each supported by a local group, and the project involved 75 people.
Rock Paper Scissors	A collective shop opened for time-limited periods. This linked the local L'Arche group with other local makers, involving 61 people in two shopping opportunities.
The Stitch	A regular meeting for people who wanted to knit, sew, tailor, upholster and craft using L'Arche's facilities, which involved 51 people.
Out in the Open	Six weeks of activity organised and publicised to encourage new engagement in Open Works.
Civic Incubator	A six-week evening programme to support residents in developing project ideas and taking them to the next stage.
Play Street	Linked to a national network of temporary street-closures to allow children to play.
Department of Tinkerers	Using abandoned electrical items from Emmaus and the local recycling centre to dismantle and create new things.
Collaborative Childcare	A workshop to explore the idea of sharing childcare.
Public Office	A network of up to 15 freelancers who used different cafes to meet and work together.
West Norwood Soup	A crowd-funding dinner held to support local projects. Half the ticket cost covered the meal and the other half was for projects that were pitched and voted on during the night. This attracted 18 people to the first event.

Source: Summary developed from information in Civic Systems Lab, 2015

idea out there and people bouncing ideas back – and that's been really good' (Civic Systems Lab, 2015, 101).

The Open Works project rested upon the labour of making and sustaining relationships and, as Laura put it during interview, 'you have to be here, you have to be having the conversations, you have to go visit people in their spaces, invite them into yours, there isn't a way round that'. What's more, 'the coincidence of conversations doesn't happen unless you're here'. Echoing the arguments about the CBC made above, and those in relation to community organising (covered in Chapter Six), there were a relatively small number of people who proved critical to making this work. Without the small number of staff who could facilitate relationships and make connections, it would not have been possible to initiate or sustain the work that was done. Moreover, the fact that Lambeth Council funded Open Works only as a short-term experiment was a major weakness of the project itself. These practices would need to be supported for the long term, as part of wider efforts to foster a more vibrant civic culture, in order to have lasting effect.[5] The Civic Systems Lab report on the project emphasised the need for this long-term investment, arguing that 'this platform approach is about making a long term commitment for institutions to work collaboratively with local residents to transform a place. The commitment to building a new system will be a minimum of three years, but this is not an approach with an exit strategy. It is about building a new type of mutual relationship for creating outcomes collaboratively over the long term' (Civic Systems Lab, 2015, 59).

Localist lessons from Lambeth

The two examples of neighbourhood working outlined in this chapter have highlighted a number of important lessons for thinking about localism in relation to the work of local authorities and other arms of the state. In Lambeth, becoming a cooperative council had involved the development of a number of projects – including the two outlined here – that exposed the need for more equal relationships between the community and council. Rather than thinking that the council had to lead all the work that goes on in the borough, the projects exposed the extent to which the community were already doing important work, and/or had the potential to create new activities on a much larger scale, without very significant council support. Indeed, both projects relied on a small number of people to facilitate relationships in the community, and between the community and the council, and it would be productive for the council to think about the investments it could make to foster this kind of capacity without having to control everything or predetermine the outcomes.

Indeed, the CBC project, in particular, exposed the extent to which the council's leadership, in line with those in charge of other publicly funded and controlled organisations, are liable to think in terms of 'commissioning' things in/with the community. At a time of limited resources, when statutory expectations are likely to absorb more than the budget allocated for services, any council or public body has to develop a different approach to its work. The case studies presented here show that, in Lambeth's case, it was possible to provide very limited resources to people in the community who were already doing important work to connect people around their shared needs, interests and ideas, and thereby strengthen that community and its capacity.

While Lambeth was not fully in control of either of the projects examined above, it was facilitating the work that was done, and following the lead of the community. This role reversal exposed the existing and potential capacity of Lambeth's community, and it highlighted a way for the council to re-imagine the work that it does. By championing the ideas and resources of its own people it could signal stronger support for work of the neighbourhood forums, and it could also fund coordinators to replicate the work developed by Open Works on a neighbourhood basis. While the outcomes of this work would not necessarily conform to the predetermined outcomes already laid down by the council (as outlined in Table 4.2 above), the activity would foster stronger relationships, increase social capital and boost the capacity needed to underpin civic life in the borough. As such, Lambeth would be fostering a cooperative culture in and between its communities and in its own relationships with residents, even if it was not in direct control of the work that was done.

Since moving towards a cooperative model, the council had already strengthened the civic infrastructure of the borough, most obviously in relationship to its support for the neighbourhood forums. In addition, however, as outlined in this chapter, the council was also developing new vehicles for civic activity in relation to particular projects such as Open Works and the ones developed to run services like libraries and the youth service. Captured in Figure 4.4, this emergent civic infrastructure highlights the way in which Lambeth experimenting to further develop its cooperative model. However, the research suggests that further strengthening independent civic organisation and activity would allow the council to stimulate local capacity, which would have lasting benefits for the borough as well as its people.

Figure 4.4: The institutionalisation of the community in Lambeth's civic infrastructure

Representative structures

Vehicles for action

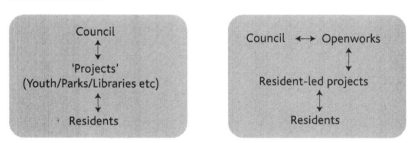

In this regard, local government can play a critically important role in providing or facilitating funding for the small numbers of people who are necessary to facilitate community projects and relationships. As demonstrated in both the examples of neighbourhood working examined in this chapter, and in the ones that follow, just a handful of people can be critical to activity at the neighbourhood scale. In the first case, the CBC, it was clear that the Tulse Hill Forum provided a mechanism through which community interests could be reflected, articulated and represented in dealing with the council. The fact that the forum included representation from other organised groups in the area (the community centre, tenants' and residents' groups and councillors) gave it authority and legitimacy. In the second case, Open Works, it was also clear that a small number of people were able to facilitate relationships and enable a number of local groups to develop their work. Both projects required limited funding in order to ensure their survival for the long term. Just as the forums received a small amount of money for their work every year, a model like Open Works needed the resources to employ a coordinator (and in future it might be possible to link this to the work of the neighbourhood forums) to maintain activity and relationships over time. This issue was similarly raised in relation to the idea of creating a parent-to-parent network for people in Tulse Hill. While the community could generate the ideas and energy to get something started, it needed the formalised relationships of the forum and the community centre to get it off the ground. Once such activities are underway, the council could provide or facilitate limited funding to support the work for the long term.

In so doing, the council would better demonstrate its cooperative principles. As one participant in the CBC explained, the council needed to 'reaffirm some of the cooperative principles that we set up a few years ago, which are still there, but which we are not necessarily living in everything that we do as an organisation ... [the] principle of co-production ... co-commissioning ... and [adding] some new insights about the strengths and assets that exist within communities ... [with an] impact on better outcomes'. The experience of Lambeth highlights the extent to which cooperative working is in keeping with localism, but it also exposes the degree to which it needs the state to work (and see) in new ways.

Notes

[1] In 2012 Steve Reed was selected as the Labour Party's parliamentary candidate for Croydon North and he won a by-election to become the Member of Parliament, being re-elected in 2015. After nearly nine years' service in Lambeth, Derrick Anderson left the council at the end of 2014. Councillor Lib Peck replaced Steve Reed as leader of the council in 2012 and Sean Harriss took over as Chief Executive in early 2015.

[2] This finding about the importance of council-led efforts to support the neighbourhood forums is reinforced by other research into the way that local councils relate to their residents, and the outcomes achieved. When Vivian Lowndes and her co-authors (2006) compared the work of eight local authorities across a range of areas and populations they highlighted the extent to which the local civic infrastructure can be critical in fostering local participation, despite differences in socioeconomy and political representation. Going on to compare levels of public participation in Hull and Middlesbrough, both of which had similar socioeconomic circumstances, exposed the importance of the political culture and the civic infrastructure that already existed. Whereas Hull had a paternalistic, patronage-based political culture and a poorly organised civil society, Middlesbrough had a more open culture with a much better-organised network of civil society groups. The research found that it was easier for relationships to develop where the community and voluntary sector had a strong coordinating infrastructure that allowed them to speak with one voice, so increasing their potential power in interactions with public and private organisations. The role of political parties was also found to be particularly important in shaping the civic offer being made. Politicians sent a 'message' to citizens about whether their participation was encouraged or not (Lowndes et al, 2006, 551). Differences in the political leadership at the council,

as well as civil society, thus helped to create space for more or less of a relationship between the state and local citizens.

3   In this regard it is interesting that the council's official view of councillors seemed to be out of line with what happened on the ground. Whereas public statements suggested that 'local councillors should continue to play a pro-active role in their local wards as community leaders; identifying problems and working with local people to tackle these' (London Borough of Lambeth, 2011, 24), the CBC project found that some councillors were less than willing to play this role and even those who were had little recognition or support for the work they were doing (and for the wider academic debate about the changing role of councillors, see Copus, 2010).

4   Civic Systems Lab is led by Tessy Britton and Laura Billings and it has led a series of projects or experiments in different parts of the country, including Lambeth, Norwich, Dudley and Essex (2015). The organisation has a mission to 'seed a local civic economy in the UK' and this is 'local, participatory and driven by people not systems'. As outlined on its website, 'Our challenge is to create the conditions and mechanisms for change to flourish ... [to] accelerate local initiatives to solve unique problems, with unique opportunities, with unique local resources. This practical and participatory localism cannot be ... a rare act performed by a few ... [it is] a different way of living our day-to-day lives in which the many become co-producers of the new local' (www.civicsystemslab.org/about/).

5   After 18 months of investment and activity the project was generating benefits for the participants and, as Laura explained, the 'outcomes are beneficial but ... [the projects] weren't designed to tackle a specific problem around employment or education or anything else. If it happens to involve education and confidence building, and skills sharing and new connections, and potentially, new opportunities, that's great but it wasn't designed to tackle an issue and there's multiple outcomes as well.'

FIVE

Institution building for localist futures

The key plank of the localism policy agenda – the Localism Act (2011) – instituted new rights to neighbourhood planning. As indicated in Chapter One, this legislation has galvanised a new wave of self-organisation in communities across the country. Many hundreds of forums have been set up in urban areas where none existed before, and many hundreds of parish councils are also widening their civic networks to develop neighbourhood plans. In contrast to the state-led localisms being developed in Poplar and Lambeth (and examined in Chapters Three and Four), neighbourhood planning has stimulated community-led localism. Rather like the permissive legislation that was so important in stimulating early local government in England (see Chapter Two), the change in the law and the statutory powers granted to neighbourhood plans have provided a new opportunity for those who are able and willing to seize the opportunity to exercise greater control over what happens in their neighbourhood. In so doing, their work has generated stronger local social networks and greater civic capacity, with ideas for projects that potentially extend far beyond planning. As the government minister for neighbourhood planning put it towards the end of the Coalition government's period in office:

> Of all the reforms that we've brought in this is the one which has the potential to completely transform our planning system, but perhaps more importantly than that, it can transform the relationships between communities and the change that happens in those communities ... Of course it's still an acorn but it has the potential to actually establish a proper sense of community control over development and over the way the community changes. (Nick Boles, MP, when Minister for Planning (DCLG), speaking at an event about neighbourhood planning in Leeds, July 2014)

As you'd expect, some people and some areas are better resourced to undertake neighbourhood planning than others and the pattern of existing activity will reflect underlying variations in the geography of civil society and civic capacity (as explored in Chapter Three). This chapter looks at the development of neighbourhood planning in three different urban areas, none of which had previous experience of community-led planning (more information about the research is provided in the appendix at the end of this book). The Exeter St James Neighbourhood Forum, in the city of Exeter in Devon was the first urban group to develop a plan and secure local support for it through a referendum in 2013. As such, the case highlights the local social organisation and civic skills that already existed in the area, allowing the group to act as fast as it did. Exeter St James also provides an example of the subsequent impact of the plan on local development and the social dynamics of the area. The group has already used its plan to contest a local planning decision, testing the extent to which its role in planning extends beyond the adoption of the neighbourhood plan. This group has also pioneered a number of community projects that developed as a result of the plan. It has set up a community trust to improve a neglected green space in the area, developing new forms of community engagement around the site and, at the time of writing, it has secured change of use from private open to public space.

In a similar vein, the example of Highgate in North London provides an example of the importance of pre-existing social connections, skills and capacity in allowing a community to mobilise around its local concerns. In this case, however, the local forum has fought for recognition of a 'natural area' that has long been divided between two different local authorities (Camden and Haringey) and overlooked by both. The Highgate Neighbourhood Forum has used the legislation to secure a stronger presence for its area in planning at a larger scale, as well as using it to launch negotiations with other key stakeholders who control transport, water management and land use in its location. In both cases, the legislation has helped the community to shift the balance of power in its relationships with government of various kinds.

The final example, Holbeck in Leeds, provides an interesting contrasting case. Holbeck is an area that has suffered from economic decline, high rates of population mobility and low levels of community organisation. In this case, the city council stepped in to initiate the formation of the neighbourhood forum, seeking to use the new legislation to help galvanise the community and develop new plans for social and economic improvement. Despite the intentions of the Localism Act, the Holbeck case actually provides another example of state-led localism, albeit that the council has had to work *with* local people to set up the forum and start the process of planning. Echoing some of the work being developed in Lambeth and outlined in the previous chapter, the city council has used the new rights to planning to try to reconfigure its working relationships with local organisations, residents and other state-funded bodies. However, the emergent Holbeck plan highlights the challenges of working in areas with weak pre-existing civic capacity. Indeed, it exposes the extent to which effective localism *requires* the kind of neighbourhood-level organisation, skills and capacity that were present in Tulse Hill in Lambeth and were evident in the way that the Exeter St James and Highgate forums have been able to develop a plan. This level of community organisation allows the local demos to be engaged on its own terms as a potentially equal partner in its work with the state. In Leeds, neighbourhood planning has allowed the city council to try to establish such infrastructure and to tap the talent that exists in the area, but more intervention would be needed to truly put the community in the driving seat of the process of neighbourhood planning.

In what follows, this chapter explores the recent history of planning before looking at the three examples in much greater depth. In so doing, I highlight the way that the permissive legislation has galvanised local people to act and thereby forged new relationships between different parts of the local community, as well as enhancing their capacity for action and change. The new rights to planning have been important in shifting the balance of power between community groups and the state, such that people have more confidence and willingness to act. As one research respondent from a planning department described it, the community has secured 'legitimacy through the legislation' and, as a result, these communities have a stronger vehicle for civic engagement, voice and action around – but beyond – planning. The relatively minor step of granting new powers to self-organised communities around planning has generated a wider range of often unexpected outcomes in local civic capacity. However, in areas where this capacity is weak, more direct intervention is needed to foster the social relationships and skills on which it depends. While the city council has tried to do this in Holbeck in Leeds, in other cases community-organising techniques have been used to identify local talent, teach civic skills and foster collective capacity, and this work is explored further in the following chapter.

Neighbourhood planning in its wider context

Historically, planning has had a hierarchical model of authority, with the power concentrated at the top of the chain. As Gallent and Robinson (2013, 5) suggest, this has meant that 'local policy actors

[are] guided by strategic decisions taken above them – an arrangement that has reduced the importance attached to local input, resulting in a system that is largely oriented towards achieving outputs fixed at higher levels'. While not fully overturning this arrangement, the new rights to neighbourhood planning have somewhat disrupted this model by granting new powers to those local citizens who are able and willing to develop a plan. Even though neighbourhood plans have to be in keeping with 'higher level' plans that are already agreed, for the first time, the local level of planning has statutory status. This means that 'the people' – and their representative bodies (parish councils and neighbourhood forums) – have been given some solid ground from which to represent themselves and their interests in the hierarchy of planning decisions. In neighbourhood planning, the plan, once passed by an independent examiner and a referendum of local residents, becomes part of the official planning framework that shapes decisions about development in the area.

While the New Labour governments (1997–2010) made similar noises about the importance of community engagement in planning, they did not grant any new rights to those working at the grassroots. As outlined in Chapter Three, local authorities were encouraged to reach out to a wider range of stakeholders and the Local Government Act (2000) made a particular demand on local authorities to produce community strategies via their Local Strategic Partnerships (LSPs). These community strategies were then to be implemented via action plans as part of the Local Area Agreement (LAA) that, in turn, influenced the Local Development Frameworks (LDFs, or what were called Local Plans after 2004). In addition, the Planning and Compulsory Purchase Act (2004, later strengthened by the Sustainable Communities Act 2007) introduced a requirement that every planning authority had to produce a Statement of Community Involvement that outlined the ways in which local people could shape the local plans that were being produced.

At that time, many parish councils took up the challenge of this work, developing their own plans that were supposed to contribute to the wider process of producing a plan, but they had no statutory power to realise these plans (Owen et al, 2007; Gallent and Robinson, 2013). Moreover, at the same time, local authorities were themselves bound to higher-level plans – Regional Spatial Strategies – that were prepared by unelected regional planning bodies in order to determine longer-term plans for infrastructure, housing and economic development. The authority of statutory planning (regional and local) and the prevailing balance of political power made it next to impossible for rural parishes to have any serious impact on the plans that were produced. As Gallent and Robinson (2013, 19) suggest, communities had 'to accept a significant degree of control, conceding power to the regions and the centre'.

If local parishes organised themselves to try to influence the planning process they often found it very difficult to be heard. Indeed, Gallent and Robinson (2013) looked at the activities of 10 different parishes in the Ashford area of Kent and found that the main impact of their work was ultimately on non-planning issues. They found very distinct differences between the parishes in relation to the strength of local community feeling, the skills available to work on the plan, the quality of relationships with officers working in the local council and the ideas being developed. However, beyond planning, they also noted that the process of engagement had 'a crucial role in triggering collective interests among residents, in local projects and in setting community priorities' (Gallent and Robinson, 2013, 181). With echoes for the lessons of neighbourhood planning that are outlined later on in this chapter, the research found that engaging people in planning allowed them to develop ideas for social action such that 'the process of plan production is often more important than the product, focusing local energies, bringing groups together and building new ties' (Gallent and Robinson, 2013, 188).[1]

There is, of course, a much longer history of community-led planning initiatives in the United Kingdom and much of this activity has been directed against the state over unwelcome decisions and/or unwanted development.[2] In one of the most well-known examples, the organised communities based in London's docklands launched their own People's Plan to oppose the planned development of the area during the 1980s, conducting very large-scale consultation around an alternative agenda for change (Brownill, 1990; Colenutt, 1991; Pile, 1995). As such, 'the people' were fighting to have their plan considered alongside state-led plans that were laid down from on high, and local citizens were generally left outside the rooms where decisions were made. In this context, neighbourhood planning is highly significant because it grants the community the right to set its own ambitions in the print of the plan, albeit that any community needs to be sufficiently organised in order to be able to develop a plan.

As Richard Lee from the campaigning group Just Space, which comprises a network of local groups with interests in spatial development and planning issues in London, put it during interview, 'There's always been an interest among community groups about producing their own visions and plans. It's not something that's just come in with the Localism Act … [but the law] has obviously given it a new dimension and a new push.' Thus the Localism Act has put new powers into the hands of local people to set out what they want to see happen in their local area. Whereas there were efforts made to move in this direction under the New Labour governments, planning remained firmly in the hands of professionals. In contrast, the new rights to neighbourhood planning have empowered a growing number of citizens who are able and willing to take up the cudgels of planning in order to try to influence what happens in their locality.3

Research in three different locations

As intimated above, I have explored the emergent neighbourhood forums and their plans in three very different parts of the country: Exeter, London and Leeds (Figure 5.1 and Table 5.1; see also the research appendix at the end of this book). The neighbourhoods concerned vary in size from just 3,000 people in Holbeck (Leeds) to as many as 18,000 in Highgate. Exeter St James and Highgate are both desirable residential communities in their urban locations, although the former has been affected by increased levels of student accommodation that reduced the stock of family housing available and reconfigured the demographics of the area, providing a key motivation for getting a forum established. In contrast, Holbeck is currently much less prosperous. Situated on the edge of the city centre, it has a proud history of being at the centre of Yorkshire's industrial revolution but has been blighted by de-industrialisation, motorway development around the edge of the area and years of neglect. The area comprises an area of back-to-back housing where an estimated one in six of the properties are empty, several social housing estates and a significant number of industrial units. Many respondents described the area as being 'low rent' and as having 'a transient population'. Indeed one respondent described Holbeck as being a place where 'people come in for a few months and then move somewhere else'. One of the local councillors similarly noted that 'there's such cheap housing [that new arrivals] go to the cheap housing and then they move on. As soon as they get a job, as soon as they get the wherewithal, they move. Then another lot come.' In contrast to Exeter and Highgate, where the communities were already firmly established and relatively well organised to act for themselves, the civic ground from which to develop neighbourhood planning was far less fertile in Holbeck.

Figure 5.1: Map of the case study neighbourhood forums

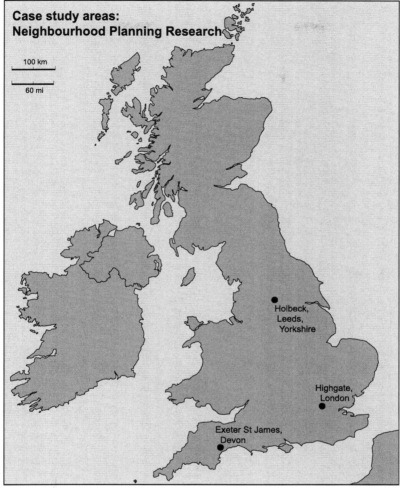

The forum in Exeter St James was one of the first set up in the country (in May 2011) and it worked fast to develop its plan, securing a successful referendum result in May 2013. The forum was able to draw on the skills of its members in planning, design, information technology and governance, and, with the help of a planning consultant, it drew up a relatively short, snappy plan stretching to 37 pages of text. In focusing on its shared vision for the area, the forum included plans to develop a better hub for the community, it listed a number of identified sites for development, advocated improved access to the area, protection for green spaces and better traffic management, as well as five community projects that were to provide a focus for the forum once the plan was adopted. The plan was designed 'to ensure that St James is a vibrant neighbourhood with a balanced and diverse community. It will be a great place to live and work close to the city centre and University and will support Exeter's character, identity and cultural life. St James will become known by people at all stages of their lives as one of the best parts of the city in which to live' (Exeter St James Forum, 2013, 13).

Table 5.1: Background to the case study neighbourhood forums

Area and 'character'	Population total (households)	Key dates	Key issues
Exeter, St James Inner city, largely residential, next to the university	6,891 (2,366) (53% full-time students, up 11% from 2001)	Started May 2011 (with frontrunner funding). Designated 2012. Referendum May 2013 (92% support)	Sustaining a balanced community (restricting houses in multiple occupation); supporting the residential community; local economic development; fostering community projects.
Highgate, London Suburban village, large green areas, largely owner-occupied, expensive property	18,000 (8,100); 1/3 under 20 and 1/3 over 60 years old; 30% born abroad	Started January 2012. Designated 2012. Draft plan 2015; rewrites and final consultation late 2015	Linking two LA areas (Camden and Haringey); representation to official bodies (transport, water); fostering community projects.
Holbeck, Leeds Inner city, old industrial, brownfield, transient rental market, some longer-term residents and business	3000 (n/a)	Started June 2012 (with frontrunner funding). Designated March 2014. Initial draft plan late 2015.	Initiated by the city council to attract investment and development and develop a new approach to planning.

In Highgate, North London, the forum was founded a year later than the one in Exeter (in early 2012), but it had to change national legislation in order to get permission to straddle the geographical boundaries of two local authorities. Indeed, part of the motivation for the Highgate plan was to overcome the legacy of being split down the middle by a local authority boundary such that 'Highgate is an area, in planning terms, which is split between a number of London boroughs and has never benefitted from a cohesive and singular set of development guidelines that recognise and seek to preserve the unique character and needs of the neighbourhood area' (Highgate Neighbourhood Forum, 2015, 6). The ambitious draft plan, published in early 2015, stretched to 100 pages and declared its ambition that 'Highgate should grow and prosper as a united community across the artificial boundary between the London Boroughs of Camden and Haringey. It should be a vibrant place that protects its unique character and heritage, while embracing new ideas and beneficial change. It should be home to a community that can work together to meet local needs, while respecting its differences and diversity. It should be a neighbourhood that complements and connects with neighbouring communities. All of these factors combined should make Highgate a better place to both live and work' (Highgate Neighbourhood Forum, 2015, 19). The plan then introduced five core objectives (covering social and community needs, economic activity, traffic and transport, open spaces and public realm, development and heritage), with 17 more specific sub-objectives that formed the basis of the proposed new planning policy for Highgate for the next 15 years (2015–2030). The document also identified five 'key areas' where new developments were possible, with specifications of the 'types and level of development that can be delivered and accommodated on the site' (Highgate Neighbourhood Forum, 2015, 73). As in Exeter, the plan also included an action plan for the community, identifying as many as 36 different areas for action that could improve the area beyond the process of planning.

At the time of writing the Holbeck neighbourhood forum did not yet have a published draft plan. It had a vision to make Holbeck 'a more attractive and healthier place for everyone, it will have a thriving local centre with a range of community facilities, a choice of quality but affordable housing, a variety of local job opportunities, all set in a green environment, respecting the heritage of the area, and well connected to the city centre and adjoining neighbourhoods' (Holbeck Neighbourhood Forum website). The forum was holding regular meetings and consulting people around the themes of housing, environment, traffic and transport, heritage, economy and employment, community facilities and services. In line with the other forums, it had secured some funding from national government schemes to hire professional help in drafting its plan. As in Highgate, the team in Holbeck had started work in 2012, but it had taken almost two years to secure designation and the process of drafting the plan was a much slower affair.

As elaborated further below, the process of neighbourhood planning had allowed these communities to identify and galvanise talent, skills and ideas among the local population. Moreover, the process of thinking about their communities and what they wanted them to become had proved to be a catalyst to new activity that was already making a difference to the social and physical fabric of the areas. Some members of the forums were meeting council and transport officials, discussing planned developments and acting as mediators between the state and the people. Beyond this, the forums were also building relationships across the community, identifying areas of need and potential grounds for action in future.

Galvanising community capacity

In all three of the study areas, the leading activists involved in developing the neighbourhood forums were already involved in local community organisations and/or activity prior to setting up a forum and creating a plan. In a number of instances, the participants had previously worked in related fields (in public services and community relations in planning) before taking up the challenge of neighbourhood planning. In Exeter, for example, the first chair of the forum, Jo Hawkins, had a career as a community relations advisor to developers before she turned her hand to galvanising the team in Exeter St James. Similarly, in Highgate, the first chair of the forum, Maggy Meade-King, had prior experience in community activity as a school governor and relevant skills through her previous employment in lobbying government. The second chair, Rachel Allison, who took over in 2014, had previously been a councillor in Haringey, and she brought a wealth of political experience into the work of the forum. In Leeds, too, the first chair, Dennis Kitchen, was active in his residents' association, was a governor at the local primary school, was leading a team of volunteers who were keeping the local working men's club open, belonged to Holbeck in Bloom and was active in a local Christian fellowship group.

Thus the forums were chaired by local people who already knew how to take the initiative to make things happen and they were capable of galvanising other people to act. In addition, however, particularly in Exeter and Highgate, the forums were able to draw upon a number of existing organisations and local social networks to foster support for the idea of a neighbourhood plan. In 2011, Maggy Meade-King took the initiative to explore the idea of setting up neighbourhood planning in Highgate, and even before the forum could be established Maggy and contacts from the Highgate Society had to lobby Parliament to change the law and allow a neighbourhood forum to straddle two boroughs. In so doing, they also had to work with six borough councillors –

three from each of the boroughs and, at that time, from three different political parties (Labour, Liberal Democrat and Green). Maggy had a meeting with them and won their support at the start of the process and then engaged them in the subsequent work of the plan.[4]

By January 2012, Maggy invited all potentially interested parties in the Highgate area, including local community groups and the six councillors, to a meeting to start the work of the forum, and as many as 80 people turned up. By drawing on the existing social infrastructure of the area, Maggy was able to get representation from a wide range of local groups – many of whom did not already know each other – to attend that first meeting. In reflecting on this experience she highlighted the different pockets of organisation in the area, contrasting the Highgate Society, which has a long history of work to protect the area and its heritage, with an active group supporting the local park, faith groups and schools, and the 20 residents' associations that later got involved, as well as individuals who had never been involved with any local group. The forum brought these people together around a shared interest in developing the neighbourhood plan. The forum was able to build upon the existing social infrastructure of these local networks, sending out newsletters and conducting consultation activities through each organised group, as well as having the new channels set up by the forum.

Similarly, in Exeter, Jo Hawkins and others started to galvanise support by contacting the six residents' associations that were already active in the ward, and when a community meeting was called in May 2011 as many as 90 people attended. In contrast, however, in Holbeck, the city council took a more prominent role in the work to establish the forum. While the forum similarly drew on the existing organisational networks of local residents associations' and social groups, these were relatively weak in the area of Holbeck itself. Dennis Kitchen, the chair, lived just outside the area, as did a number of others involved in the forum. The local groups that were active in the area (Holbeck in Bloom, Holbeck Gala, a group running the soup kitchen, a Christian fellowship, a group called Mosaic Church, and a team of volunteers running the local working men's club) were also often led by people who lived outside the area and, in this context, getting the neighbourhood forum established would have been very difficult without additional outside support. As Dennis explained, it all started off 'with an approach from the council ... [and] without their involvement, we wouldn't have got this far'. Ian McKay, the city council's Neighbourhood Planning Officer, chaired the steering group that predated the forum and he facilitated extra support. In addition, the forum was supported by a number of volunteers from Planning Aid England as well as by a retired planner who lived in the city and who worked with the group to develop their plan.

The Labour-led city council in Leeds had decided to support neighbourhood planning in a number of areas and, while Holbeck was the first, there were fledgling groups in Seacroft, Little Woodhouse, Hyde Park, Headlingly, Kirkstall and Beeston.[5] Ian MacKay argued that the council wanted to balance the designation of forums that already covered the richer suburban and rural parishes on the edge of the city. It also saw the new law as a way to bolster community-level organisation and give it a better chance to engage with local people over the issue of planning. In early 2012, Ian contacted the three existing residents' groups in the area of Holbeck and he then worked with them to submit an application for 'frontrunner' status that provided additional funding from national government to cover the work. He recalled that it 'took a lot of work to do that, people needed convincing', and even once they'd agreed to act, the steering group needed a lot of extra support.

In this regard, Ian chaired the group prior to its formal designation in April 2014. The city council also facilitated a number of planning workshops to help focus the ideas being developed in the plan. These were attended by a wide range of council officers from the teams responsible for regeneration, conservation, traffic and transport, health and well-being. Whereas in the other areas covered by my research the forums were meeting on their own, developing their own ideas and then taking the initiative to contact local council officers and a range of stakeholders, in Holbeck, the city council's planning team was taking the lead. In many ways, the forum provided a way for state-funded organisations to better coordinate what they were already trying to do. While the community was part of the forum, and it was involved in consultation over the development of ideas for the plan, the city council staff were largely driving the process.

The Leeds example thus seems to confirm the view that neighbourhood planning (and localism more broadly) will take off only where there are sufficient numbers of middle-class people and/or existing community organisations to lead in the work. Indeed, one of the councillors who represented the area was rather dubious about the idea to undertake this work in Holbeck because the area lacked the 'professional people who could have done it on their own'. Moreover, it made extra demands on the small number of people – herself included – who were already doing remarkable amounts of local community work. One of the councillors in Exeter also raised this issue, saying that 'The communities most likely to get themselves organised are ones like St David's, St James and Alphington where there's probably quite a high proportion of people with professional jobs, kind of middle-class people, early retirees with time on their hands. There's a danger that if there is money to be dished out it would go to those best able to organise themselves quickest and the wards that, by definition, the Labour councillors are more likely to represent will find it more difficult because they don't have that level of skill [and] even if they've got the skill, they don't have the time, they're busy keeping body and soul together.' In this regard a number of councillors and officers referred to a risk of the 'usual suspects' and 'usual places' taking the lead in this work.

Certainly, the cases of Exeter and Highgate demonstrate the importance of having skilled, professional people who were able to take the lead in the work of the forum. As Jo Hawkins, the first chair in Exeter, put it, 'there are not many wards in Exeter which could have done this. We are very fortunate that we have the people with the expertise, interest and time.' In addition, it seemed particularly important that some of the people in both Exeter and Highgate had just retired. Di Boston, the second chair in Exeter, who had just retired from her professional job, reported that she had missed the 'level of professional respect' she'd experienced at work and 'being chair gives me some of that in return'. In contrast, the existing social organisation and capacity in Holbeck were too weak to have catalysed a neighbourhood forum without external support. While the city council was helping to support the forum and nurture its work, council staff were trying to fill a vacuum in local civic capacity and it was not clear whether this was going to be sufficient to generate the independent civic organisation that would be needed to realise the ideas being developed as part of the plan. Moreover, it is not clear that the people living in Holbeck would have put neighbourhood planning at the top of their 'to do' list if they had been in a position to organise themselves to sort out local concerns. In places like Holbeck – just as was highlighted in relation to Poplar in Chapter Three – there is a case for additional funding to try to organise the community so that it is in a position to engage in localist work.

Developing a vision for the people and place

A key part of the work of neighbourhood planning involved efforts to consult the local community about their feelings about their area and their ideas for improvements. During the summer of 2012 the Highgate forum distributed questionnaires to every household in the area, backed up with online access to the survey, asking people what they liked and disliked about the area, with space for additional comments and a chance to sign up to stay in touch with the forum. The survey generated hundreds of responses and, in its own summary, the forum emphasised the extent to which people appreciated the 'village atmosphere', the built environment, local amenities and green spaces. Echoing Sampson's (2012) findings about the importance of community efficacy in Chicago, it also found that people appreciated the fact that it was the kind of place where 'people care about what happens'. The forum identified traffic, parking, transport provision, retailing and the protection of green spaces as areas for improvement, and these have been key to the plan. The forum subsequently revisited the community to explore more detailed ideas about these concerns and, following the publication of the draft plan in 2015, a second round of consultation also helped to increase local engagement in the work it was doing.

Of course, such consultation generated conflict, and in Highgate, where as many as 50 people were involved in different groups working on the different parts of the plan, tensions sometimes arose. As Maggy remarked, 'it's not all sunshine and light. There are people frustrated that other people won't do what they want them to do and don't agree with them about what the policies should be and all that sort of thing.' It was a community project, and there was no one in the forum able or willing to exercise the authority that might have helped to speed things along. The planning groups had to work things out and reach a compromise, however long this might take.

In contrast, the team in Holbeck started from a very different position. Its area had been the focus of intensive periods of council-led planning and local consultation in the past and, in testimony to the arguments made in Chapters Two and Three, the area had been the focus of a lot of activity during the New Labour years. Local residents' groups had each sent representatives to a local Community Association Group (CAG) that worked with the council to oversee local regeneration, including the development of a Private Finance Initiative (PFI) to build new housing in the area. Dennis Kitchen and Anne Hooper, another member of the forum, had sat on the CAG for Holbeck for as long as seven years and much of their work had been overturned by the subsequent collapse in the market for housing. When they were approached to get involved in the neighbourhood plan, it felt like a continuation of this previous work. They were used to working with the council to try to shape development in the area, and neighbourhood planning was more of the same. Although the forum was supposed to be led by 'the people', there was insufficient independent community self-organisation for this to happen, and the council stepped in to continue its work.

The neighbourhood forum galvanised a small number of community representatives to work with city council officials to consult local people and try to develop a plan. Dennis argued that they wanted to make Holbeck 'a place not just to pass through but to become a destination … we want to make it into more of an area',6 but, given the scale of the problems they faced, it was essential for state-funded organisations to lead in this work. The forum was keen to explore options for valuing the industrial heritage of the area and seeing the potential to make more of the old buildings and infrastructure that had fallen into decline and disuse. Indeed, the area had developed as an industrial centre in the early 19th century, when it became famous for its mills, ironworks and machine making. The man who later became the first mill-owner to sit in Parliament, Sir John Marshall, built a six-story water-powered flax mill in Holbeck in 1791. Next door, in 1836 he built a larger, Egyptian-style mill that stretched over two acres and still stands today, with little left of its roof. At its height, this factory grazed cattle on the meadow on top of the roof. Yet much of this remarkable industrial heritage is left unremarked. An old viaduct built in blue brickwork (and founded in 1879) that runs through the area is unprotected and largely ignored. As a result, the neighbourhood forum was trying to make more of this history in the work of its plan.

Of course, these projects might have been developed by the officers of the city council without the work of the forum, but neighbourhood planning was providing a way for officers to work more closely with local people and to plan things together. For Ian MacKay, it was also a way to foster relationships between the professionals who were already working in Holbeck. As he put it, the critical relationships are 'not just between the council and the people in Holbeck, it's actually within the council and in many ways, you could argue that's the most critical part of the jigsaw'. Indeed, steering investment and the necessary regeneration activity in an area like Holbeck made planning extremely difficult unless the different professions and their organisations were working together. The existence of the neighbourhood forum and efforts to hold regular planning workshops that included community representatives as well as professional groups made this much easier to do than had been the case in the past.

In other areas, however, it was clear that the forums were developing ideas and activities that would *not* have been advanced by local government in the absence of the forum. In Exeter, a team of volunteers had focused on improving a green space called Queen's Crescent Garden that had been neglected for years. Indeed, Jo Hawkins reported that the area – once called a pleasure garden when it was created in the 19th century – had not been maintained since 'at least 1930'. The two ward councillors also reported previous efforts to maintain the area that had failed to progress. For Jo Hawkins, the first chair in Exeter, the forum and plan had galvanised people to improve Queen's Crescent Garden by giving them the sanction to act. The neighbourhood plan included a section on the garden (policy EN3) and in early 2014 the forum held some design workshops with local people to develop their ideas for the space. People were keen on getting rid of the walls around the area, opening up the space, adding a children's playground, some new planting and a hard-standing area that could be used for events. As part of this work, the forum also established a Friends of Queens Crescent Garden group that allowed it to 'bring in new blood'. The project had also allowed the forum to forge closer links with the mosque and the primary school adjacent to the site and it was keen to widen the group of people involved.

In October 2014, the forum took this work further by launching a new community benefit society, called Exeter St James Trust Ltd, that was designed as a vehicle for implementing its plan for the site. Members of the community were invited to buy a minimum of five shares (costing £1 each) and they had sold 2,305 shares by the time of the first public meeting held on 16 January 2015. The four-strong board of directors (all from the steering group of the neighbourhood forum) was elected by the 60-strong meeting and it outlined its plans to raise funds to support the development and make the case to the council for planning permission. Once agreed, this would allow the council to then make a compulsory purchase order for the site and lease it to the trust for a minimal fee.

In addition to the work at the garden, the forum was establishing close relationships with a number of important local organisations as part of its activity to support the work of the plan. Early on it had forged close relationships with local businesses, and John Lewis – the local department store on the edge of the ward – had sponsored its campaign during the referendum in 2013. It had also established a liaison panel with the university to look 'at the long term issues and the university's ambitions'. It was working closely with senior people from the university but was also including the students' union and the neighbourhood partnership from the neighbouring ward of St David's, which also adjoined the university's grounds. A similar initiative was being developed in relation to transport to ensure that the local community had a voice in plans to redevelop the bus garage and reorganise bus routes. While one of the councillors argued that it would have more power to lead on these issues if it became a parish council, the forum was, in some ways, already acting as a community council, representing local people and their interests with agents of government such as the council, transport bodies and the university.

Similarly, in Highgate, the forum had galvanised a group of people to secure a green area called The Bowl. The Friends of Highgate Bowl was set up in 2014 to protect the site from development, with the aim of raising the funds to buy it and then develop it further for community use. This was one of a number of community activities reported at the fourth Annual General Meeting (AGM) of the Highgate neighbourhood forum in May 2015. By working together on the basis of shared interests in the protection and development of the local area, the forum had identified nine different action groups, and at the AGM the ex-chair, Maggy Meade-King, went through them, explaining the focus of their work and asking people to get more involved. This list included: developing opportunities for local volunteering; support for local businesses (including the need to protect premises from increasing rents, and the potential for fostering synergies between them and the local community); advocating for the needs of pedestrians and cyclists with local authorities and Transport for London (TfL); ongoing work with TfL to improve local bus routes (including the provision of better east–west connections); looking after small open spaces; activity to support renewable energy; heritage and the public realm. Many of the 80 people present were already engaged in this work and others signed up to take part.

Questions of power in the process of planning

Respondents from each of the areas argued that neighbourhood planning was reshaping the way things were done in their localities. In all three areas, the key protagonists told me that in the past local residents had often complained about things rather than feeling able to do things themselves. As Di Boston in Exeter reflected, 'I used to hate going to residents' association meetings because people would moan all the time about all the things that I was fed up with too. But nobody would do anything.' Similarly, Dennis reported of the residents groups: 'People are very quick, especially in these residents' groups, to come along and moan about what's not been done. This has not been picked up or that's an area that's not been looked after, and they come with all their moans but not any constructive things, you know, positive things. It's all looking at the negatives. And [now through the forum] they've got to try and make Holbeck into a positive area to live.' In each case, the forums welcomed the chance to exercise control over planning and development, but in Exeter and Highgate, where the process was furthest advanced and the initiative lay with the community rather than the council, some planning professionals raised a number of concerns about the process of neighbourhood planning. One officer suggested that while neighbourhood planning was positive in stimulating community organisation, he argued that it had given local people a false sense of their own powers in planning. Indeed, once a neighbourhood plan becomes part of the local authority's local development plan, the forum has no continued formal involvement. Thus, in Exeter the council staff felt that the Exeter St James Forum had failed to understand its limited role in the future of planning. As one planning officer put it, 'I think one of the problems with the system is that ... the community probably thought they were going to become the Planning Authority, that they would have a greater discretion in applying the policies. The reality is [that] whilst they produced the policies and obviously, we helped them do that, the reality is it's our judgement as to whether something complies with the policy, and with so many planning policies, they are questions of degree.' This question of judgement was also raised by officers in North London, who highlighted the scope for conflict over the interpretation of the policies laid down in the draft Highgate plan.

This issue actually came to a head in Exeter during 2014, when the forum clashed with the council over its interpretation of the plan in regard to the proposed development of an old pavilion on a cricket ground in Exeter St James. The plan was to demolish the pavilion (built in 1904) and put up four multi-storey blocks for 159 students. When this planning application came forward, the forum objected on the grounds that it was against a specific policy in the neighbourhood plan, but the council's planning committee made its own decision *against* the views of the forum. The Exeter St James Forum then initiated a judicial review against the council. In this context, the planning authority and the developer then acted to reach a compromise by going back to the applicant, who made some amendments to the design that were accepted by the council and the forum. The officer involved reported having 'discussions about how we handle things in future to try and make sure that they [the forum] feel their views are given weight', but it was clear that the forum had tested the balance of power. Indeed, a representative from the Exeter St James Forum welcomed a change in relations after this case, reporting that now 'the council agreed that although we were not a statutory consultee ... this could have been handled a lot better and in future, when we meet developers or major applicants, especially if is related to policies ... a case officer ... will come and then have a separate meeting with us to find out what we thought about things so that we don't reach the stage where we either have to start or threaten litigation again. It was a compromise but that was an achievement.'

Following this experience the forum had strengthened its planning and design panel so that it would be better able to defend the plan be 'more assertive' in future. It was this body that would liaise with developers as well as with the council, and the forum was anticipating further conflict over the development of the local football ground that would further test its mettle in the months ahead. In this regard, one planning officer in North London reflected that in the past 'we produce a plan, we consult [and] you tell us what you think of it but this is the opposite. You're doing a plan, you come to us, you show us what you've done and we comment on it and we're helping you, so it reverses that relationship.' While he anticipated conflict over the interpretation of the plan once it was adopted, he also recognised the significance of this shift in the balance of power, saying that 'it is a significant transfer of power ... you have the chance to have a plan that has teeth that is written by you, it is a big thing ... Ultimately, their plan has the same weight as our plan.' As such, the legislation has started to reconfigure the balance of power between organised community groups and local authorities. However modest this is in practice, it represents an opportunity to forge new relationships with local government and developers, and this provides an incentive for engagement for local people who want to secure local change.

An emerging infrastructure for localism?

There is a long history of local communities organising themselves to defend their interests, often in the face of a perceived threat of some kind. In what E.P. Thompson (2009) would call 'reactionary radicalism', people have always organised to defend what they have, often deploying very radical tactics against forms of change. For Roger Scruton (2006 [2000]), a large part of English identity and culture is rooted in exactly this sense of local people getting together to create new organisations for getting things done. While this might be a reaction to change and an attempt to defend what exists, it is equally about meeting a perceived local need. As he suggests, 'From the guilds to the trade unions, from the cathedral chapters to the colliery brass bands, from the public schools to the Boy Scouts and the Women's Institute, from the Worshipful Company of Farriers to the Institute of Directors, you will find the same "clubbable" instinct, which prefers custom, formality and ritualised membership to the hullabaloo of crowds, and which imposes a quiet and genial discipline in place of spontaneous social emotion' (Scruton, 2006, 14). Neighbourhood planning has similarly offered people the opportunity to try to defend what is valued in the locality while developing positive ideas for reform. The top-down permissive change in the law has opened the door to bottom-up initiatives and, rather than being a defensive protest movement, neighbourhood forums are an institutional mechanism that can allow urban communities to take some initiative and bear some responsibility for the development of their locality.

There are certainly opportunities for these emerging neighbourhood forums to take on a wider role in governing their local communities. In Exeter, the city council was already looking to work more closely with citizens in running local parks, allotments and libraries, and the forums were obvious places to go to explore these ideas. Devon County Council was similarly looking to train volunteers to act as snow wardens and road wardens, and it needed to find people who could take the lead in clearing their streets of snow and filling in potholes. However, as in Lambeth (and reported in the previous chapter), there was a tendency for the city and county council officers to come and talk to the community when they wanted something doing. Rather than establishing a working relationship in advance, they were convening meetings only when they wanted the community to take on some work. As Di Boston in Exeter put it in relation to the council's efforts to hand over the parks, 'if you get all the communities together for the first time, the first thing you don't ask them is to take something on', although that was what they had done. Rather than asking them what they would like to do and how the council and community could work together in general, the council focused on the parks and 'it just looks like they're just interested in it because of saving money. They can't afford to do things so they're going to off-load it!' Rather than seeing the community as an equal partner in the development of the local area, there was still a tendency for local government to put its own interests above those of a sustainable partnership with organised local groups.

At the national scale, government ministers have been encouraging neighbourhood forums to become parish councils so that they can manage a share of the benefits of development (through the Community Infrastructure Levy) and raise a precept in order to provide new services and make local improvements. In Highgate the forum's website has a space where residents can make suggestions about how such money would be spent and it includes ideas for an adventure playground, improved planting and green spaces, improvements to bus stops and cycle-ways, investments to assist local businesses and create green energy, as well as better signage. If the forum had a budget, it could decide how to spend its money in the local area and, as Rachel Allison suggested, very simple things like improving the crossings and pavements outside a residential home could make a dramatic difference to the quality of life for some local people. Moreover, the forum could listen and act much faster than the local authority had done in the past. Having a relationship with local people would also make it easier to publicise the benefits of the money that was being spent.

However, many of those involved in the work of the forums were concerned about becoming more formalised and politicised. Reflecting on the future of the forums in London, Richard Lee argued that 'the parish council is part of an established system and … what most community groups find attractive about the neighbourhood forum is not that you elect some representatives to speak for you over a period of time, but that actually you have a more participatory approach rather than a representative approach. Parish councils are part of a representative system. Parish councils are serviced by an administration, similar to the chief executive and the returning officer of the local authority, obviously on a much smaller scale, but you still have an administrator with that kind of function, basically to guide the parish councillors in terms of their function, their duties, what they can do legally, what their relationship is with the bigger authority and all of that.' As such, there was concern that neighbourhood forums would become more rigid and formal if they became parish councils, but many were also worried that political parties would get more involved. As Jo Hawkins in Exeter suggested, 'As soon as you start things like parish councils you bring in party politics and we've kept party politics successfully out of it.' This desire to retain a non-partisan culture, with a strong connection to the local population, was a major reason for deciding not to take up the option of becoming a parish council in the cases I looked at.

In this regard, it is highly significant that this desire to remain independent of political parties is now also being reflected in the work of some existing parish and town councils across the country. The campaigns undertaken by small groups of people in Frome, Somerset and Liskeard, Cornwall, have become something of a beacon for others looking to improve the political culture of their local council, to better reflect the interests of the local community and to take new initiatives (Harris, 2015; MacFadyen, 2014). In addition, a number of the new parish councils that have been recently established in urban areas have sought to defend their non-partisan culture, and I return to the example of the Queen's Park community council at the end of this book. Effective local government is likely to be non-partisan government, and the pioneers of neighbourhood forums, as well as the activists now trying to re-energise existing parish and town councils, are reflecting a genuine desire to represent the interests and concerns of local people – rather than political parties – in the work that they do.

This chapter has highlighted the way that new rights to neighbourhood planning have provided the impetus to create new neighbourhood-level, community-wide institutions in urban areas where none had existed before and, with parallels to the work of the English parishes (introduced in Chapter Two), these new bodies have been concerned to communicate with local people, to develop ideas for improving the area, to look after green spaces, support local businesses and represent their interests to other organisations. These forums have started by galvanising the minority who are able and willing to act, and from there they have organised activity that identifies new people who are interested in getting involved and further increases local capacity. Even in the case of Holbeck, where the city council took the initiative in starting the process, those involved were able to then reach out to others over their plans to make change. In all three cases, people reported that they enjoyed meeting their neighbours and this was a key motivation for staying involved. Once established, the new bodies generated new opportunities to engage, and a new round of activity that often went far beyond the issue of planning.

Notes

[1] It is significant that some of the parish councils that have been able to develop neighbourhood plans were those that had completed work during this earlier phase. As an example, the Upper Eden neighbourhood plan, the first to be agreed in England, built on prior work that had been done during the 1980s (see Sturaker and Shaw, 2015).

[2] There is also an important literature about more collaborative endeavours in planning but they have often relied on the goodwill of professional planners and the vagaries of the political context (see Geddes, 1915; Fagence, 1977; Sandercock, 1998, 2004; Sandercock and Lyssiotis, 2003; Healey, 2006, 2012).

[3] Although it is not the position adopted in this chapter, there is a growing body of scholarship that dismisses initiatives like neighbourhood planning on the grounds that they reflect and reinforce neoliberal political economy (see, for example, Allmendinger and Haughton, 2013). Critics argue that citizen-led planning initiatives are being supported in order to roll back the state as part of a wider

neoliberalisation of public policy, eroding the role of local government and cutting public expenditure (Peck and Tickell, 1994; 2012).

[4] In the early days of its efforts to establish a neighbourhood forum the group encountered great hostility from officers in Haringey Council. The Labour Cabinet was not open to the idea of neighbourhood planning and this influenced the approach of the staff. However, this improved as time went on, not least because the officers in Haringey began to work alongside more helpful people from Camden (also Labour controlled).

[5] Although it might seem rather unusual for a local authority to initiate a new urban forum, a larger research project conducted in 2014 found that as many as a quarter of forums were initiated by the local authority (Parker et al, 2014, 18).

[6] This phrase is particularly significant when we consider that civic activity is positively related to what John and his co-authors (2011) call 'neighbourhood affect', by which they mean feelings about the neighbourhood. In their statistical analysis of data from the 2005 Citizenship Survey they found that civic activity was positively related to feelings about the neighbourhood, as well as being related to lower levels of trust in government, while being un-associated with moral beliefs and/or social norms. In trying to improve the area of Holbeck and make it what he called a 'destination', Dennis was trying to shape the way local residents felt about the place where they lived.

SIX

Community organising: past, present and future

Thus far, this book has explored new forms of neighbourhood-level civic organisation that have emerged – directly or permissively – through the actions of government. As outlined in the previous chapters, national legislation has opened up the space for people to organise around planning, and local authorities and other state-funded bodies have also developed new ways to engage with community partners at the neighbourhood scale. This chapter now looks in more detail at the issue of community organisation and capacity. People have always built and supported organisations around their own particular interests such as religion, politics and sport, as well as their need for self-help. As already outlined in Chapter Three, people are differentially engaged in such organisations and there is an uneven distribution of organisations between different locations. In this regard, there have long been efforts to foster more community development in the poorest parts of the country (Twelvetrees, 2008; and for the example of the Community Development Project established in the 1970s, see Chapter Three). Such community development is variously envisaged as a way to strengthen social relationships, to provide better services and to foster local capacity (Wyler, 2009). Once it is established, there is further scope for local organisations to work with each other to strengthen the collective voice, representation and capacity of the local community (Saegert, 2006).

These efforts have been captured in concepts such as 'community capacity' (Chaskin, 2001), 'local effectivity' (Cooke, 1989), 'localities as agents' (Cox and Mair, 1991) and 'collective efficacy' (Sampson, 2012). Such concepts reflect the way that the geography of social organisation shapes the potential for political change (Agnew, 1987). As Chaskin (2001, 295) puts it, community capacity reflects 'the interaction of human capital, organisational resources, and social capital existing within a given community that can be leveraged to solve collective problems and improve or maintain the well-being of a given community'. Neighbourhood planning has exposed the existence and potential of this kind of capacity in Exeter St James and Highgate, and its absence was evident in relation to the NCB project in Poplar.

The fact that communities are differentiated by their existing and potential civic capacity has been a recurring theme in this book, and it remains the key challenge for localist statecraft and citizenship in England today. Indeed, if, as outlined in Chapter One, the future of policy making is to be increasingly dependent on local civic capacity, localism is likely to reinforce existing spatial divides. The places that face the greatest challenges will be the ones least able to mount a response. In this situation, it may be relatively easy for local state-funded organisations to step in and fill the political space, but, as has been evident in the cases of Poplar and Holbeck (and was similarly true in relation to the projects developed during the New Labour years), this will not necessarily generate the community organisation and civic capacity necessary for people to organise around their own interests on their own terms. As in Poplar, state-funded organisations will default to consultation, or as in Holbeck, they will work with key collaborators who try to represent the local community, but neither approach is sufficient to generate the independent capacity on which localist statecraft depends. Indeed, localism requires the creation of independent and self-organised community groups that have the authority to conduct their own organising activity, to develop an agenda, to lobby for change, to represent and negotiate for the community and, when necessary, to mobilise in order to secure the power needed to get a result. Such a body would have authority only if it represented the broad range of local community interests, was inclusive and proved able to attract new people to get more involved. This is a tall order, and it is remarkable how many communities do show signs of being able to organise in this way.

The focus of this chapter, however, is to look at what can be done when such pan-community organisation does not yet exist and it is necessary to try to build such connections from scratch. While community development will obviously be critically important in such locations, this chapter looks at a particular model of community intervention that has been developed to link existing community organisations and their members to the political sphere. Broad-based community organising is designed to work with local people, through the organisations to which they already belong (such as schools, faith organisations, community centres and trade union branches), and then engage them in political life around a set of locally determined shared goals (Walls, 2014; Bretherton, 2015; Schutz and Miller, 2015).

This model of politics has a strong track record in building power and securing change in poor communities in North America, and it provides important lessons for thinking about the way to foster greater civic capacity in poor communities in England today. Moreover, the history of its development has particular salience for understanding the challenge of localism; it was developed to allow people living in the poorest parts of the city of Chicago to win a place at the negotiating table and shape the changes taking place in their city during the 1930s and 1940s. As such, this tradition highlights the kinds of interventions that are necessary to allow people to organise and develop the civic skills required to engage successfully in political life.

In what follows, I look back at the history of this approach in order to consider the lessons for localism and the creation of the Big Society today. The first sections of the chapter trace the history of this approach back to the University of Chicago's School of Sociology in the early years of the 20th century. As a new generation of scholars and their students mapped the prevalence of social problems in the fast-changing city, they also developed interventions that were designed to help people to solve their own problems. In an early manifestation of arguments for the Big Society that are being made today, a number of academics set up the Chicago Areas Project to build alliances to develop indigenous leadership in some of the poorest parts of the city. These alliances were then supported to deploy social research methods to identify shared problems and develop ideas for solutions. One of the first of these alliances, in the neighbourhood called Back of the Yards, located next to the stockyards and meat-packing factories on the south side of the city, went on to generate a model of community politics that spread across the US and then further afield. Looking at that early example highlights the potential for alliance building around shared interests – and the potential gains to be made – at the neighbourhood scale (Alinsky, 1941, 1946, 1971).

This chapter looks at the way in which this model of politics has evolved since those early days in Chicago and it draws on original research conducted with the broad-based community alliance called Citizens UK and its work in East London, to explore the wider implications for localism (full details of the research are provided in the appendix at the end of this book). While the Conservative Party has recognised the potential to use community organising to support community development and capacity building to underpin localist statecraft and citizenship, its support for community-organising activity between 2011 and 2015 has not proved sufficient to reconfigure the situation in the poorest parts of the country (although there were positive outcomes from the project as evaluated by Cameron and Rennick, 2015). Much greater investment would be needed to do this, and in so doing it would be important to think about the model of community organising most likely to succeed in this work.

To this end, I end the chapter by highlighting the limits of both of the models of community organising currently being deployed in this country. I argue that one (led by Locality) operates by targeting individuals in a way that is too piecemeal to effect wider change, but that the other (led by Citizens UK) is too dependent upon a base of shrinking civil society organisations and operates at too large a scale to fill this political space. A model that sits in the middle ground between these current positions would better suit the requirements of localist policy making and practice today. Organisers would need to focus on creating and connecting residents' organisations with the other community groups that already operate at the neighbourhood scale. As recognised by the pioneers of community organising in Chicago in the 1930s and 1940s, as well as those involved in neighbourhood forums today, this is the scale at which it is possible for people to forge meaningful relationships with each other in order to engage in ongoing activity around a common agenda.

Chicago, sociology and Back of the Yards

The tradition of broad-based community organising has its roots in the city of Chicago in the early 20th century. While the model is most strongly associated with the launch of the Back of the Yards Neighbourhood Council in Chicago in 1939, its roots lay in the newly established School of Sociology at the University of Chicago. The School was established in 1892 and the first generation of professors started to develop a new approach to understanding the city. Shaped by the philosophical tradition of pragmatism that was developing in the country at that time, this first generation sought to ground their academic scholarship in the social life of the fast-changing city that was growing around them (Jackson, 1984; Barnes, 2008; Harney et al, 2016). Robert Ezra Park (1864–1944) and one of Chicago's first graduate students, Ernest W. Burgess (1886–1966), were particularly important in developing this new approach to urban research. From 1916, they shared an office, taught and wrote together, and argued that the city of Chicago was a laboratory for understanding urban social life and culture. Deploying new sources of research data and research techniques that included the social survey, personal life histories and ethnography, these scholars sought to map social problems, patterns of local culture and emergent social organisation. As Burgess and Bogue (1964, 5) later put it when reflecting back on the tradition they had helped to develop, these sociologists had 'an ambition to understand and interpret the social and economic forces at work in the slums and their effect in influencing the social and personal organization of those who lived there. Although the objective was scientific, behind it lay a faith or hope that this scientific analysis would help dispel prejudice and injustice and ultimately would lead to an improvement in the lot of slum dwellers.'

Their programme of research – described as 'the City as a sociological laboratory' (Burgess and Bogue, 1964, 5) – reflected this mix of research, analysis and action. The small group of academics gradually attracted funding and greater support across the university, and the resulting body of work comprised three key activities: mapping the spatial distribution of social problems; linking these maps to social practices and cultural phenomena (in what became known as 'natural areas'); and then using this research to develop practical interventions to improve social life in the city.

Through this work Park and colleagues developed an argument that population movement, rapid industrial change and new methods of mass communication were causing social disorganisation among the people who moved to the city. As traditional forms of social organisation and solidarity were disrupted by national and international migration, Park and colleagues explored the new forms of social organisation that were starting to emerge in the city. Most obviously demonstrated in relation to youth delinquency and criminal gangs, such organisation could be deleterious to the wider society, but they explained such trends as products of differential opportunity and geography rather than individual pathology. As such, their identification of 'natural areas' or neighbourhoods in the city was particularly important to their approach. They argued that neighbourhoods were the crucible in which new immigrants sought to build a life and, as a community, they then had the potential to generate new forms of social organisation: the neighbourhood was the scale at which people learned to live with each other, gradually developing the social and cultural forms, and sentiment, that then shapes what is possible and what people become (for an updated version of this argument about neighbourhoods in Chicago today, see Sampson, 2012).

As Park put it as early as 1915: 'Proximity and neighborly contact are the basis for the simplest and most elementary form of association with which we have to do in the organization of city life. Local interests and associations breed local sentiment, and, under a system which makes residence the basis for participation in the government, the neighborhood becomes the basis for political control' (reproduced in Park et al, 1925, 7). While they identified 'great differences between the various neighborhoods of the city' (Burgess and Bogue, 1964, 6), these scholars also realised that the nature of local community organisation and civic capacity made a tremendous difference to the evolution of social practices and outcomes in these neighbourhoods.

In this regard, Park and colleagues were exercised about the official agencies, professionals and organisations that were attempting to set the tone for local neighbourhood life. Park was acutely aware that most professional people were 'physically or in imagination, abroad most of the time' (in Park et al, 1925, 113), and he argued that the burgeoning civic and governmental sector (including the probation service, school organisations, the Boy Scouts and the YMCA) had done little to reduce social problems. In this political space, Park and colleagues called for a 'new parochialism' (Park et al, 1925, 122) whereby would-be social reformers should seek to galvanise 'right-thinking' people in the local area in order that they might solve their own problems. This was a political argument to defend the power of democracy over the well-intentioned interventions being made by government, professionals and philanthropists. Reflecting the influence of John Dewey, his university teacher and old colleague at the newspaper *Thought-News* (in 1892), Park had a firm belief in the power of people to solve their own problems (Matthews, 1977).

This approach was also strongly supported by Ernest Burgess, who by 1924 was advocating the social science of 'neighbourhood work', whereby an organiser would identify the local people who could help a local community to solve their own problems. He suggested building relationships with 'all the local dynamic personalities, including gang leaders, pool hall proprietors, leaders of all the neighbourhood organisations, and of all the professional persons, like representatives of social agencies, physicians, lawyers, clergymen, at work in his locality ... [and identifying] the basic interests, the driving wishes, and the vital problems of the men and women, the youth and children, living in the community' (in Park et al, 1925, 153–4). This approach built on his earlier efforts to promote the 'social survey' whereby the sociologist similarly worked as something like a community organiser to bring together a local committee of people who were: (1) trained to lead a community survey; (2) thereby educated about the social problems in the area; and (3) supported to develop solutions (Burgess, 1916).

Building on his experiences in leading this kind of community surveying work at the University of Kansas and in Columbus, Ohio, Burgess worked with Park to lead a course in field studies that encouraged their students to do the same in Chicago (Bogue, 1974). For Burgess, the social survey was a research method that allowed the sociologist to better understand society while also making a contribution to social change. Indeed, by training local people and developing their capacity for action, Burgess argued that sociology had a role to play in democracy itself and this vision was further developed through his work in Chicago. As early as 1916, he was clearly committed to this path, arguing for 'an organic transformation of habits of sentiment, thought, and action of the American people … [that] cannot be efficiently effected upon a nation-wide scale; it must take place on a community basis' (Burgess, 1916, 500). This was a powerful argument that sociology had a role to play in realising the capacity of the people to engage in the democratic life of the nation (see also Fisher and Strauss, 1978).

A number of the graduate students from Chicago subsequently took up this challenge. Most notably, in his role directing the emergent research programme at the Illinois Department of Public Welfare's Institute for Juvenile Research from 1926, Clifford R. Shaw (1896–1957) and his colleague Henry D. McKay pioneered this spirit in their research and associated interventions in the field of criminology (Shaw, 1930; Shaw and McKay, 1931; Shaw et al, 1938). Shaw sought to develop practical experiments in order to try to reduce the problem of crime. From 1932, he worked closely with Burgess to set up the Chicago Areas Project, which established three new initiatives in tough neighbourhoods in inner-city Chicago (Russell Square, the near North Side and the near South Side). Their vision was to find the local talent and leadership that could 'coalesce into an effective neighborhood organisation – completely indigenous, completely independent, and fully self-determining' (Burgess and Bogue, 1964, 316). Once formed, these 'community committees' were trained and supported to draw on the resources of local institutions such as 'churches, societies and clubs' (in Bogue, 1974, 82) in order to provide support and new facilities to young people. In the Russell Square area this involved a new community-led boys' club, a summer camp, kerbstone counselling and mediation with the authorities. These activities had widespread – if somewhat contested – local support and, although it was not officially trumpeted, rates of youth offending fell by two-thirds (Schlossman and Sedlak, 1983).

Echoing the approach developed at the University, the Chicago Areas Project was based on the analysis that 'juvenile delinquency is essentially a manifestation of neighbourhood disorganization … [and] only a programme of neighbourhood organization can cope with and control it. The Juvenile Court, the probation officer, the parole officers, and the boys' club can be no substitute for a group of leading citizens of a neighbourhood who take the responsibility of a program for delinquency treatment and prevention' (Burgess and Bogue, 1964, 310). The theory was that by identifying local leaders and winning the support of the local institutions, 'the entire community can be involved cooperatively in working out its own salvation' (Burgess, in Bogue, 1974, 88). The new community committees were encouraged to reach out across their neighbourhoods and to develop their own newspapers to win over the local population in support of the work. They were also encouraged to evaluate all that they did in order to improve its impact and effectiveness (Schlossman and Sedlak, 1983).

In 1938, Saul D. Alinsky (1909–72), another graduate from the School of Sociology at the University of Chicago, who had also been working in the field of criminology, was appointed to lead a new area project that was being established in the neighbourhood called Back of the Yards (Horwitt, 1992; Engel, 2002). In following the established model, Alinsky developed a committee that included representatives from the Catholic Church, the Meatpackers' Union, the Chamber of Commerce, Chicago Park district, the American Legion, social and sports clubs. In April 1939 the Back of the Yards Neighborhood Council was founded at a large public meeting under the banner 'We the people will control our own destiny'. The local leadership established eight different committees looking at infant and adult welfare, the development of a community centre and housing, a credit union, jobs and new experiences for young people, dental services, green spaces, community events and youth organisation. Their statement of purpose explicitly linked this work, and the relationships upon which it was built, to the nature of democracy: 'This organization is founded for the purpose of uniting all of the organizations within the community known as Back of the Yards, in order to promote the welfare of all residents of that community regardless of their race, color or creed, so that they may all have the opportunity to find health, happiness, and security through the democratic way of life' (Alinsky, 1941, 800).

The Back of the Yards Neighborhood Council went on to take its own initiatives to improve local facilities and services, as well as to challenge the established vested interests in the meat-packing industry, government and public services. Indeed, Alinsky's encounter with the organised trade union movement in the Back of the Yards was particularly significant for the development of community organising as he fused the lessons of urban sociology – most notably, an understanding of the importance of locally rooted social networks and indigenous leadership – with an appreciation of the power of collective organisation (Horwitt, 1992; von Hoffman, 2011). On the back of these experiences Alinsky developed a battery of principles and techniques for changing the balance of neighbourhood power and, although he didn't acknowledge it, even in his best-selling books *Reveille for Radicals* (1946) and *Rules of Radicals* (1971), the legacy of his mentors at the University of Chicago was clearly evident in all that he did.

Echoing the ambition of Park, Burgess and their colleagues, the Back of the Yards Neighborhood Council began to change the sentiment and culture of the area. The opportunity to forge personal relationships and work together for shared goals altered local expectations and, as Alinsky (1941, 805) described it, 'leaders in various interest and action groups have learned to know one another as human beings rather than as impersonal symbols of groups which, in many cases, appeared to be of a hostile nature. The personal relationships which have been developed have to a large degree broken down that urban anonymity characteristic of all such communities. Furthermore, we today find an independent philosophy developing in Back of the Yards which can best be described as a people's philosophy' (see also Billson, 1984; Reitzes and Reitzes, 1992). While Alinsky probably took a more explicitly political position than his mentors would have liked (Engel, 2002), he was clearly enacting the vision that had been developed by Park, Burgess and Shaw.

Since its development in Chicago, this tradition of politics has evolved significantly. Alinsky himself set up a national organisation, the Industrial Areas Foundation (IAF), that was designed to train and provide organisers who could work in neighbourhoods to build new connections and establish programmes of action. He was subsequently invited to organise in other areas of Chicago (most notably in Woodlawn (von Hoffman, 2011)) as well as Rochester and Kansas City (Schutz and Miller, 2015). Following Alinsky's unexpected death in 1972, community organisers sought to make stronger connections to the institutional traditions of local groups, and particularly so in relation to faith organisations (Warren, 2001), but they also started to operate at a much larger scale. Rather than embedding the organisation in the social life of a relatively small geographical area – and the Back of Yards Neighborhood Council covered only one square mile of the city – these newer alliances tended to comprise a metropolitan-wide network of institutions that focused on challenging city and even county-level officials rather than on developing local projects in which the local community had leadership roles.

In the main, these newer community-organising alliances have become less concerned with helping people to solve their own problems and more focused on mobilising the community in order to challenge the key power holders in any jurisdiction (including large employers, government officers and elected politicians) as well as to hold them accountable for the decisions they make. While IAF alliances will put some concrete ideas on the table in order to tackle local concerns (such as the call for a living wage, a model for affordable housing, changes in schooling and so on), the ambition is to work with official bodies and elected officials to realise these goals. To this end, local alliances deploy the established techniques of listening, action research and relationship building, but much of the collective energy is spent on mobilising very large numbers to turn out for major public events. Through the organisation of people in a manner more akin to a traditional social movement, impressive gains have been made in relation to school standards (Stone et al, 2001; Warren and Mapp, 2011), urban infrastructure (Warren, 2001), affordable housing (Gecan, 2004) and living wages (Fine, 2006). Along the way, the experiences of those taking part in these campaigns and the related negotiations can be critical for a minority of the participants, giving them the chance to learn the civic and political skills required to change other aspects of life.

Today, there are a variety of national networks that promote different forms of community organising across the US, including the IAF, People Improving Communities through Organizing (PICO), the Direct Action and Research Training Centre (DART), the Gamaliel Foundation, National People's Action (NPA) and USAction. These networks and their affiliated organisations all operate in the spirit of the first experiments in Chicago, albeit that some organise only faith institutions, others are more focused on political campaigns and some build new organisations from scratch (as practised by the now largely disbanded network called the Association of Community Organizations for Reform Now (ACORN) (Atlas, 2010). Since the 1940s this model of politics has become established as a way of engaging people in American democracy by organising them across their membership affiliations at the city-wide scale (Fisher, 1984; de Filippis et al, 2010). Its ubiquity is reflected in the fact that the current president of the United States, Barack Obama, and his would-be successor, Hillary Clinton, both worked as community organisers before going on to more mainstream political life.

Community organising, the English way

This model of politics came to England in 1989. Neil Jameson attended IAF training during the late 1980s and he then went on to set up the Community Organising Foundation to promote and initiate community organising in the UK. The first wave of development involved the establishment of a number of local organising alliances (in Bristol, the Black Country, Liverpool, North Wales and Sheffield) before he started organising in East London during the early 1990s (Warren, 2009). Although the early alliances all subsequently left the network – some of them folding and others sustaining themselves as independent organisations – the London work took deeper and more sustained root. The East London alliance was officially launched in 1996, with later expansion to South London (2004), West London (2005) and North London (2011), with the scope to also operate across the city at large (under the moniker London Citizens). During this period the wider network was renamed Citizens UK and alliances were subsequently created in Birmingham, Milton Keynes, Nottingham, Cardiff and Leeds. The organisation has spun off a national Living Wage Foundation on the back of its living wage campaign and this establishes the living wage rate (in London and the rest of the country) and accredits employers who pay the wage to their in-house staff and to those who are sub-contracted but working on site (Wills and Linneker, 2014). As such, a community-organising effort that started in London has spawned an arm's-length organisation that allows it to act more like a traditional social movement campaign.

My own employer, Queen Mary University of London, was the first in the sector to sign up to the living wage (in 2006) and the campaign prompted my own School (Geography) to join the alliance. As an 'insider', I have conducted a number of research projects to explore the reasons why local organisations join Citizens UK, the nature of local relationships and the impact this has on the individuals and organisations that engage in the work (more information is provided in the research appendix at the end of this book). This research raises important insights about the state of local community organisations, the potential for forging relationships between different groups, the prospects for engaging local people in political life and the extent to which it is possible to organise people to solve their own problems. As explicated in the final part of the chapter, the research highlights the potential to use existing organisations as a means to reach local people, but it also queries whether traditional forms of civil society organisation are sufficiently representative and embedded to provide the main vehicle for doing this work. Many faith and labour organisations are only poorly connected to the communities in which they are located. In addition, rates of population mobility are eroding the membership base that they already have. The research suggests that there may be greater potential to reach people through local neighbourhood organisations that incorporate tenants' and residents' groups (as witnessed in the development of neighbourhood forums and discussed in the previous chapters).

The desire for local relationships at the neighbourhood scale

My research in East London has exposed the extent to which respondents from a wide gamut of affiliates all valued the opportunity to forge relationships with local organisations from different traditions. As the Buddhist respondent put it, the advantage is 'just meeting with people from other communities that we wouldn't really come across in any other way. I think that's really important ... for us as individuals ... as an institution, and I think it's important for society at large.' Being a member of Citizens UK (CUK) provided a safe framework or platform for this kind of basic relationship building. As a representative from the East London Mosque put it, 'CUK gave us the opportunity to meet other people, work together with others and before that, we didn't have any sort of common platform to work from. CUK provided this platform where people from very different backgrounds came together, it is something very interesting and encouraging, and something unique.'

A representative from another Muslim organisation called Darul Umma similarly emphasised the basic desire to forge local relationships saying, '[We joined] to be able to make relationships with other institutions locally', and he contrasted this with the kind of relationships they had tried to forge in the past. Darul Umma had been able to forge particularly strong relationships with people who belonged to the other local churches in membership of CUK (St Paul's Shadwell, St Mary's Cable Street and E1 Community Church), such that 'The relationship that we have now is more based on love and respect and common ground ... than before ... It's not just like a ceremonial kind of relationship.' During Ramadan members of Darul Umma were teaming up with local Christians for nightly patrols of the area 'to reduce anti-social behaviour. What happens a lot is that young people say they're going to the mosque for Ramadan but it's an opportunity for them to go and hang about in the streets, you know, and not come to attend the mosque.' Recognising the risks that drugs and gang violence posed to young people in their communities, the mosque and churches were using their existing relationships to try to tackle the problem. Young people were directed towards local youth clubs in the churches and mosques.

The idea that CUK provided a safe framework for engaging with others was raised by a number of respondents who valued the opportunity to build relationships in circumstances where they wouldn't be judged and would not have to worry about upsetting people who were very different to them. As one Catholic priest explained, 'It's made us much more open to each other, [it's] much easier to engage with other people, [and we are] less fearful about, you know, getting things right or wrong.' Another priest also emphasised the importance of working together over shared concerns with respect for one another's religious traditions. As he explained, 'We can work together and we can witness together, even if we can't worship together.'

In addition, however, beyond the importance of relationship building, all the religious affiliates were able to point to their religious heritage as a major part of their motivations to join the alliance. Representatives from a range of Christian denominations, the two Muslim representatives and a member of staff at the Buddhist Centre all highlighted the way in which the core teachings of their religion emphasised the importance of fostering local relationships. As the representative from the East London Mosque explained, 'Islam teaches that we should work for the common good, cooperate with each other in virtues and good deeds ... Whoever is doing good work, we are encouraged to cooperate with them ... [Islam teaches not to] be good and stay in your own areas but to pass this goodness to others. You are concerned about humanity, about your community and you can't just stand by yourself.'

In contrast, the Buddhist representative focused on their teachings about the alleviation of suffering and the importance of loving-kindness in a world in which everything is connected. As he explained, 'if we were enlightened, we'd see the connectivity, between human beings and between all things, and how actually everything is linked, spatially and temporally ... [which] can translate very powerfully with forming community, forming relationships'. For him, being in relationship with other local people was important to demonstrate connections and loving-kindness in practice.

This emphasis on the practical manifestation of religious belief was common across the Christian denominations. The two Methodist interviewees − one representing a network of community centres in Newham and the other a church in Stratford − both highlighted the importance of the 'social gospel', which emphasises the manifestation of faith through good works in the wider community. As one minister put it, 'John Wesley said there's no holiness that's not social holiness and it was very much about not just converting people but going into prisons and he got involved in the [anti-]slave[ry] campaign. Right from the beginning there was that aspect of Methodism that was very different from the Church of England ... there is that edge to Methodism that is very much about social action.' Indeed, in this regard one of the Anglican respondents noted that they got their 'power not from being a mass movement but from the quality of connections to power'. As the established church, the Church of England already had access to power, but it still needed an authentic connection to the people who lived in the parish.

The Catholic respondents (from churches in Canning Town, Forest Gate and Bethnal Green, as well as a secondary school in Woodford Green) all emphasised the importance of Catholic social teaching, which urges Catholics to 'work for the common good'. As the head teacher based at a large, successful secondary school in Redbridge explained, '*Rerum Novarum* is a seminal document, the church was now saying that the condition of the poor in the inner cities is a matter of grave injustice. Workers have rights!' Citing the examples of the Good Samaritan and Dickens' *A Christmas Carol*, he argued that Catholics had a duty to act when they had the opportunity to do the right thing. He was able to use CUK's living wage campaign as a way to teach his students about the importance of taking responsibility for the plight of the poor. Rather than leaving things to the market, he saw the campaign as a way to demonstrate the power of people to do the right thing.

For another Catholic respondent, joining CUK was a way to rebuild a largely forgotten tradition of Catholic engagement in politics in the East End of London. Growing up in the area, he had witnessed the political leadership of people he knew in his parish. For him, CUK was a way to try to re-engage people in political life and, especially, around the parish surrounding each church (Coriden, 1996).[1] The Catholic community – and at the time of his childhood this was largely Irish, Italian and German – had played a significant part in the emergent trade union movement and the formation of the Labour Party, providing organisers and councillors who went on to govern the borough. Indeed, the Catholic social teaching now celebrated in the wider Catholic community is largely credited to the initiative of Cardinal Manning, following his experiences during the great dock strike in East London in 1888. Citing this as a 'local legacy', this respondent supported CUK's idea of 'creating leadership' as a way to revive this tradition of Catholic engagement in political life. For him, this would help the church to look outwards, and he remarked that 'When you are parish-based you can be very parochial, just focused on the school and the church roof, and many churches are like that.' Following in the footsteps of earlier generations, this priest noted that 'Catholic social teaching encourages us to engage and use ... the principles of the Gospel and the teaching of the church to engage in the world in which we live.'

From a very different perspective, some of the trade unionists made a similar point. They were attracted to CUK because it provided a means to engage people in political life in a way that the trade unions were rarely able to do. As one respondent explained, 'it's an ironic thing that the sort of things CUK is doing used to be done by the Left. My background is in the Communist Party and ... I sometimes sit back and say that it's bloody awful leaving it to all these religious people. They are doing things that the Left ought to be doing but I'm grateful that somebody's doing them.' Although this union leader supported the work of CUK as a vehicle for greater local engagement, it is striking that very few of her fellow union activists and none of the branch members took up the opportunity of local engagement. While CUK was trying to organise, it was clearly not appealing to large numbers of people in her trade union branch and she reported that 'most people join a union like an insurance. If something goes wrong at work, I've got someone to defend me. People don't see it as something that involves them unless the union is operating in a way that does involve them and most of the time we don't.' Given this passivity, and the fact that many of the members lived a long way away, membership of CUK had little meaningful impact on the life of the 3,000 people in the union branch. While she was keen to join so as to offer support, membership had little purchase on the day-to-day work of the union branch (and I return to this issue in greater detail later on in this chapter).

One Catholic priest put particular emphasis on the politics of CUK's approach to personal development as his motivation for getting involved. As he explained, 'The religious order I belong to ... came with the intention of working among the poor ... most religious orders have what we call a solidarity with the poor and for me that was never just sort of learning about them and praying for them and maybe supporting them in some way, it was much more about being involved. Citizens really provided that real involvement, you know, actually engaging with the people and working with them rather than for them ... And the thing that won it for me is that whenever they engage, even though the initial engagement may be a bit hostile, the aim is to actually build friendships and relationships and not make enemies. And for me ... that's precisely what we're called to do as Christians.'

Belonging to CUK had allowed him to work in solidarity with the poor, particularly over the demand for a living wage and related calls for affordable housing.

It is significant that the only other organisation that highlighted the importance of engaging in local politics as a key motivation for joining the alliance was the Salvation Army in Stepney Green. It had a very unusual organisational model and had built a network from scratch without having a building as the base for its work. The husband-and-wife team had moved to the Ocean Estate in 2003 and they started by making new contacts from which to develop their work. They built relationships with local people through a cricket group, an old people's lunch club, a parent-and-toddler group, schools, the community farm, and by organising activities in local spaces, including a kids' club, youth club, baby song, knitting group and football sessions that were held at the local mosque's community centre, the youth and scout centres and other spaces on the estate. One of the captains leading this work told me that 'the whole community was our building', and while he knew that '[there are] loads and loads of people … in the community who would never realistically come to a Salvation Army event … we do have a relationship with them … not just in terms of sort of friendship but … we see ourselves in some ways as sort of community chaplains because … you become … an advisor in a sense.'

Over time, this Salvation Army network had grown and developed its presence such that it encompassed up to 100 local families. When they were asked to join CUK, they were attracted as much for the political angle as for the relationships they'd be able to make. As the captain explained, 'I'd say [that before] we weren't particularly switched on in terms of politics, local politics and how it worked. So even though we were very involved with people and the community we hadn't done a lot in terms of relating to politicians and how you could bring about change. So I think we really got the relational bit, but maybe the other bit, that's what's been filled in by being part of organising … [It] gave us the tools to think about how to make things happen.'

In contrast, the schools were much more careful in their justification of membership in CUK, not least because they were vulnerable to charges that the staff were indoctrinating the children. While a number of schools had joined the alliance it was often difficult to get them involved without having a route into the life of the school. During the 1990s Norlington Boys' School in Leyton had set up a CUK group within the school and a number of its most talented pupils used the techniques of community organising to lobby for improvements at the school and to improve community safety. While the head teacher reported that he was not comfortable about some of the more obviously political sides of the work of CUK (citing a demonstration that had been held to support the demand for a living wage), he could see the advantages of his students' learning how to achieve significant change. In relation to their efforts to improve street safety and secure living-wage jobs as part of the legacy of the Olympic Games in 2012, CUK had helped to 'put our students into relationship with the most powerful people in the country'.

Emphasising the skills that were learned through this work, there was also a feeling that being part of CUK granted them the scope to do things that would ordinarily never be possible. This was also true for the trade union representatives who already thought of themselves as politically active and politically connected. Commenting on the audacity of some of the living-wage campaigning techniques, one trade unionist described her experience of being at the House of Commons to launch a document for socially responsible contracting as an example of 'Chuzpah ... it is monumental cheek ... the idea of this little community organisation in East London [being] there at the heart of power'. Belonging to the alliance increased a sense of collective efficacy in what was possible, encouraging local people to take their concerns to those who held power.

Having the chance to engage and learn

Recent research suggests that experience is particularly important in shaping attitudes toward civic and political engagement, rather than the other way around (Quintelier and van Deth, 2014). Using panel data to capture the political experiences and attitudes of more than 3,000 young Belgians when aged 16, 18 and 21, this research shows that 'being politically active makes young citizens "better" democrats, especially in terms of political attitudes and normative considerations' (Quintelier and van Deth, 2014, 154). While explanations for patterns of civic behaviour have tended to focus on socioeconomic class – and it has long been known that income and education levels are strongly associated with political engagement, levels of volunteering and civic participation (Pattie et al, 2004; see also Chapter Three) – this is clearly not the whole story. The way in which local community organisation and civil society institutions shape opportunities for engagement is also important. In this regard, CUK is playing a very important role in providing opportunities for local people to engage in political life. The thousands of people who belong to the membership organisations in CUK have the chance to take part in the campaigns being run by the alliance and, over the decade covered by this research, these campaigns have included the call for a living wage, regularisation for irregular migrants, properly affordable housing, better community safety and access to living-wage jobs.

Although many of the people involved were not directly touched by it, the living wage campaign proved particularly significant for the Salvation Army in Stepney Green. One of its members worked as an estate cleaner for a housing association that was not paying the wage and, on the initiative of his church, CUK led a campaign to ask his employer to adopt the new rate of pay. This man was supported to speak out in public, confident that he had the support of his church and the wider alliance. Moreover, following its success, the Salvation Army saw a more concrete reason for belonging to the alliance and, as the captain described it, '[This] was when organising made sense for us. It was a real pivotal moment. Seeing a family, [and] his life, essentially transformed by having a better wage, and just seeing how we could make something happen. [It] was really amazing to think that you could do that and have an influence.'

Going on to reflect on his wider experiences of collective action with CUK, this Salvation Army captain argued that this kind of politics was a manifestation of 'humanity at its best. It just shows what it can be and everybody knows that it can be better … it's in those moments, and something goes like that [clicks fingers] and people get it for that moment … Sometimes it feels like a hassle to get to that point and there's so many barriers … but once they're there … I think that's what we get out of it: it's that feeling of being a part of this bigger thing, that it's not all doom and gloom.'

Other respondents similarly highlighted the impact of shared experiences on those who took part. For one of the Methodist ministers I interviewed, the campaigns generated 'the sort of solidarity you would never experience with people from other faiths otherwise … unless you're actually working on something together, you don't get a working relationship with people.' This minister had led a campaign to secure a set of ethical guarantees as part of the preparation for the Olympics in 2012 and she argued that her campaign experience had changed her view of power. As she told me, 'It's a lesson in power and that we can have some power. Ordinary people can have some power and we do matter … and can have some effect.'

CUK provided this opportunity for personal development through shared political experience. As one of the trade union respondents suggested, this was about 'the means being more important than the end', such that people had to solve their own problems and would be changed in the process. This was certainly true for some of those involved with the Salvation Army, and I have witnessed the same for some of our students who engaged in a campaign over road safety on campus during 2014 and 2015. It seems to be the organisations that have the strongest focus on personal relationships (such as the Salvation Army) that have been most able to help their members to make the most of these opportunities. In large, less personal organisations, many members knew little about the work of CUK and the leaders had little capacity to encourage them to get more involved. Thus, while one of the Catholic priests told me that 'faith is about human development' and 'there is a real joy in being able to work with people who are ... on the edge of society, and just see them grow, there's a joy in that', it was often difficult to realise this potential in the largest churches and mosques. The full-time leadership and even the organisers working for CUK rarely had the necessary time to spend in meeting with individuals to support their development as part of this work.

It is significant that rather than just challenging the authorities over a particular problem, CUK would generally try to put something more concrete on the table, with a view to joint working to effect social change, and many of the East London respondents welcomed this constructive approach. Indeed, the head teacher at Norlington Boys' School argued that this was what they had done in their work to improve the safety of the children coming to school. He reflected that the recommendations were all about what 'we will do rather than what they will do'. While they were in dialogue with the police, the local council and politicians, they were trying to emphasise the power of working together to secure the changes they wanted to see.

In the same spirit, the respondent from the Buddhist Centre argued that he valued the emphasis on taking responsibility rather than expecting others to act. As he explained, 'Buddhism throws the responsibility back on the individual and says, well, "What are you going to do? How can you be more loving, kinder, more aware, more compassionate, more giving?"' It is this spirit that allows communities to try to engage in solving their own problems rather than just demanding that others act for them.

The challenges of sustaining engagement

There were, however, major challenges in sustaining this work. Most of the organisations involved in CUK were already engaged in a range of other local activities and many were struggling to find the people they needed to keep things afloat. The Methodist church in Stratford, for example, had a core congregation of about 100 people on a Sunday, but it was also running a community centre and a homeless hostel as well as a range of other events and activities. As the minister explained, CUK sat alongside this other community work, such that 'it's not the beginning and the end of everything in our church: it's one of the things that we do'. She reported that they had struggled to get people to engage in any meaningful way and, while 10 to 15 people would turn up for the large public assemblies during election periods, fewer were willing to take up the offer of training or the chance to develop their own leadership through the activities on offer with CUK (and at that time there were ongoing campaigns for the living wage, including the demand for an ethical Olympics that was to be held very close to the church).

Similarly, the respondent from the Buddhist Centre explained that supporting CUK was 'quite problematic because it's not necessarily at the forefront of what we're doing'. At the time of our interview, the Centre had been in Bethnal Green for 30 years and the community of Buddhist leaders were running regular open sessions for people who wanted to learn more about meditation. They were also supporting a number of businesses, including a cafe and a health centre. They had a number of other community relationships, including a partnership with Tower Hamlets council (to provide events for carers), a link with St Joseph's Hospice (to provide volunteers to visit) and a project at the Royal London Hospital, where they were providing meditation classes for staff. For him, CUK was 'not the only way that we're trying to work in the community' and it was not necessarily the most important part of their community work. Indeed, they had struggled to get people to attend CUK's training, meetings and events, and this made it hard to sustain their membership for the long term. There was little concrete benefit, beyond the relationships, for the Buddhist Centre to sustain its membership, especially when it was already well established in the area and had a network of other local connections.

The schools took a very similar approach to their membership of CUK, treating it as an additional arm to their programme of work, but it was very much secondary to the core business of teaching. As the head teacher of a Catholic school in East London explained, 'I'm the head teacher at a school and my main job is to get the best possible deal for the children in my care. It's a balancing act … We learn a lot from CUK and it has made a significant contribution to our citizenship work … [But] my real contribution to social justice is to make sure the children here get a good deal.' Indeed, for another school-based respondent, the pressures from government and the expectations of parents made it very difficult to engage in additional community work.

As indicated in Figure 6.1, many of the organisations involved in CUK were thus already supporting a range of local community activity within and beyond their own organisations. This included providing services for different sub-communities of their own, and this was particularly common in the Catholic churches, as indicated in relation to the congregation at Our Lady of the Assumption in Bethnal Green. In addition, many of the member groups were also developing their own local projects that helped to forge connections with a wider network of people. This was particularly important in relation to the work being done at St Peter's church in Bethnal Green, where they sought to take their faith out to the community, rather than expecting people to turn up in church. As the vicar explained, 'We sometimes talk in church about the Kingdom of God drawing near and that to my mind [means] the people will smell and touch and see and sense the effects of the drawing close to the Kingdom of God, and it ... needs to begin somewhere.' By sending their people out 'as disciples' into the local community they were bearing witness to the Kingdom of God and, in so doing, fostering new links between the church and the local community. This church had grown considerably since being re-founded in 2010 and its local projects were a particularly important part of its work.

Figure 6.1: Models of community being developed by faith organisations in Tower Hamlets Citizens

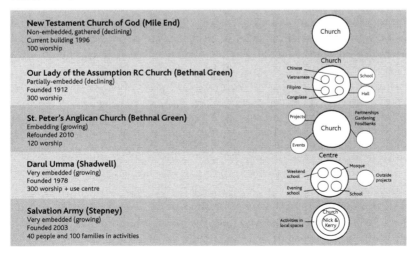

Not surprisingly in this context, a number of the faith organisations also highlighted the challenge of finding sufficient people who were able and willing to engage in their ongoing community work. As a respondent from the East London Mosque put it, the 'people who are capable are already very busy', and, as in the trade union branches, if they spotted potential talent, the existing leadership would look to further develop those people to help bolster their own activity, rather than encouraging them to put their energies further afield. In this regard, many member organisations reported relatively low levels of engagement in the wider network of CUK. Moreover, while people might be willing to turn out for occasional large public assemblies, they were much less likely to engage in the ongoing campaigns.

The research thus exposed a degree of tension between the needs of each member group in relation to the needs of the wider collective. Each organisation needed to keep itself going, and CUK sat 'on top' of this work.[2] As one of the trade union representatives reported: 'people get it up to a point but it isn't their top priority and they've got a million other things [to do]. They've got other political issues coming in and it then becomes something that is dispensable. It's optional rather than saying this is the core of what we want to be doing.' Added to the fact that some trade union members were uncomfortable about the religious tone of some of the meetings, such that one respondent noted that 'a lot of active trade unionists are also active atheists', this further eroded the motivation for working together (see also Holgate, 2015).

Thus, while a few of the Buddhists engaged in activities during the period when the Buddhist Centre was in membership, it was only 'a handful of individuals ... and typically what happens is that people do it for a few years and then move on in some way'. Furthermore, those who engaged tended to be people who were already committed to this kind of work in some way. For many of the leaders whom I interviewed, joining CUK chimed with their pre-existing ideas about faith, citizenship, politics and community. They were able to take part because it fulfilled some of the ideas they already had, and CUK was less good at developing people who had not previously engaged in this kind of work. For one Methodist minister, for example, the training and experience on offer was not sufficient to build the confidence and skills needed to widen the capacities of most of her members. As she explained, 'I think empowering people who are not very empowered is a long process and I think CUK training is helpful but I don't think it's everything. There's a lot of other things that need to happen as well.'

In addition, in the context of intense urban development, rising house prices and rents in East London, many of the member organisations were suffering from increased rates of population mobility. In the face of population churn it often proved difficult to keep track of their own people and sustain their own organisations, let alone contribute to the wider alliance. A Catholic priest in Bethnal Green reported seeing a 50% turnover in the parish congregation in just under nine years, and while some congregants returned every Sunday, it also made it very hard to know who was taking part in the life of the church. Similarly, the Anglican vicar at St Peter's church in Bethnal Green described the 'fragile social ecology' of the area, which was being undermined by rising rents and new developments that changed the demographic dynamics.

This was a particular problem for the Salvation Army, which had built its own community from scratch and was at risk of losing people as fast as it secured new recruits. As the captain described it, the situation felt 'very fragile ... you think it could all fall apart any minute. There's a family who came very early on, really the first people who kind of joined us, [and they] are moving next week up to Birmingham ... That's four people who are really involved and very reliable, who get the whole history, have been with you ... And there are lots of people I'd say in that situation, they're moving because they can't afford to be here ... For us that's really gutting because they do really want to be here and they love this community and they would want to stay if they could.' Later on he expressed his frustration at the way that market forces were constantly undermining their community work. As he put it, 'I don't think we can realistically resist the market and gentrification ... of the area, and ... if I project forward 20 years that is the challenge. What will the Salvation Army look like?' Following this interview, his own church decided to move him and his wife to another part of London, further eroding the remarkable work they had done.

One faith organisation in membership was not really able to engage in any community work. The New Testament Church of God, a Pentecostal church in Mile End, had become a gathered church. It served a community of about 100 people but most of its members had moved further away to find affordable housing and they then came back to church on a Sunday. The respondent I met had engaged in a CUK project to establish a Community Land Trust in Tower Hamlets on a site close to the church, but this link had been made due to his professional work in the building industry as much as on account of his connection to the area. His wife had three generations of her family still living in the borough and Sunday was about coming back to meet their family and worship together. As he explained, 'You almost get a sense that ... this church community wants to be a community because we all live so far afield we hardly meet anyway.' In this context, and despite previous efforts, the church was not able to sustain local community work. People lived too far away and were stretched too thin to do more than attend church on a Sunday. Given the high rates of mobility in the area, this was likely to become a more common experience across the other faith organisations that belonged to CUK at the time that I did the research.

Furthermore, during the period of this research a number of the clergy in the Anglican, Methodist, Catholic and Salvation Army churches as well as some of the other key leaders in the organisation had moved away or retired. Of the communities reported upon in this chapter, one of the schools and the Buddhist Centre, and the local trade union branches in the health sector, had all decided to leave CUK. While the organisation had grown, particularly among London's schools, sustaining and growing the alliance was very hard work. It demanded considerable organiser time and resources and they had to battle against the social forces that were constantly undermining their work.

The ongoing importance of scale

While CUK – in tandem with its sister organisations in the US and elsewhere – has created an alliance that can operate at the scale of the borough, the wider East End, the whole city of London, and even the nation, the leaders interviewed for this research were largely driven by a desire for better relationships with other local organisations. Fostering meaningful relationships, however, required that people had the opportunity to meet and work together on a regular basis, and, in reality, much of CUK's activity actually took place a rather long way away. A number of respondents argued that this made it harder to engage their own people, as the alliance seemed too remote to the work they were doing. One Catholic sister who had tried to engage some of the hundreds of people who attended mass at her church in Forest Gate every Sunday reported that she thought the lack of a local focus and activity comprised the key barrier to or had little motivation for getting people involved. As she reported, 'we always talk about building local teams but we need to have local actions which are consistent with that', and without this, people saw little purpose in getting involved.

The vicar at St Peter's church similarly explained that they had to face the reality that 'we are a series of villages ... and ... we're in the northern bit of the village of Bethnal Green and that's really the only bit that we're interested in. I mean yes, we are interested in the Borough and we know we should ... love people in Poplar, but we don't really know them ... It's going to take a lot for me to travel on the bus and the DLR [Docklands Light Railway] ... [to] get there. I don't know where I'm going. I don't really have a relationship with these people ... I think that's quite a hard ask.' In relation to the arguments of the sociologists at the Chicago School, it was what they would call the 'natural areas' of the borough – such as Bow, Limehouse, Mile End, Poplar, Shadwell, Stepney, the Isle of Dogs, Wapping and Whitechapel – that would really make sense to the people who lived in the borough. Moreover, if local residents were to have the chance to get to know new people, identify shared interests and act over common concerns, it could only really happen at a neighbourhood scale with people who shared the same space. As demonstrated by the case of Darul Umma's successful relationships with the local Christian churches in Shadwell, the physical closeness of the organisations and their members helped to sustain their relationships and generate shared activities in a meaningful way.

This issue of geography becomes very obvious when looking at the scale of the borough. As illustrated in Figure 6.2, the 23 member groups that belonged to CUK in Tower Hamlets in 2015 included a broad gamut of faith organisations (Christian and Muslim), educational establishments (primary and secondary schools as well as the School of Geography at the local university), one trade union branch, one housing association and one community centre (Toynbee Hall), but they were often a considerable distance apart. Going back a decade, to early 2005, just three of these organisations were in membership (East London Mosque, the New Testament Church of God and Toynbee Hall), and at that time the alliance operated at the scale of East London, stretching across the five boroughs of Hackney, Newham, Tower Hamlets, Waltham Forest and Redbridge. Over time, the number of paid organisers had grown, such that CUK was able to recruit sufficient organisations to operate at the scale of the borough, but as is clear from the map in Figure 6.2, membership is still too distantiated for most of the organisations to make local links. While there was a cluster of members in the west of the borough, there were large areas with no local representation at all. Increasing the density of membership such that neighbourhood alliances became possible would allow the organisation to deepen its roots, and, ultimately, its impact as well.

In addition, the fact that broad-based community organising depends upon forging relationships between the existing islands of social capital in any area necessarily excludes those who do not belong to such groups. It is likely that the most vulnerable and marginalised people are the least connected (Rowson et al, 2010), and these are the people who need politics the most. More locally oriented neighbourhood organising would be better able to reach out and develop such people, but, as indicated by the work of the Salvation Army in Stepney, this is resource-intensive work that is constantly undermined by the processes of urban change and population migration. Despite the current policy emphasis on localism, it is not clear where the resources will come from to do such important neighbourhood work.

Figure 6.2: Membership map of Tower Hamlets Citizens (2015)

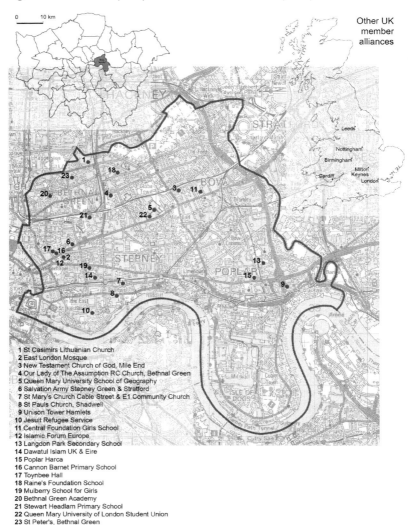

1 St Casimirs Lithuanian Church
2 East London Mosque
3 New Testament Church of God, Mile End
4 Our Lady of The Assumption RC Church, Bethnal Green
5 Queen Mary University School of Geography
6 Salvation Army Stepney Green & Stratford
7 St Mary's Church Cable Street & E1 Community Church
8 St Pauls Church, Shadwell
9 Unison Tower Hamlets
10 Jesuit Refugee Service
11 Central Foundation Girls School
12 Islamic Forum Europe
13 Langdon Park Secondary School
14 Dawatul Islam UK & Eire
15 Poplar Harca
16 Cannon Barnet Primary School
17 Toynbee Hall
18 Raine's Foundation School
19 Mulberry School for Girls
20 Bethnal Green Academy
21 Stewart Headlam Primary School
22 Queen Mary University of London Student Union
23 St Peter's, Bethnal Green

Partly due to contact made between individuals in the Conservative Party and CUK in the run-up to the general election in 2010, a number of national politicians made a commitment to support community organising that was subsequently featured in the Coalition agreement (see Chapter One). Following the election, ministers at the Office for Civil Society organised a tendering process to secure the training of up to 5,000 community organisers who would work across England and Wales. CUK was unsuccessful in its bid and the contract was awarded to Locality, which has a long history of community development work. Locality recruited and trained hundreds of new organisers who were hosted by a wide variety of local community organisations for up to two years. These hosts included the housing association Poplar HARCA, which was introduced in Chapter Three, and the Hightrees Community Development Trust (CDT) in Lambeth, which was introduced in Chapter Four. For Margaret Pierre-Jarrett, the Director of Hightrees CDT, these local community organisers provided a way to reach out to some of the thousands of people living in its area with whom it had no prior contact. The organising activity provided better intelligence about the local community, while also procuring the additional contacts that it needed to further develop its community work (see also Cameron and Rennick, 2015, for an evaluation report).

This kind of grassroots relationship building is absolutely essential to identifying – and developing – the new people who are able and willing to get more involved in community life. Indeed, basic organising activity is essential to any attempt to create new organisations or to grow those that already exist. At any time, in any location, the full range of local civil society organisations such as churches, mosques, sports clubs, residents' associations and reading groups will each be looking for new people to get more involved. While this largely depends on lay organisers who aren't paid for the work and who do it for love, some organisations such as trade unions, political parties and community centres have had the funds to create paid posts to lead on this work, and, even if this is not possible now, this is how they were built in the past. Indeed, the work of professional organisers has been critical to the past development of all our important civil society traditions such as the labour movement, faith organisations, social movements and community centres.

Today, similar organisers are needed to create new organisations, as well as to strengthen those that already exist. As we have seen in this chapter, many existing civil society organisations are struggling to secure their own organisations, let alone being able to reach out to others in a broader alliance. In this regard, it is noticeable that the forums introduced for neighbourhood planning (covered in Chapter Five) and the bodies initiated by local authorities as in Lambeth (introduced in Chapter Four) have largely worked with local residents' groups to get off the ground. They did not rely on the more established civil society organisations – and particularly the churches and other faith organisations – that might have been expected to play more of a role in local community life. As Mary Atkins, one of the councillors in Tulse Hill, Lambeth reported, 'church groups only represent church groups. I'm not saying I wouldn't work with them on some things, like the local vicar had a peace march through Tulse Hill a couple weeks ago, but on the specific changes needed [here] I wouldn't go to a church group because they don't live there. On the whole, they don't live in the area. They might come together for something but they don't live there.' Thus Mary explained why tenants' and residents' groups were more important to getting local things done. Faith organisations were often poorly rooted in the local community and, at best, they represented only a small minority of local residents, who were also likely to move (for a similar pattern in the US see Farnsley, 2000; Sampson, 2012).

Going forward, it would seem that some amalgamation of Locality's focus on grassroots community development work with CUK's broader networked approach could be better aligned. There is a need to employ organisers who can identify individuals and make connections from scratch – as was done by the Chicago Area Project organisers when they first started out – but to do this in order to help people identify their shared interests and develop their capacity for civic campaigns. Localism provides an opportunity to do something that merges the strengths of both strands of work at the neighbourhood scale: to use new and existing community organisations as a base from which to reach people and to build new neighbourhood alliances that are simultaneously linked to wider networks of organisation and civic campaigns. Moreover, greater investment in this kind of organising activity will be essential to fostering civic capacity in the areas that need it the most.

Notes
[1] This focus on the work of the church in the parish reflects the fact that the parish has always been the foundational scale of ecclesiastical organisation (Coriden, 1996). As outlined in Chapter Two, after the Reformation, the Church of England carried this over from the Catholic Church, and it became key to early forms of government and administration in England.

2   Elsewhere, I have written about the way in which membership of CUK can be thought of as a superordinate identity category that sits 'on top' of other sets of identities and relationships (Wills, 2010). This gives it a strength, as very diverse groups of people can easily affiliate without having to compromise their beliefs. However, it is also a weakness, as no one group has the alliance at the heart of its work.

SEVEN

A localist future?

This book has explored localism as a new policy paradigm in relation to the history of government in England while also considering its implications for the political geography of statecraft and citizenship in the 21st century. I have located localism as both an elite and a popular project; it is driven by a healthy, 'top down' recognition that the world cannot be run from Westminster and Whitehall and it is providing opportunities for people and organisations to act on the ground. As such, localism is about the political establishment making a new civic offer to its colleagues in 'lower tiers' of government as well as to the wider citizenry. It is about the pluralisation of political decision making through greater decentralisation.

In this regard, however, the outcomes of localism depend on a wide range of actors taking up the new opportunities on offer to them. In Chapter One I characterised localism as a form of 'liberal institutionalism'; it is designed to free up local capacity but, in so doing, it will expose the importance of having the institutions through which people are able to act. While the permissive legislation to support localism is liberal, allowing people to act if they want to – and this is particularly obvious in relation to neighbourhood planning – the existing distribution of civic capacity will shape the ability of people to take up this work. The uneven distribution of people with the skills and interest in localism, as well as the variable strength of local civil society organisations, will shape what happens on the ground. This means that localism is likely to widen existing spatial divides, and those places that need localism the most are the least likely to be able to mount a response. As such, this book has argued that much greater attention needs to be paid to the creation of the civic infrastructure and related capacity that will be necessary to underpin localism. At present, policy is rather ad hoc, but if a sustained localism is to be possible, much more investment will be needed to create the appropriate civic infrastructure that will allow this to happen.

In this book I have highlighted the way in which the emerging technologies of localist statecraft have already prompted the creation of neighbourhood-level institutions that facilitate people's entry into the arena of local decision making. However limited at present, national-level reform has opened up space for new institution building and activity at the neighbourhood scale (for parallel examples from the period of Scottish devolution see Raco, 2003). Indeed, despite the fact that I designed my research to explore four *different* forms of localism, all of them exposed the importance of having some kind of a neighbourhood forum for getting things done. From the outset, these examples each looked like very different formulations of localist practice – the NCB, the work of a local authority, neighbourhood planning and community organising – and yet, as it unfolded, the research exposed the importance of having some kind of organisational infrastructure at the neighbourhood scale in *every* case. Without a legitimate structure to represent the diversity of local people, to identify shared issues and concerns, to articulate and mobilise around these and to negotiate with other power brokers in the locality, localism could not be sustained. In my examples it was neighbourhood forums that were best fulfilling this role, through a combination of both representative and participative democracy. People were putting themselves forward to represent the local population but the work of the forum then allowed a much larger group of people to participate in activities and get further involved.

This kind of activity was most obvious – and predictable – in relation to neighbourhood planning. As explored in Chapter Five, people have used the new right to neighbourhood planning to set up a forum in an urban area where none existed before. While those living in rural areas are already covered by parish and town councils that can lead on this work, as many as three-quarters of the population do not currently have access to this level of government (NALC, 2015). In this context, neighbourhood planning has stimulated the formation of new civic institutions in a minority of urban neighbourhoods across the country. The research highlighted the challenge of extending these forums to areas where people are less able or interested to develop them, and, while the local authority was trying to fill this gap in Holbeck in Leeds, the wider challenge is to develop the civic skills of local residents to take up this work. In something of a chicken-and-egg situation, it is difficult to do this without the kind of local activity that might demonstrate the value of organising, attracting new participants and giving them the chance to learn the skills needed to take up this work, but without such local capacity it is possible to develop it only through some sort of intervention from the outside. There is scope for thinking more carefully about the kind of intervention that might allow this to happen, and the work of community organisers might be particularly important in this respect.

Neighbourhood forums were not expected to be important in relation to the local authority case. As outlined in Chapter Four, my research focused on the efforts being made by the London Borough of Lambeth to become a cooperative council and I looked at ongoing efforts to develop reciprocal relationships with local community groups. However, the council had facilitated the creation of arm's-length, semi-independent forums in 10 different neighbourhoods across the borough. These bodies had volunteer chairs and they provided coordination and communication across the different groups already operating in the neighbourhood while also attracting residents who were keen on getting involved in particular projects. In the example covered in my research – in Tulse Hill in Lambeth – the forum had provided leadership for the community and it was becoming the 'go to' organisation for the council and statutory bodies in the area. This forum had also begun the process of neighbourhood planning and was keen on widening the scope of its work, especially as this granted it statutory powers in dealing with the council over planning concerns. Ironically, the ability to challenge the council as an independent partner was recognised as being critically important in establishing more reciprocal relationships with the local authority. Many council officers were slow to understand and reflect more cooperative ways of working, and this was a significant problem for local community groups. The thinking was that by taking up neighbourhood planning the forum would increase its statutory weight and its ability to challenge the council.

It is significant that even the research into community organising highlighted the need for organising efforts to be focused on the neighbourhood scale. Although the leading body promoting community organising in England today, the broad-based alliance CUK, does not prioritise organising at the neighbourhood scale, my exploration of the history of this form of politics exposed its origins in efforts to foster neighbourhood councils in the city of Chicago during the 1930s and 1940s. The history of community organising points to the importance of creating neighbourhood-scale alliances of local civil society groups in order to develop the leadership and generate the collective power to allow citizens and their communities a place at the table of government. Linked to the School of Sociology at the University of Chicago, this form of community organising was all about a 'new parochialism' whereby residents were connected to democracy via their local institutions and the neighbourhood council, through which residents had the opportunity to learn the political skills necessary to shift the balance of political power.[1]

My research into the work of CUK in East London, covered in Chapter Six, highlighted the potential for this form of organising to focus anew on the neighbourhood scale. This is partly due to the greater scope for building meaningful social relationships at a relatively small scale, but also because the civil society organisations on which the organisation is currently based are often in decline, struggling to meet their own need for capacity and sometimes only thinly connected to the geographical communities in which they are situated (and this is a particular issue in relation to churches in areas where rising house prices have forced people to move and they come back only to worship on Sunday). A return to the scale of the neighbourhood would allow organisers to focus on the people living in the area, to engage with tenants' and residents' groups and to widen the brief to include individuals who have the potential to develop their capacity to contribute to the good of the local community. As such, community organising would make a stronger contribution to democratic culture than it does at the present time, strengthening the creation of civic capacity at the neighbourhood scale.[2]

In this regard, it is important to note that Locality, the organisation that won the government's tender to provide community organisers as part of the creation of the Big Society in 2010, has a stronger track record of working at the neighbourhood scale. Formed from a merger of the settlement movement with the Development Trusts Association in 2010, Locality is a network of 492 community organisations. These member organisations hosted the community organisers for the government-funded project and, with greater long-term investment, it would be possible to build on this work to direct community organisers to help create and support neighbourhood forums in areas that currently lack them, increasing civic capacity for the long term.

The key finding of this research is thus that the creation of a parish-like infrastructure across urban areas is needed to underpin localism. The neighbourhood has emerged as the critical scale through which people can organise themselves to engage with each other as well as with the state (and for an insight into the history of debate about the salience of the neighbourhood in the USA see Mumford, 1954; Miller, 1981). Indeed, in the example of the NCB in Poplar, East London, covered in Chapter Three, it was the *absence* of this kind of local organisation that meant the project was not able engage with local people in any meaningful way. If the state is being encouraged to make a new civic offer to its citizens, then those citizens need the infrastructure to allow this to happen at the neighbourhood scale. Moreover, neighbourhood planning points to the importance of taking an 'emergent' approach to this process. Rather that drawing lines on the map in the office or standardising the units to be used, the existing legislation has allowed communities to draw their own boundaries through debate and negotiation about the size of area that makes sense, the way people feel about their community and where the lines are best drawn. In the examples I have looked at, the resulting neighbourhoods often reflected established ward boundaries, but they also varied in size from just 3,000 people in Holbeck in Leeds (where the forum used the ward boundary already in use by the local authority) to 18,000 in Highgate in London, where people were anxious to create an area that made sense to the people who lived there. Most 'natural neighbourhoods' are likely to be somewhere in the middle of this range in terms of their size.

The challenge for localism is to encourage the creation of more neighbourhood forums and to grant them greater recognition as part of the geo-political infrastructure of English government. In time, this will mean the ad hoc planning forums becoming more formal neighbourhood councils in line with the 9,000 parishes that already exist (largely in rural parts of the country, NALC, 2015). The government will need to make it easier for forums to become councils in urban areas. It will also need to make such bodies less formal, more dynamic and more creative. While the National Association of Local Councils (NALC) reports that some 250 new councils have been founded since the turn of the century, national reforms could make it easier to set up a council and, once secured, to make it more enticing to get more involved.

As outlined in Chapter Five, there is also scope to learn lessons from areas where local people have put together a non-partisan slate based on a shared desire to improve the operation and impact of the local council (Rustin, 2010; MacFadyen, 2014). In towns like Frome in Somerset and Liskeard in Cornwall, local democracy has been revitalised by residents organising themselves to stand on non-partisan platforms in order to secure control of the council. By wresting control from candidates who are elected on the basis of their national party affiliations, groups like Independents for Frome are using the structures of representative democracy to galvanise the local community and get things done. This form of non-partisan, place-based political organisation had largely died away during the 20th century – partly as a result of the processes of centralisation described in Chapter Two – but there are signs that localism is now stimulating a revitalisation of non-partisan local politics. Taking control of existing structures is one way to do it, but in most parts of the country people need to organise themselves to create the civic structures through which they might then be able to act.

In this regard, the story of Queen's Park Community Council in West London is particularly instructive for thinking about the next phase of localism in England. With parallels to the work of the Hightrees Community Development Trust in Tulse Hill that was covered in Chapter Four, the Paddington Development Trust (PDT) was created in 1997 to support the local community, and it has since pioneered a number of important projects in relation to community health, economic development and active citizenship.[3] During the 2000s, the PDT created neighbourhood forums in three areas of its patch – Church Street, Queen's Park and Westbourne – in order to allow elected representatives to develop and sustain new working relationships with the statutory and voluntary sectors that were active in its part of London. In each area, six residents were elected to work alongside six representatives from statutory organisations like the NHS, housing organisations and the police, as well as with six representatives from the voluntary sector. When PDT lost the funding it needed to support this work in 2010, the elected residents in Queen's Park were keen to keep the work of the forum alive. They recognised the need to retain the formal infrastructure of the forum, as it allowed them to coordinate activity, lead projects and manage communications with local residents, and without some formal arrangement things would likely collapse over time.

Having discovered the little-known and never-used legislation that allowed people to create an urban parish council in London that had been passed by the New Labour government via the Local Government and Public Involvement in Health Act (2007), the Queen's Park forum members sought to win support to create a new council. They launched their campaign in early 2011, but it ended up taking as long as 3½ years to get the new council set up. Under the legislation they had to demonstrate the support of at least 10% of local residents in order to request a governance review from Westminster Council. Westminster's councillors and officers then decided to call a referendum to see if local people really did want to set up a council and, once that was done, they then waited to hold the necessary elections as part of wider council elections already agreed for May 2014.[4] In the event, 12 new councillors were elected, 7 of them women, all of them working, from a wide range of backgrounds. Since coming into office, these councillors have had to grapple with the formal requirements of being a community council and the rules and regulations required. However, the precept (an additional charge on the council tax) has generated just over £100,000 a year, and the councillors are using this money to support their administration by employing a clerk, to coordinate their own local events that include a music festival and fireworks night that had previously been run by the forum and to set up a new initiative to provide grants for local organisations. The processes involved in setting up the new body as well as in supporting ongoing efforts to secure a neighbourhood plan have involved regular consultation with local residents and businesses, and the council also produces a quarterly newsletter.[5] Keeping this level of organisation and activity going would not have been possible without a formal structure, and becoming a community council has also provided limited funds to further enable the work.

When I interviewed the council chair, Angela Singhate, and the councillor leading on the neighbourhood plan, Gill Fitzhugh, they highlighted the struggle they had faced to set up the council, to maintain momentum over the years and to then make it work. For them, this was still an experiment and they were unsure about what was possible by becoming a formal community council. However, being a statutory body meant that Westminster Council had to take them more seriously and having a budget gave them the independence and autonomy they needed to organise things as they saw fit. They were keen to change the prevailing culture of local government and to make their council more open, and were appealing to local people to get more involved. They were also resolute about keeping political parties out of the frame. As Gill put it, 'it is much stronger for being apolitical', meaning that they were being non-partisan in the work they were doing. When asked what they would do to improve the work of the council, Angela and Gill highlighted the need for more training for councillors, and they also advocated the need to make things less formal. In addition, reform to council tax benefit had reduced the size of their budget and this was being raised at the national level in the ongoing work led by NALC.

The long history of neighbourhood work in Queen's Park had helped to generate the strong social and civic capacity needed to set up the council. The local protagonists had good working relationships with each other, they had already shared a lot of experience in organising at this scale, and they understood the wider context in which they were working. Without this, it would be much harder to establish this kind of council and additional support would be needed to get things set up and to sustain it for the long term (for a similar argument in relation to the neighbourhood councils operating in poorer neighbourhoods in Los Angeles, USA, see Jun and Musso, 2013).

Recognising the importance of institutional renewal in the ongoing story of democracy, Fukuyama (2014) reminds us that the English journey to develop democracy took hundreds of years, leading up to the achievement of the full franchise in 1928. Moreover, this history highlights the extent to which there is nothing inevitable about the particular institutions through which we practise democracy in England today. As John Dewey (1954 [1927]; 1987 [1937]) remarked, democracy is akin to a mission; it always has to be renewed, as circumstances change over time. Thus we can argue that localism is one of the ways in which politicians and citizens are currently trying to reconfigure the way our democracy works. To date, localism has prompted the ad hoc development of neighbourhood forums, but much more could be done to support this and to provide extra assistance to the areas that face the greatest challenges in making this happen. Doing so could potentially connect localism to the wider network of 9,000 parish and town councils that already exist, building on the geo-history of our representative structures by responding to the desire for greater local involvement today.

This certainly chimes with ongoing calls to revitalise this tier of government and to increase its power, authority and funding as part of the shift towards the devolution of political power in England today (NALC, 2015). The creation of, and greater support for, civic infrastructure at the scale of the parish or neighbourhood would help to ensure that the new devolution deals forged between the Treasury and the largest cities in the country don't simply move power from Whitehall and Westminster to a range of town halls. As Justin Griggs from NALC put it to me during interview, 'the government need to decide how much they support parishes, how much they really subscribe to them being the backbone of democracy, how important they are to service delivery and whether they want them to do more'. This is a key challenge now to be faced by those involved in our national and local government: to what extent do they want to create and sustain the civic infrastructure and related capacity required to underpin localist statecraft and citizenship? And if they want to do this, how will it be done?

In this regard, the research outlined in the bulk of this book should have something useful to say. However, the main conclusion – that neighbourhood-level civic infrastructure is crucial to the practice and outcomes of localism – remains rather counter-cultural, particularly in relation to academic debates. Not surprisingly, in a world characterised by globalisation, increased rates of population mobility and the obvious importance of social networks, many commentators have suggested that the local scale has lost its social and political importance today (Wellman, 1979; Wellman et al, 1997). As our geographical fixity has taken on less salience in our social lives and we manage our complicated social relationships across very wide distances, it has been logical to assume that geographic location has become less important in public life, politics and government too. Indeed, from their very beginnings, the social sciences have reinforced this view of the world. Early sociological analysis counterpoised the 'Gemeinschaft' of the small-scale rural community in which face-to-face relationships were established over time with the 'Gesellschaft' of the urban society in which people lived anonymous lives spread across space (Tönnies, 1936 [1887]). The automatic solidarity of the former was argued to be replaced by anonymised processes associated with industrialisation and urbanisation in ever more complex divisions of labour (Durkheim, 1933 [1893]). The old 'Great Communities' in which local publics could form and determine their mind were replaced by the 'Great Society' in which mediated publics operated across a much larger scale in a largely disorganised way (Dewey, 1954 [1927]).

Yet, despite the fact that our geographic communities have become more spread out across space and we now form many relationships without spatial propinquity (Calhoun, 1998), it does not mean that geographical place has lost its importance in the question of government and the practice of politics. There is a danger in conflating the social with the spatial, when each are important in their own right (Agnew, 1987; Sampson, 2012). Indeed, while the scale of social life has been extended dramatically, the role of geographical place has been reconfigured rather than overturned. Practitioners in my own discipline of human geography have highlighted the way in which particular scales of political decision making have taken on greater or lesser importance in the context of wider shifts in global political economy (Brenner, 1999; Swyngedouw, 2004; Morgan, 2007). Place still matters, even if its role and contribution have changed.

In his efforts to understand the interconnection between place and politics in political life nearly 30 years ago, John Agnew (1987) argued that place has a three-fold salience for politics. First, as the space in which people live, shaping the microsociology of everyday life. Second, and relatedly, as the arena in which local people generate a sense of shared identity connected to place, which he calls a 'sense of place'. And third, as a geographic location in the macro-order of things, being about relationships to other locations. Given this triad of factors, place is *always* constitutive of social and political life, shaping identity, activity and possibility, even if such geographical factors are also a product of non-local relations (see also Savage, 1987; Johnston and Pattie, 2006). Indeed, as documented in regard to the localist experiments explored in this book, each place had a very particular set of local possibilities based on its historical inheritance, the nature of the local community and the presence (or otherwise) of civic institutions and people who were able and willing to act, as well as being shaped by the wider dynamics of political change.

In many ways, this seems a rather obvious point to make and it seems odd that place is often disparaged in relation to understanding the world. Even in my own discipline of human geography, an attachment to the constitutive role of place is sometimes read as a product of naïve nostalgia for the world of 'Gemeinschaft' that no longer exists. Contemporary analysis tends to see places as intersections or nodes in spaces of flows that are unbound and fluid, providing weak foundations for political life (Amin, 2002; 2004; Massey, 2005; Clarke, 2013). There is little acceptance for the idea that place remains a significant space for organisation, action and the potential for fostering change. While human geographers used to emphasise the uniqueness of place, with little to say about the connections between places and the wider process of change, the development of this more sophisticated approach to understanding our geography has sometimes meant that any focus on place itself has got lost.[6]

John Tomaney (2013) has recently mounted a defence of parochialism, arguing that local places remain critical to everyday life by shaping experience, identity and behaviour and providing a set of perspectives on the rest of the world. For him, 'A parochial outlook values the local, its culture and solidarities, as a moral starting point and locus of ecological concern and a site for the development of virtues including commitment, fidelity, civility and nurture' (Tomaney, 2013, 659). While Tomaney develops this position in relation to the creation of art, a similar position can be developed in relation to civic organisation and politics. While any civic institutional infrastructure and local politics will reflect a diversity of interests and positions, and the balance of local relations of power, it cannot be rejected as necessarily exclusionary or reactionary simply on the basis of scale. While researchers need to attend to the dynamics of politics at work at *any* given scale, it is not possible to negate the importance of the local or place in advance of studying the situation concerned.

In this light, it is possible to understand localism as reflecting the persistent importance of geography in providing the motivation and potential capacity for political organisation and agency (Jupp, 2012). Indeed, the emergent neighbourhood forums being developed in Lambeth and via neighbourhood planning in Exeter, London and Leeds were found to provide a civic platform to develop local voice, identify shared interests, demand recognition and develop the capacity to negotiate with the people able to help effect local change. These forums also provided the means to find other local people who wanted to act over a range of concerns. Through stimulating the creation of new institutions, localism was generating new potential for collective organisation, self-government and new forms of political authority that could then contribute to the wider good of the whole (Frug, 1999; 2014; Magnusson, 2005a; 2005b; 2012).

Once established, such neighbourhood organisations and related activities have local effects which can generate lasting and path-dependent change over time. As Sampson (2012, 21) puts it in relation to his work in Chicago, 'We react to neighborhood difference, and these reactions constitute social mechanisms and practices that in turn shape perceptions, relationships, and behaviours that reverberate both within and beyond traditional neighborhood borders, and which taken together further define the social structure of the city.' These neighbourhood effects are always at work and my research exposed the extent to which they made a difference to areas as diverse as Exeter St James, Holbeck in Leeds, and Highgate, Poplar, Tulse Hill and West Norwood in London. The research suggests that localist statecraft has generated new opportunities for politicians, state-appointed officials and citizens to act in relation to place. These opportunities are likely only to increase further in future, and efforts to create a more permanent civic infrastructure at the neighbourhood scale will prove critical in determining the outcomes secured.

Notes

[1] A more recent version of this argument was made by Berger and Neuhaus in the 1970s (1985 [1977]). They highlighted the importance of nurturing the institutions that mediate relationships between citizens and the state, arguing that these bodies remain critical to the functioning of democracy as well as to social well-being. Their argument focused on four different kinds of mediating institution: family, faith, charity and neighbourhood. In relation to the latter they argued that 'The goal of making and keeping life human, of sustaining a people-sized society, depends upon our learning again that parochialism is not a nasty word. Like the word parish, it comes from the Greek, *pura* plus *oikos,* the place next door ... we all have a great stake in the place where we live, it is in the common interest to empower our own places and the places next door' (Berger and Neuhaus, 1985 [1977] 176). In the spirit of de Tocqueville before them and Putnam after them, they argued that policy should focus on nurturing these institutions, thereby empowering local citizens to engage with the state (see also Bacqué and Biewener, 2013).

[2] At present, CUK operates at a larger scale and focuses on mobilising for public assemblies at which politicians are asked to meet particular demands and are held to account for their actions in relation to those demands. While this is valuable, it is a step removed from the day-to-day work needed to coordinate civic capacity at the neighbourhood scale. Indeed, CUK relies on existing member organisations (churches, schools, community groups) to provide the institutional foundation for

its organising and mobilising efforts (Wills, 2012). This model makes it easier to mobilise large numbers of people but it does not focus on developing unaffiliated people, nor on coordinating new structures from scratch.

3   The Community Development Trusts in Tulse Hill and Paddington both belong to the network coordinated by Locality mentioned above and in Chapter Six.

4   The referendum took place from Wednesday, 9 May 2012 to Friday, 25 May 2012. All Queen's Park ward residents on the electoral register received a ballot paper in the post and were given the opportunity to vote on whether or not they supported the creation of the Queen's Park Community Council. To help residents decide, supporting information was provided alongside the ballot paper. Residents were able to vote by post, internet, telephone and SMS (text). On a 20% turnout, almost 70% of the votes were in favour and the new council was elected 18 months later, in May 2014.

5   The ward of Queen's Park includes about 12,500 people living in 5,000 households. The newsletters are delivered door to door by a network of volunteers and the community council has also had space on the high street to help it communicate with local people about their needs and the work the council is doing.

6   There are, of course, a good number of scholars who have retained an attachment to ideas about the constitutive power – and political potential – of place (see, for examples, Entrikin, 1991; Castree, 2004; DuPuis and Goodman, 2005; Manzo and Perkins, 2006; Jones, 2009; Sampson, 2012; Jones and Wood, 2013; Tomaney, 2013). In his philosophical topography, for example, Jeff Malpas (1999) draws on Heidegger's notion of 'dasein' to highlight the necessary relationship between place and 'being-in-the-world'. As he explains, 'Heidegger's fundamental conception of human existence as "being in the world" implies the impossibility of properly understanding human being in a way that would treat it as only contingently related to its surrounding and to the concrete structures of activity in which it is engaged' (Malpas, 1999, 8). For Malpas (1999, 32), 'place is integral to the very structure and possibility of experience' and it is fundamental to understanding the world. In this reading, it is place that makes politics possible and, as Malpas (1999, 198) explains, '[T]he complex structure of place, its resistance to any simple categorisation or characterisation, its encompassing of both subjective and objective elements, its necessary inter-connection with agency, all suggest that the idea of place does not so much bring a certain politics with it, as define the very frame within which the political itself must be located.'

Appendix: Research design and methods

The research presented in this book was developed as part of a Major Research Fellowship funded by the Leverhulme Trust between and 2012 and 2015 entitled Place and politics: Localism in the United Kingdom. The fellowship aimed to 'explore the reasons why the local is being mobilised and prioritised at this particular time; consider people's attitudes towards place and whether they want to take a greater role in political life and the conditions in which they do so; chart the outcomes of top-down and bottom-up localism; and determine whether localism is a viable route to democratic renewal.' The project coincided with the election of a new Conservative-led government that made a full and public commitment to pursuing localism. As such, the research was well placed to track the unfolding localist agenda of the government, focusing on the particular policy measures adopted (such as NCBs and neighbourhood planning) while also taking a broader perspective. Given the growing interest and activity around localism, it has been impossible to be comprehensive, but the aim has been to look at a series of case studies in the context of the wider policy change.

The research presented was conducted via four separate projects of varied design, duration and content, and the research conducted is summarised briefly below.

1 Poplar Neighbourhood Community Budget, 2012–13 (Chapter Three)

I was involved in the learning and evaluation of the pilot NCB in Poplar, East London, from June 2012 until the submission of a final report in March 2013. While analysts at the DCLG conducted a light-touch evaluation of all the pilots and later published a comprehensive report (Rutherfoord et al, 2013), each of the 12 project teams was urged to include its own learning and evaluation activity, and a number similarly developed links with academic researchers. The staff running the Poplar Neighbourhood Community Budget (PNCB) appointed me as an evaluator and I worked with Erica Pani to: record and assess the processes involved in developing the PNCB; identify success (particularly in relation to community consultation and co-design); and highlight any obstacles and the ways they could be overcome. From the outset, the PNCB team was aware and supportive of the overlaps between this evaluation activity and the larger research project written up in this book. Being evaluators gave us open access to the project and its protagonists, and we had complete freedom to design our interview questions and develop our analysis as we saw fit.

The evaluation comprised a three-part methodology. First, background, desk-based research included a review of all the relevant documents produced and provided by partners, various consultants and DCLG. We also looked at all the secondary data provided by the partners, including observational notes and minutes from various partner and briefing events, notes from one-to-one partner meetings involving the programme consultant and/or manager, notes from a group session on shaping the community engagement strategy and various e-mails. Overall, the background research helped to capture the nature of existing service provision and partner attitudes. It also helped to shed light on the size and complexity of developing the PNCB.

The second stage involved primary research. Eight one-to-one, semi-structured interviews were held with the key stakeholders identified by the PNCB team, including all the core partners and consultants (Table A1). The interviews were digitally recorded and transcribed for analysis to capture interviewees' reflections on the process, their experiences in developing the various aspects of PNCB and, importantly, what they had learned. The final part of the research design comprised participant observation. We attended various partner, community and co-design events. Observing and participating in the dynamics of the partnership gave us a better understanding of the work and the sort of relationships being developed over this time.

Table A1: Interviews conducted with the Poplar NCB team

Organisation	Role	Date(s)
Poplar HARCA	Project consultant	12.07.12
	Project manager	14.07.12 and 21.01.13
	Project support worker	21.07.12
The Bromley by Bow Centre	Director of strategy	17.11.12
The GP network	General practitioner	21.11.12
Andrew Mawson Partnerships Consultancy	Consultant	31.10.12
St Paul's Way Trust School	-	
Kaizen (the organisation that led the community consultation)	Consultant who led on the PNCB work	2.08.12

Following this research, a learning and evaluation report was presented to the PNCB that also contributed to the overall research conducted by staff at DCLG (Rutherfoord et al, 2013). The research materials were then re-used for further analysis in writing this book.

2 Lambeth Council's Community Based Commissioning project, 2014–15 (Chapter Four)

I was involved in the evaluation of Lambeth's Community Based Commissioning (CBC) project between November 2014 and June 2015. This work was conducted as part of a wider programme of evaluation of a range of policy initiatives and projects being developed across the council and our research team was charged with collating qualitative information about the work of the project. I worked with Dr Andrea Gibbons and James Scott on this project and we attended most of the team meetings and two of the four community events that were held as part of the project (Table A2). Interviews were conducted with all the key participants and three people were interviewed twice in order to capture their thoughts and experience at the start and end of the project (as indicated in Table A3). This book draws on the interview material and notes taken during team meetings to explore the evolution of the project, the implications for the role and activities of ward councillors and the learning that has wider significance for the future of council operations and culture. In most cases the quotations used have been anonymised, but in relation to the councillors and community representatives this proved more difficult to do and they have agreed to being named in the text.

This chapter also describes some of the work that was done through the Open Works project based in West Norwood, Lambeth, funded by the council, between 2014 and 2015. The findings presented in this part of the chapter include material from an interview with Tessy Britton and Laura Billings from Civic Systems Lab who led the work in West Norwood, which was conducted on 15 July 2014. I have also drawn on the evaluation work that was funded by the Lankelly Chase Foundation and published in a large report in late 2015 (Civic Systems Lab, 2015). I was also able to develop a better understanding of this work by attending a workshop incorporating a number of projects involved in similar local experiments, hosted by Civic Systems Lab, held in Norwich in January 2015.

Table A2: CBC team meetings and events

Date	Meeting/event	Key focus/activity
4.11.14	*Officers meet councillors*	*Explain CBC and present background information about ward that included data from community surveys and information about educational performance, youth offending, loneliness, benefit claiming and levels of deprivation. Councillors identified 2 key issues.*
12.11.14	CBC team meeting	Meeting focused on the need to collect more data about the 2 key issues identified by councillors as important in Tulse Hill (gangs and social isolation). Team also noted post-election change in political leadership of the council, and the decision of the CEO to leave.
25.11.14	CBC team with councillors	Councillors decided which of the 2 issues to focus on – based on their interest and community support. CBC team provided more information. Mary put forward the idea of a parent-to-parent support network (as a follow-up to the issue of gangs).
17.12.14	CBC team	Despite major efforts it was reported that the Ferndale councillors could not be engaged. Debate about 'working with the willing' in future.
24.1.15	First community meeting [event 1]	Community Centre, Tulse Hill Estate (11am–1.30pm), 10 parents, 3 officers, 2 councillors and children. Led by Erica from forum with powerful testimony and support. No clear follow-up steps but focus on community support for raising children.
29.1.15	CBC team	Debate about next steps, the potential for more meetings to reach more people. Mary could work on getting funding with the Forum. Meeting told that Cllr Imogen Walker (Cabinet) had asked for the CBC to be wrapped up as soon as possible. The team discussed how to make the most of the project, despite the short time.
12.2.15	CBC team	Following up – recognising the need to identify responsibility for the network, going forward; the team was keen to try and make the best of the work that had already been done. They talked about meeting again with the parents who attended event 1.
26.2.15	CBC team	Some concern about the CBC piggy-backing on the event at Hightrees on 7 March, especially as there was to be a new person in charge. Similarly for the pampering event on 28 March, about which even less was known by the team. Debate focused on shutting down the CBC project and trying to make the most of it.
7.3.15	Engagement in community meeting at Hightrees [event 2]	Event to celebrate residents' completing a course called 'community in action'. Core group of 8 parents, 2 officers, 2 staff from centre, 2 councillors. A member of the CBC team introduced the idea of the parents' network and gathered ideas, finding broad support for the idea.

Date	Meeting/event	Key focus/activity
24.3.15	CBC team	Brief preparation for the 3rd event. Focus on how to learn from the project. Wanted to test: (1) if possible to achieve local-level outcomes better and cheaper (not really done this, as not part of commissioning process); (2) readiness of councillors to engage (have done this); (3) community appetite and capacity (have partially done this).
28.3.15	*Engagement in community-pampering event in TH [event 3]*	*The CBC team attended a councillor-led event to provide pampering activities to local people. Collected information from a questionnaire about priorities, potential contributions, ideas, skills/talents and engagement*
23.4.15	CBC team	Focus on learning from the CBC in regard to member development; understanding among officers; taking forward the parents' network (and funding); sharing learning.
(6.6.15	*Stand-alone community event to discuss the parent network idea [event 4]*	*Community Centre, Tulse Hill estate, 11 parents and community leaders, 1 councillor, 2 members of the CBC team. Discussed linking their networking to a planned day trip to Margate organised by the Tulse Hill Forum. Plans made for a short course about housing and a 'conference with a difference' to support the network.*
25.6.15	Evaluation meeting	CBC and Open Works learning and plan for sharing.

Note: The events in italics were not attended by our researchers.

Table A3: Interviews conducted with the key protagonists of the Lambeth CBC

Name	Role	Date(s)
Council staff		
Anna Randle	Head of Strategy and equalities (project manager)	12.11.14 and 23.04.15
Hannah Jameson	Assistant Director Policy and insight (ex-Head of Strategy and equalities; involved at start of the project)	4.04.15
Paula Royal	Policy, equalities and performance officer	19.11.14
Salome Simoes	Senior policy, equalities and performance officer	3.12.14
Sarah Coyte	Capacity building officer, Active Communities	12.11.14 and 20.04.15
Sheleena Powtoo	Intelligence and assurance officer	26.02.15
Sherilyn Dossantos	Senior policy, equalities and performance officer	12.11.14
Susan Sheehan	Senior policy officer (link to Ferndale)	12.11.14
Tony Blume	Cooperative council implementation lead	24.02.15
Tom Barrett	Strategy manager	25.11.14

Name	Role	Date(s)
Councillors		
Lib Peck	Leader of the Council (Labour)	4.06.14
Marcia Cameron	Ward Councillor, Tulse Hill (Labour)	3.02.15
Mary Aktins	Ward Councillor, Tulse Hill (Labour)	19.11.14 and 5.05.15
Community leaders		
Erica Tate	Chair, Tulse Hill Forum	5.05.15
Margaret Pierre-Jarrett	Director, Hightrees Community Development Trust, Tulse Hill	13.05.15

3 Neighbourhood planning in Exeter St James, Devon, Holbeck in Leeds, and Highgate in London, 2013–15 (Chapter Five)

The information used in this chapter was collected over a number of visits to the three study areas. This involved conducting interviews with some of the leading protagonists and their partners in the local authority and attending a number of key meetings held by the forums (including public events, planning meetings and AGMs). Key meetings included the 2014 and 2015 forum AGMs in Highgate and an event on neighbourhood planning organised by Leeds City Council at which the Minister for Planning, Nick Boles MP, was a speaker, held in July 2014. Quotes from the interviews are used in the text and the dates when they were conducted are indicated in Table A4. Given the impossibility of anonymising these cases, the names of interviewees are listed here and some people are cited (with their permission) in the main text.

The three cases were selected on the basis of providing good urban comparisons at the time when I started this part of the research in 2013: Exeter St James because it was the first urban forum to get its plan accepted and, as such, allowed the fullest exploration of the impact of neighbourhood planning in the time allocated for this research; Highgate as an area with strong civic traditions in London; and Holbeck as an area where the city council was taking the lead. Given that hundreds of forums have been established in urban areas across the country where none existed before, this research is but a small drop in the larger ocean of emergent neighbourhood planning, and it cannot be understood as fully representative in any way. However, there are now additional research projects underway that have sought to capture the wider experience (see especially Parker et al, 2014, 2015) and my research findings are not out of line with the indications from this larger body of work.

Table A4: Interviews conducted to explore neighbourhood planning in Exeter St James (Exeter), Highgate (London) and Holbeck (Leeds)

Interviewees	Role/activity	Date
Exeter St James		
Jo Hawkins	First Chair, Neighbourhood Forum	18.02.14 and 4.09.14
Di Boston	Second Chair, Neighbourhood Forum	18.02.14
Richard Short	Planning, Exeter City Council	18.02.15
Jill Day	Planning, Exeter City Council	18.02.15
Kevin Mitchell	Ward Councillor (Lib Dem), Exeter City Council	19.02.15
Kevin Owen	Ward Councillor (Labour), Exeter City Council	18.02.15
Rachel Sutton	Councillor with brief for planning (Labour), Exeter City Council	18.02.15
Jill Owen	Local Councillor (Labour), Devon County Council	18.02.15
Highgate		
Maggy Meade-King	First Chair, Neighbourhood Forum	20.01.14
Rachel Allison	Second Chair, Neighbourhood Forum	12.01.15
Richard Lee	Coordinator of Just Space – a community-led network involved in planning across London	9.05.14
Brian O'Donnell	Strategic Planning, Camden Council	19.01.15
Holbeck		
Dennis Kitchen	Chair, Neighbourhood Forum	23.04.14
Ian MacKay	Planning, Leeds City Council	28.01.15
Angela Gabriel	Ward councillor (Labour), Leeds City Council	28.01.15

4 Citizens UK, 2001–15 (Chapter Six)

The material used in Chapter Six was collated over a longer period of time than the data presented in earlier chapters. I developed a research relationship with Citizens UK when it launched a living wage campaign in East London in 2001 and have since engaged in a variety of research projects, student-led activities and teaching that relate to its work. The material presented in Chapter Six explores the history of this model of politics as well as drawing on two phases of original research work conducted in East London. In this regard, I have used some of the 14 interviews that were conducted for a previous research project between 2005 and 2006 (Table A5). These interviews were conducted with leaders in participating organisations, as well as with the Director of Citizens UK, as part of the ESRC's Identities and Social Action programme for a project on the living wage campaign (and the results of this work are published in Jamoul and Wills, 2008; Wills, 2008; 2009a; 2009b; 2010; 2012). In addition, I conducted a number of interviews especially for this project on localism during 2014, focusing solely on the leading faith groups in membership of Citizens UK in Tower Hamlets (Table A5). I have drawn on quotes from these interviews in the text in Chapter Six, with the respondents' consent.

Table A5: Interviews conducted with participants from the key membership institutions in East London and Tower Hamlets Citizens, 2005–06 and 2014

Name	Role and organisation	Date
Adewale Adenekan	Parishioner, Parish of the Divine Compassion, Newham	6.05.06
Revd Jan Atkins	Minister, Bryant Street Methodist church, Stratford, Newham (6 additional interviews were also conducted with members of this church during 2006)	24.11.05
Father John Armitage	Priest, St Anthony's RC church, Forest Gate, Newham	27.01.06
Paul Doherty	Head teacher, Trinity Catholic High School, Redbridge	21.12.05
Jean Geldart	Branch secretary, UNISON, Tower Hamlets Council	5.05.05
Neil Jameson	Director, Citizens UK	13.04.05
Janavaca	Leader, Buddhist Centre, Tower Hamlets	2.02.06
Dilowar Khan	Director, East London Mosque, Tower Hamlets	16.12.05
Deborah Littman	Head office support, UNISON	12.05.05
Sister Una McCreesh	St Anthony's RC School and parish, Forest Gate, Newham	9.02.06
Neil Primrose	Headteacher, Norlington Boys' School, Waltham Forest	9.02.06
Revd Paul Regan	Methodist minister, Newham	28.04.05
Revd Angus Ritchie	Director, Contextual Theology Centre, Tower Hamlets	17.03.05
Richard Zipfel	St Thomas More RC church, Hackney	23.01.06
Revd Adam Atkinson	Vicar, St Peter's church, Bethnal Green	16.10.14
Captain Nick Coke	Captain, the Salvation Army, Stepney	17.04.14
Colin Glenn	Member of the New Testament Church of God, Mile End	2.12.14
Father Tom O'Brien	Priest, Our Lady of the Assumption, Bethnal Green	27.03.14
Nurul Ullah	Member of staff, Darul Umma, Shadwell	26.03.14

References

Adamson, D and Bromiley, R, 2013, 'Community empowerment: learning from practice in community regeneration', *International Journal of Public Sector Management*, 26, 3, 190–202

Agnew, J, 1987, *Place and politics: The geographical mediation of state and society*, Boston: Allen and Unwin

Alinsky, S, 1941, 'Community analysis and organization', *American Journal of Sociology*, 46, 6, 797–808

Alinsky, S, 1946, *Reveille for radicals*, London: Vintage

Alinsky, S, 1971, *Rules for radicals: A pragmatic primer for realistic radicals*, New York: Random House

Allmendinger, P and Haughton, G, 2013, 'The evolution and trajectory of English spatial governance: "neoliberal" episodes in planning', *Planning, Practice and Research*, 28, 1, 6–26

Almond, G, and Verba, S, 1963, *The civic culture: political attitudes and democracy in five countries*, Princeton: Princeton University Press

Amin, A, 2002, 'Spatialities of globalisation', *Environment and Planning A*, 34, 385–99

Amin, A, 2004, 'Regions unbound: towards a new politics of place', *Geografiska Annaler*, 86B, 33–44

Amin, A, 2005, 'Local community on trial', *Economy and Society*, 34, 4, 612–33

Anderson, D, no date, *A new way of thinking and a new way of working – the Cooperative Council*, presentation available from the author

Andrews, R, Cowell, R and Downe, J, 2011, 'Promoting civic culture by supporting citizenship: what difference can local government make?', *Public Administration*, 89, 2, 595–610

Arnstein, S, 1969, 'The ladder of civic participation', *Journal of the American Institute of Planners*, 35, 4, 216–24

Ashford, D E, 1989, 'British dogmatism and French pragmatism revisited', in C Crouch and D Marquand (eds), *The new centralism: Britain out of step in Europe?* 77–93

Atkinson, D, 2004, *Civil renewal: Mending the hole in the social ozone layer*, Studley, Warwickshire: Brewin Books

Atlas, J, 2010, *Seeds of change: The story of ACORN, America's most controversial antipoverty community organizing group*, Nashville: Vanderbilt University Press

Bacqué, M-H and Biewener, C, 2013, 'Different manifestations of the concept of empowerment: the politics of urban renewal in the US and the UK', *International Journal of Urban and Regional Research*, 37, 6, 2198–213

Bagehot, W, 1867, *The English constitution*, London: Chapman and Hall

Bailey, N and Pill, M, 2015, 'Can the state empower communities through localism? An evaluation of recent approaches to neighbourhood governance in England', *Environment and Planning C*, 33, 289–314

Baine, S, 1975, *Community action and local government*, Occasional papers on Social Administration, 59, London: G Bell and Sons

Baker, J and Young, M, 1971, *The Hornsey plan: A role for neighbourhood councils in the new local government*, London: Association for Neighbourhood Councils

Barber, BR, 2003 [1984] *Strong democracy: Participatory politics for a new age*, Oakland: California University Press

Barber, B R, 2013, *If Mayors ruled the world: Dysfunctional nations, rising cities*, New Haven, CT: Yale University Press

Barnes, M, Newman, J, Knops, A and Sullivan, H, 2003, 'Constituting 'the public' in public participation', *Public administration*, 81, 2, 379-399

Barnes, M, Newman, J and Sullivan, H, 2007, *Power, participation and political renewal: Case studies in participation*, Bristol: Policy Press

Barnes, T, 2008, 'American pragmatism: towards a geographical introduction', *Geoforum*, 39, 4, 1542–54

Barnett, C, 2005, 'The consolations of "neoliberalism"', *Geoforum*, 36, 1, 7–12

Barnett, C, Cloke, P, Clarke, N and Malpass, A, 2010, *Globalizing responsibility: The political rationalities of ethical consumption*, London: John Wiley & Sons

Barron, D J and Frug, G E, 2005, 'Defensive localism: a view of the field from the field', *The Journal of Law and Politics*, XXI, 261–91

Barrow, C, Greenhalgh, S and Lister, E, 2010, *A Magna Carta for localism: Three practical steps to make localism real*, London: Centre for Policy Studies

Bartels, K, 2013, 'Public encounters: the history and future of face-to-face contact between public professionals and citizens', *Public Administration*, 91, 2, 469–83

Bennett, RJ, 1990 (ed) *Decentralization, local governments and markets: Towards a post-welfare agenda*, Oxford: Clarendon Press

Berger, PL and Neuhaus, RJ, 1985 [1977] 'To empower people: from state to civil society' [second edition], M Novak (ed) *To empower people: From state to civil society*, Washington DC: AEI Press, 157–208

Berry, D, 1987, 'The geographic distribution of governmental powers: the case of regulation', *Professional Geographer*, 39, 4, 428–37

Bevan, A, 1952, *In place of fear*, London: William Heinemann Ltd

Bevir, M and Rhodes, RAW, 2006, *Governance stories*, London: Routledge

Billson, JM, 1984, 'Saul Alinsky: The contributions of a pioneer clinical sociologist', *Clinical Sociology Review*, 2, 1, 7-11

Blair, T, 1971, 'Golborne: beginning of a revolution?' Article available from ChronicleWorld.org

Blears, H, 2003, *Communities in control: Public services and local socialism*, London: Fabian Ideas 607

Blond, P, 2010, *Red Tory: How Left and Right have broken Britain and how we can fix it*, London: Faber

Blond, P and Morrin, M, 2015, *Restoring Britain's city states: Devolution, public sector reform and local economic growth*, London: Respublica

Boaden, N, Goldsmith, M, Hampton, W and Stringer, P, 1982, *Public participation in local services*, London: Longman

Boddy, M, and Fudge, C (eds), 1984, *Local socialism?*, London: Palgrave Macmillan

Bogdanor, V, 2009, *The new British constitution*, Oxford: Hart Publishing

Bogue, D (ed), 1974 *The basic writings of Ernest W Burgess*, Chicago: University of Chicago Press

Bohman, J, 2010, *Democracy across borders: From demos to demoi*, Cambridge, MA: MIT Press

Boltanski, L and Chiapello, E, 2007, *The new spirit of capitalism*, London: Verso

Boyle, D and Harris, M, 2010, *The challenge of co-production: How equal partnerships between professionals and the public are crucial to improving services*, London: New Economics Foundation

Boyle, D, Coole, A, Sherwood, C and Slay, J, 2010, *Right here, right now: Taking co-production into the mainstream*, London: NESTA

Boyte, H, 2004, *Everyday politics: Reconnecting citizens and public life*, Philadelphia: University of Pennsylvania Press

Brenner, N, 1999, 'Globalisation as reterritorialisation: the rescaling of urban governance in the EU', *Urban Studies*, 36, 3, 431–51

Bretherton, L, 2015, *Resurrecting democracy: Faith, citizenship and the politics of a common life*, Cambridge: Cambridge University Press

Brownill, S, 1990, *Developing London's docklands – another great planning disaster?* London: Paul Chapman

Bryson, JM and Crosby, B, 1992, *Leadership for the common good: Tackling public problems in a shared-power world*, San Francisco CA: Jossey-Bass

Bulley, D and Sokhi-Bulley, B, 2014, 'Big Society as big government: Cameron's governmentality agenda', *The British Journal of Politics and International Relations*, 16, 3, 452–70

Bulpitt, T, 1983, *Territory and power in the United Kingdom*, Manchester: Manchester University Press

Bulpitt, J, 1989, 'Walking back to happiness-conservative party governments and elected local-authorities in the 1980s', *Political Quarterly*, S56-S73

Burden, R, 2013, 'Why it matters: A new social contract', *Fabian Essays* http://www.fabians.org.uk/why-it-matters-a-new-social-contract/

Burgess, EW, 1916, 'The social survey: a field for constructive service by departments of sociology', *American Journal of Sociology*, 21, 4, 492–500

Burgess, EW and Bogue, D J, 1964 (eds) *Urban sociology*, Chicago: University of Chicago Press

Burke, E, 1968 [1790], *Reflections on the Revolution in France: And on the proceedings in certain societies in London relative to that event*, London: Penguin

Calhoun, C, 1998, '*Community without propinquity revisited: communications technology and the transformation of the urban public sphere*', *Sociological Inquiry*, 68, 3, 373–97

Cameron, D, 2009, 'The Big Society', the Hugo Young lecture to the *Guardian*, 10 November, film available from: www.theguardian.com/politics/video/2009/nov/10/david-cameron-hugo-young-lecture

Cameron, D and Clegg, N, 2010, 'Foreword', in *The Coalition: Our programme for Government*, London: Cabinet Office and HM Government

Cameron, D and Rennick, K, 2015, *Community organisers programme: Evaluation summary report*, London: IPSOS Mori, available from https://www.gov.uk/government/uploads/system/uploads/attachment_data/file/415860/Community_Organisers_Programme_Summary_Report.pdf

Castells, M, 1983, *The City and the Grassroots: A Cross-Cultural Theory of Urban Social Movements,* Oakland CA: University of California Press

Castree, N, 2004, 'Differential geographies: place, indigenous rights and "local" resources', *Political Geography,* 22, 9, 133–67

Chaskin, RJ, 2001, 'Building community capacity: a definitional framework and case studies from a comprehensive community initiative', *Urban Affairs Review*, 36, 3, 291–323

Chwalisz, C, 2015, *The populist signal: Why politics and democracy need to change*, London: Rowman and Littlefield

Civic Systems Lab (2015) *Designed to scale: Mass participation to build resilient neighbourhoods*. Available from: http://www.theopenworks.org/ (last accessed 2.11.15)

Clark, G, 1984, 'A theory of local autonomy', *Association of the Annals of American Geography*, 74, 2, 195–208

Clark, G, 2012, *Decentralisation: An assessment of progress*, London: HM Government

Clark, G and Mather, J (eds), 2003, *Total politics: Labour's command state*, London: Conservative Policy Unit

Clarke, N, 2013, 'Locality and localism: a view from British human geography', *Policy Studies*, 34, 5–6, 492–507

Clarke, N, 2015, 'Geographies of politics and anti-politics', *Geoforum*, doi: 10.1016/j.geoforum.2015.04.005

Clarke, N and Cochrane, A, 2013, 'Geographies and politics of localism', *Political Geography*, 34, 10–23

Clifford, D, 2012, 'Voluntary sector organisations working at the neighbourhood level in England: patterns by local area deprivation', *Environment and Planning A*, 44, 1148–64

Coaffee, J and Healey, P, 2003, '"My voice, my place": tracking transformations in urban governance', *Urban Studies*, 40, 10, 1979–99

Coats, D, with Johnson, N and Hackett, P, 2012, *From the poor law to welfare to work: What have we learned from a century of anti-poverty policies?* London: The Smith Institute

Cochrane, A, 1993, *Whatever happened to local government?* Buckingham: Open University Press

Cole, GDH, 1947, *Local and regional government*, London: Cassell

Colenutt, B, 1991, 'London Docklands Development Corporation – has the community benefited?', in M Keith and A Rogers (eds), *Hollow promises: Rhetoric and reality in the inner city*, London: Mansell, 31–41

Columb, C and Tomaney, J, 2015, 'Territorial politics, devolution and spatial planning in the UK: results, prospects, lessons', *Planning Research and Practice*, doi: 10.1080/02697459.2015.1081337

Conyers, D, 1984, 'Decentralization and development: A review of the literature', *Public Administration and Development*, 4, 2, 187-197

Cooke, G and Muir, R (eds), 2012, *The relational state: How recognising the importance of human relationships could revolutionise the role of the state*, London: IPPR

Cooke, P (ed), 1989, *Localities: The changing face of urban Britain*, London: Routledge

Copus, C, 2004, *Party politics and local government*, Manchester: Manchester University Press

Copus, C, 2010, 'The councillor: governor, governing and the complexity of citizen engagement', *British Journal of Politics and International Relations*, 12, 569–89

Copus, C and Sweeting, D, 2012, 'Whatever happened to local democracy?' *Policy and Politics*, 40, 1, 21–38

Coriden, JA, 1996, *The parish in Catholic tradition: History, theology and common law*, New York: Paulist Press

Cornwall, A and Coelho, V S (eds), 2007, *Spaces for Change? The politics of citizen participation in new democratic arenas*, London: Zed.

Cox, E and Jeffery, C, 2014, *The future of England: The local dimension*, Manchester: IPPR North

Cox, E with Thurley, A, Davies, B and Harrison, M, 2013, *Love thy neighbourhood: People and place in social reform*, Manchester: IPPR North

Cox, E, Henderson G and Raikes, L, 2014, *Decentralisation decade: A plan for economic prosperity, public service transformation and democratic renewal in England*, Manchester: IPPR North

Cox, K and Mair, A, 1991, 'From localised social structures to localities as agents', *Environment and Planning A*, 23, 2, 197–213

Crick, B, 1998, *Education for citizenship and the teaching of democracy in schools*, Final report, 22 September 1998. London: Qualifications and Curriculum Authority

Crossey, C, 1974, *Building better communities*, Fabian Tract 429, London: Fabian Society

Crouch, C and Marquand, D (eds), 1989, *The new centralism: Britain out of step with Europe?* Oxford: The Political Quarterly Publishing Company and Basil Blackwell

Cruddas, J and Rutherford, J, 2014, *One nation: Labour's political renewal*, London: One Nation Register

Dahl, R, 1989, *Democracy and its critics*, Newhaven: CT, Yale University Press

Dahl, R and Tufte, ER, 1974, *Size and democracy*, California: Stanford University Press

Davies, H, 1990, 'Mrs Thatcher's third term: power to the people or camouflaged centralisation?', in R J Bennett (ed), *Decentralization, local governments and markets: Towards a post-welfare agenda*, Oxford: Clarendon, 194–206

Davies, J, 2008, 'Double-devolution or double-dealing? The Local Government White Paper and the Lyons Review', *Local Government Studies*, 34, 1, 3–22

Davoudi, S and Madanipour, A, 2013, 'Localism and neo-liberal governmentality', *Town Planning Review*, 84, 5, 551–62

DCLG, 2006, *Strong and prosperous communities: The local government white paper*, Cm 6939-I, London: HMSO

DCLG, 2008, *Communities in control: real people, real power*, Cm 7427, London: HMSO

DCLG, 2011a, *Community budgets prospectus,* London: DCLG

DCLG, 2011b, *The 2009–10 Citizenship Survey: Community spirit in England,* London: DCLG

Deas, I, 2013, 'Towards post-political consensus in urban policy? Localism and the emerging agenda for regeneration under the Conservative government', *Planning, Practice and Research*, 28, 1, 65–82

De Filippis, J, Fisher, R and Shragge, E, 2010, *Contesting community: The limits and potential of community organising*, New Brunswick, NJ: Rutgers University Press

De Sousa Briggs, X, 2008, *Democracy as problem solving: Civic capacity in communities across the globe*, Cambridge, MA: MIT Press

DETR, 1998, *Modern local government: In touch with the people*, London: HMSO

De Vries, MS, 2000, 'The rise and fall of decentralization: a comparative analysis of arguments and practices in European countries', *European Journal of Political Research*, 38, 193–224

Denhardt, RB and Denhardt, JV, 2000, 'The new public service: serving rather than steering', *Public Administration Review*, 60, 6, 549–59

Dennis, N, 1958, 'The popularity of the neighbourhood community idea', *Sociological Review*, 6, 2, 191–206

Dewey, J, 1954 [1927] *The public and its problems*, Athens, OH: Swallow Press and Ohio University Press

Dewey, J, 1987 [1937] 'Democracy is radical', in J Boydston (ed), *John Dewey, The later works volume II, 1935–1937*, Carbondale and Edwardsville: Southern Illinois Press

Dewey, J, 2000 [1935] *Liberalism and social action*, New York: Prometheus Books

Dicey, AV, 1885, *Law of the constitution*, London: Macmillan and Co

Dinham, A, 2005, 'Empowered or over-powered? The real experiences of local participation in the UK's New Deal for Communities', *Community Development Journal*, 40, 3, 301–12

Dorey, P and Garnett, M, 2012, 'No such thing as the Big Society? The Conservative party's unnecessary search for "narrative" in the 2010 general election', *British Politics*, 7, 4, 389–417

DuPuis, EM and Goodman, D, 2005, 'Should we go "home" to eat? Toward a reflexive politics of localism', *Journal of Rural Studies*, 21, 359–71

Durkheim, E, 1933 [1893] *The division of labour in society*, New York: The Free Press

Durose, C, 2013, *Towards transformative co-production of local public services*, Swindon: AHRC

Durose, C and Rees, J, 2012, 'The rise and fall of neighbourhood in the New Labour era', *Policy & Politics*, 41, 1, 39–55

Elden, S, 2007, 'Governmentality, calculation and territory', *Environment and Planning D: Society and Space*, 25, 562–80

Engel, LJ, 2002, 'Saul D Alinsky and the Chicago School', *Journal of Speculative Philosophy*, 16, 1, 50–66

Entrikin, N, 1991, *The betweenness of place: Towards a geography of modernity*, Baltimore: Johns Hopkins University Press

Evans, SM. and Boyte, HC, 1992, [1986] *Free spaces: The sources of democratic change in America*, University of Chicago Press

Eversole, R, 2011, 'Community agency and community engagement: retheorising participation in governance', *Journal of Public Policy*, 31, 1, 51–71

Exeter St James Forum (2013) Exeter St James Neighbourhood Plan, available from: http://www.exeterstjamesforum.org/home (last accessed 2.8.15)

Fagence, M, 1977, *Citizen participation in planning*, Oxford: Pergamon Press

Farnsley, A, 2000, *Rising expectations: Urban congregations, welfare reform, and civic life*, Bloomington: Indiana University Press

Farole, T, Rodriguez-Pose, A and Storper, M, 2011, 'Human geography and the institutions that underlie economic growth', *Progress in Human Geography*, 35, 1, 58–80

Featherstone, D, 2015, 'Revolt on Clydeside? Space, politics and populism', *Geoforum*, 62, 193–5

Featherstone, D, Ince, A, MacKinnon, D, Strauss, K and Cumbers, A, 2012, 'Progressive localism and the construction of political alternatives', *Transactions of the Institute of British Geographers*, 37, 177–82

Fesler, J, 1965, 'Approaches to the understanding of decentralisation', *The Journal of Politics*, 27, 3, 536–66

Fine, J, 2006, *Workers centers: Organizing communities at the edge of the dream*, Ithaca, NY: Cornell University Press

Finlayson, A, 2012, 'Cameron, culture and the creative class: the Big Society and the post-bureaucratic age', *The Political Quarterly*, special issue on the Big Society, 82, 35–47

Finlayson, G, 1994, *Citizen, state and social welfare in Britain 1830–1990*, Oxford: Clarendon Press

Fisher, B and Strauss, A, 1978, 'The Chicago tradition: Thomas, Park and their successors', *Symbolic Interaction*, 1, 2, 5–23

Fisher, R, 1994, *Let the people decide: Neighbourhood organizing in America*, New York: Twayne Publishers

Fishkin, J S, 1991, *Democracy and deliberation: New directions for democratic reform*, New Haven, CT: Yale University Press

Flinders, M, 2012, *Defending democracy: Why democracy matters in the twenty-first century*, Oxford: Oxford University Press

Foot, M, 1973, *Aneurin Bevan a biography, Volume 2: 1945–1960*, London: Davis-Poynter

Foucault, M, 1991 [1978], 'Governmentality', in G Burchell, C Gordon and P Miller (eds), *The Foucault effect: Studies in governmentality*, Chicago: University of Chicago Press, 87–104

Freeman, TW, 1968, *Geography and regional administration, England and Wales: 1830–1968*, London: Hutchinson University Library

Frug, GE, 1999, *City making: Building communities without building walls*, Princeton NJ: Princeton University Press

Frug, GE, 2000, 'Against centralization', *Buffalo Law Review*, 48, 31–38

Frug, GE, 2014, 'The central–local relationship', *Stanford Law and Policy Review*, 25, 1, 1–8

Fukuyama, F, 2014, *Political order and political decay: From the Industrial Revolution to the globalization of democracy*, London: Profile Books

Fung, A and Wright, E O, (eds) 2003, *Deepening democracy: Institutional innovations in empowered participatory governance*, London: Verso

Gallent, N and Robinson, S, 2013, *Neighbourhood planning: Communities, networks and governance*, Bristol: Policy Press

Game, C and Leach, S, 1996, 'Political parties and local democracy', in L Pratchett and D Wilson (eds) *Local democracy and local government*, Basingstoke: Macmillan, 127–49

Gauntlett, D, 2011, *Making is connecting: The social meaning of creativity from DIY and knitting to YouTube and Web 2.0*, Cambridge: Polity Press

Gecan, M, 2004, *Going public: An organizers guide to citizen action*, New York: Anchor Books

Geddes, M, 1915, *Cities in evolution: An introduction to the town planning movement and to the study of civics*, London: Williams

Gibson-Graham, JK, 2006, *A post-capitalist politics*, Minneapolis: University of Minnesota Press

Giddens, A., 1994, *Beyond left and right: The future of radical politics*, Stanford: Stanford University Press

Giddens, A., 2001, *The global third way debate*, Cambridge: Polity Press

Glaeser, E, 2012, *The triumph of the city*, London: Macmillan

Glasman, M, 2010, 'Labour as a radical tradition', *Soundings*, 38, 31–41

Glasman, M and Norman, J, 2012, 'The Big Society in question', *The Political Quarterly*, special issue on the Big Society, 82, 9–21

Goldsmith, MJ and Page, EC, 1987, 'Britain', in EC Page and MJ Goldsmith (eds), *Central and local government relations: A comparative analysis of West European unitary states*, London: Sage, 68–87

Goodin, R, 2003, *Reflective democracy*, Oxford: Oxford University Press

GLA (Greater London Authority), 2013, *Raising the capital: Report of the London finance commission*, available from www.london.gov.uk/sites/default/files/Raising%20the%20capital.pdf

GLA, 2014, *London Borough Council Elections 22 May 2014*, London: Greater London Authority

Greater Manchester Combined Authority, no date, 'Greater Manchester City Deal', available from: https://www.gov.uk/government/uploads/system/uploads/attachment_data/file/221014/Greater-Manchester-City-Deal-final_0.pdf, last accessed 6.3.2015

Green, DG, 1996, 'Community without politics – a British view', in M Novak (ed), *To empower people: From state to civil society by P L Berger and R J Neuhaus* [second edition], Washington DC: AEI Press

Green, T H, 1885, *Works of Thomas Hill Green, Volume 1, philosophical works*, London: Longmans, Green and Co

Griffith, J A G, 1966, *Central departments and local authorities*, London: Allen and Unwin

Guarneros-Meza, V and Geddes, M, 2010, 'Local governance and participation under neoliberalism: comparative perspectives', *International Journal of Urban and Regional Research* 34, 1, 115–29

Gyford, J, 1976, *Local politics in Britain* [second edition], Beckenham: Croom Helm

Gyford, J, 1985, *The politics of local socialism*, London: Allen and Unwin

Hain, P, 1980, *Neighbourhood participation*, London: Temple Smith

Hall, P, 1999, 'Social capital in Britain', *British Journal of Political Science*, 29, 417–61

Hambleton, R and Hoggett, P, 1987, 'The democratisation of public services', in P Hoggett and R Hambleton (eds), *Decentralisation and democracy: localising public services*, Bristol: SAUS, 53–83

Hansard, 1894, speech available from: http://hansard.millbanksystems.com/people/mr-henry-fowler/1894 (last accessed 23.3.16)

Harney, L, McCurry, J, Scott, J and Wills, J, 2016, 'Developing "process pragmatism" to underpin engaged research in human geography', *Progress in Human Geography*, 40, 3, 316–33

Harris, J, 2015, 'How flat-pack democracy beat the old parties in the People's Republic of Frome', *Guardian*, 22 May, available at www.theguardian.com/politics/2015/may/22/flatpack-democracy-peoples-republic-of-frome (last accessed 21.12.2015)

Hatcher, R, 2011, 'The Conservative–Liberal Democrat Coalition government's "free schools" in England', *Educational Review*, 63, 4, 485–503

Hayek, JA, 2001 [1944] *The road to serfdom*, London: Routledge

Hays, RA, 2015, 'Neighborhood networks, social capital, and political participation: the relationships revisited', *Journal of Urban Affairs*, 37, 2, 122–43

Healey, P, 2006 [1997], *Collaborative planning: Shaping places in fragmented societies* [second edition], Basingstoke: Palgrave Macmillan

Healey, P, 2012, 'Re-enchanting democracy as a mode of governance', *Critical Policy Studies*, 6, 1, 19–39

Held, D, 2006, *Models of democracy* [third edition], Cambridge: Polity Press

Heller, P, 2001, 'Moving the state: the politics of democratic decentralization in Kerala, South Africa, and Porto Alegre', *Politics and Society*, 29, 1, 131-163

Herbert, S, 2005, 'The trapdoor of community', *Annals of the Association of American Geographers*, 95, 4, 850-865

Heseltine, M, 2012, *No stone unturned: One man's vision*, HM Government, available from https://www.gov.uk/government/uploads/system/uploads/attachment_data/file/34648/12–1213-no-stone-unturned-in-pursuit-of-growth.pdf (last accessed 13.7.2015)

Hickson, K, 2013, 'The localist turn in British politics and its critics', *Policy Studies*, 34, 4, 408–21

Highgate Neighbourhood Forum (2015) Draft neighbourhood plan, available from: http://www.highgateneighbourhoodforum.org.uk/ (last accessed 2.8.15)

Hilder, P, 2006, *Power up, people: Double devolution and beyond*, London: The Young Foundation

HM Government, 2010, *Decentralisation and the Localism Bill: An essential guide*, London: HM Government

HM Government, 2013, *Government Response to the House of Commons Political and Constitutional Reform Committee Report: The prospects for codifying the relationship between central and local government*, Cm 8623, London: The Stationery Office

Hobhouse, L, 1964 [1911] *Liberalism*, Oxford: Oxford University Press

Hodge, M, 1987, 'Central/local conflicts: the view from Islington', in P Hoggett and R Hambleton (eds), *Decentralisation and democracy: Localising public services,* Bristol: SAUS, 29–36

Hodgson, L, 2004, 'Manufactured civil society: counting the costs', *Critical Social Policy,* 24, 2, 139–64

Hoffmann, S, 1959, 'The areal division of powers in the writings of French political theorists', in A Maas (ed), *Area and power: A theory of local government,* Glencoe, IL: The Free Press, 113–49

Hoggett, P and Hambleton, R (eds), 1987, *Decentralisation and democracy: Localising public services,* Bristol: SAUS

Holgate, J, 2015, 'Community organising in the UK: a "new" approach for trade unions?' *Economic and Industrial Democracy,*36, 3, 316–33

Horwitt, SD, 1992, *Let them call me rebel: Saul Alinsky, his life and legacy,* New York: Vintage

Houghton, JP and Blume, T, 2011, 'Poverty, power and policy dilemmas: lessons from the community empowerment programme in England', *Journal of Urban Regeneration and Renewal,* 4, 3, 207–17

House of Commons Select Committee on Communities and Local Government, 2009, *The balance of power: Central and local government, 6th report for the session 2008–2009,* HC33-1, London: The Stationery Office

House of Commons Select Committee on Communities and Local Government, 2011, *Localism, third report of session 2010–2012, Volume 1 Report,* HC547, London: The Stationery Office

House of Commons Select Committee on Communities and Local Government, 2014, *Devolution in England: The case for local government, first report of session 2014–2015,* London: The Stationery Office

House of Commons Select Committee on Political and Constitutional Reform, 2013a, *Prospects for codifying the relationship between central and local government, Volume 1 Report,* HC 656-1, London: The Stationery Office

House of Commons Select Committee on Political and Constitutional Reform, 2013b, *Prospects for codifying the relationship between central and local government, Volume IV written evidence from session 2010–2013,* London: The Stationery Office

Hunt, T, 2004, *Building Jerusalem: The rise and fall of the Victorian city,* London: Weidenfeld and Nicolson

Huntingdon, SP, 1959, 'The founding fathers and the division of powers', in A Maas (ed), *Area and power: A theory of local government,* Glencoe, IL: The Free Press, 150–205

Hurd, D, 1989, 'Citizenship in the Tory democracy', *New Statesman,* 29 April

Imrie, R and Raco, M (eds) 2003, *Urban renaissance? New Labour, community and urban policy*, Bristol: Policy Press

Jackman, R, 1985, 'Local government finance', in M Loughlin, M D Gelfand and K Young (eds) *Half century of municipal decline 1935–1985*, London: George Allen and Unwin, 144–68

Jackson, P, 1984, 'Social disorganization and moral order in the city', *Transactions of the Institute of British Geographers*, 9, 168–80

James, W, 2000 [1907], *Pragmatism and other writings*, London: Penguin.

Jamoul, L and Wills, J, 2008, 'Faith in politics', *Urban Studies*, 2008, 45, 10, 2035–56

Jenkins, S, 2004, *Big Bang localism: A rescue plan for British democracy*, London: Policy Exchange and Localis

Jennings, J, 2012, 'Tocqueville and the Big Society', *The Political Quarterly*, special issue on the Big Society, 82, S1, 68-81

Jochum, V, no date, *Active citizenship: A policy agenda or a reality?* London: NCVO, available from: www.observatoritercersector.org/pdf/centre_recursos/1_4_joc_01550.pdf (last accessed 13.7.2015)

John, P, Fieldhouse, E and Liu, H, 2011, 'How civic is the civic sphere? Explaining community participation using the 2005 English citizenship survey', *Political Studies*, 59, 230–52

John, P with Richardson, L, 2012, *Nudging people towards localism?* London: British Academy Policy Centre

Johnston, R and Pattie, C 2006, *Putting voters in their place: Geography and elections in Great Britain*, Oxford: Oxford University Press

Jones, A, 2007, 'New wine in old bottles? England's parish and town councils and New Labour's neighbourhood experiment', *Local Economy*, 22, 3, 227–42

Jones, M, 2009, 'Phase space: geography, relational thinking, and beyond', *Progress in Human Geography*, 33, 4, 487–506

Jones, M and Wood, M, 2013, 'New localities', *Regional Studies*, 47, 1, 29–42

Jun, K-N and Musso, J, 2013, 'Participatory governance and the spatial representation of neighbourhood issues', *Urban Affairs Review*, 49, 1, 71–110

Jupp, E, 2012, 'Rethinking local activism: "Cultivating the capacities" of neighbourhood organising', *Urban Studies*, 49, 14, 3027–44

Katz, R S and Mair, P, 1995, 'Changing models of party organization and party democracy: the emergence of the cartel party', *Party Politics*, 2, 4, 525–34

Kelly, P, 2012, 'Red or orange: the Big Society in the new Conservatism', *The Political Quarterly*, special issue on the Big Society, available online, 22–34

Kenny, M, 2014, *The politics of English nationhood*, Oxford: Oxford University Press

Kothari, U and Cooke, B (eds), 2001, *Participation: The new tyranny?* London: Zed Books

Layfield, FHB, 1976, *Local government finance: report of the committee of inquiry*, London: HMSO

Leach, S, Lowndes, V and Roberts, M, 2012, Evidence (EvW133) presented to the House of Commons Political and Constitutional Committee's enquiry into Codifying the relationship between central and local government, *Volume IV, Written evidence from session 2010–12*, London: The Stationery Office

Leeder, A and Mabbett, D, 2011, 'Free schools: Big Society or small interests?' *The Political Quarterly*, 82, s1, 133–44.

Leese, R, 2014, 'City deals and city regions', in The Smith Institute (ed) *Labour and localism: Perspectives on a new English deal*, London: The Smith Institute, 39–45

Leighninger, M, 2006, *The next form of democracy: How expert rule is giving way to shared governance ... and why politics will never be the same*, Nashville, TN: Vanderbilt University Press

Lind, M, 2014, 'The liberal roots of populism', *Demos Quarterly*, 4, available online: quarterly.demos.co.uk/article/issue-4/liberal-roots-of-populism (last accessed 20.3.16)

Lippmann, W, 1925, *The phantom public*, Piscataway, NJ: Transaction Publishers

Local Government Taskforce, 2014, *People-powered public services* (commissioned for the Labour Party Policy Review), available at http://lgalabour.local.gov.uk/documents/330956/6335671/INNOVATION+TASKFORCE+FINAL+REPORT.pdf (last accessed 13.7.2015)

Lodge, G and Muir, R, 2011, 'Localism under New Labour', *The Political Quarterly*, 82, Supplement, S96–S107

London Borough of Lambeth, 2011, *The co-operative council: Sharing power – a new settlement between citizens and state*, London: The Cooperative Council Citizens' Commission

London Borough of Lambeth, no date, *Lambeth's co-operative commissioning cycle*, paper available at https://cooperativecounciltoolkit.files.wordpress.com/2013/06/commissioning-cycle.pdf

London Tenants Federation et al, 2014, *Staying put: An anti-gentrification handbook for council estates in London*, available at http://southwarknotes wordpress com/2014/06/13/staying-put-an-anti-gentrification-handbook-for-council-estates-in-london/

Loney, M, 1983, *Community against government: The British Community Development Project, 1968–1978 – a study of government incompetence*, London: Heinemann

Loughlin, M, 1996, 'Understanding central-local Government relations', *Public Policy and Administration*, 11, 2, 48–65

Loughlin, M, 2013, *The British constitution: A very short introduction*, Oxford: Oxford University Press

Loughlin, M, Gelfand, MD and Young, K (eds), 1985, *Half century of municipal decline, 1935–1985*, London: George Allen and Unwin

Lowndes, V and Pratchett, L, 2012, 'Local governance under the Coalition government: austerity, localism and the Big Society', *Local Government Studies*, 38, 1, 21–40

Lowndes, V and Sullivan, H, 2008, 'How low can you go? Rationales and challenges for neighbourhood governance', *Public Administration*, 86, 1, 53–74

Lowndes, V, Pratchett, L and Stoker, G, 2001, 'Trends in public participation: Part 1 – local government perspectives', *Public Administration,* 79, 1, 205–22

Lowndes, V, Pratchett, L and Stoker, G, 2006, 'Local political participation: the impact of rules-in-use', *Public Administration*, 84, 3, 539–61

Lyons Inquiry into Local Government, 2007, *Place-shaping: A shared ambition for the future of local government*, London: The Stationery Office

Maas, P, 1959, 'Division of powers: an areal analysis', in A Maas (ed) *A theory of local government*, Glencoe, IL: The Free Press, 9–26

MacFadyen, P, 2014, *Flatpack democracy: A DIY guide to creating independent politics*, Bath: Eco-logic Books

MacIntyre, A, 1981, *After virtue: A study in moral theory*, Notre Dame, IN: University of Notre Dame Press

McKenna, D, 2011, 'UK local government and public participation: using conjectures to explain the relationship', *Public Administration*, 89, 3, 1182–200

McQuarrie, M, 2013, 'Community Organizations in the Foreclosure Crisis: The Failure of Neoliberal Civil Society', *Politics & Society*, 41, 1, 73–101

Macpherson, CB, 1977, *The life and times of liberal democracy*, Oxford: Oxford University Press

Magnusson, W, 2005a, 'Protecting the right of local self-government', *Canadian Journal of Political Science*, 38, 4, 897–922

Magnusson, W, 2005b, 'Urbanism, cities and local self-government', *Canadian Public Administration*, 48, 1, 96–123

Magnusson, W, 2012, *Politics of urbanism: Seeing like a city*, London: Routledge

Mair, P, 2013, *Ruling the void: The hollowing of western democracy*, London: Verso

Mallaby 1967, *Report of the committee on the staffing of local government*, London: HMSO

Malpas, JE, 1999, *Place and experience: A philosophical topography*, Cambridge: Cambridge University Press

Mansbridge, J, 1983 [1980], *Beyond adversary democracy*, Chicago: University of Chicago Press

Mansbridge, J, 1995, 'Does participation make better citizens?' *The Good Society*, 5, 2, 1 and 4–7

Manzo, L and Perkins, D D, 2006, 'Finding common ground: the importance of place attachment to community participation and planning', *Journal of Planning Literature*, 20, 4, 335–50

Marquand, D, 2004, *Decline of the public*, Cambridge: Polity Press

Martin, RL, 2010, 'Rethinking regional path dependence: beyond lock-in to evolution', *Economic Geography*, 86, 1, 1–27

Massey, D, 2005, *For space*, London: Sage

Matthews, FH, 1977, *Quest for an American sociology: Robert E Park and the Chicago School*, Montreal: McGill–Queen's University Press

Michelleti, M, 2010, *Political virtue and shopping: Individuals, consumerism and collective action*, Basingstoke: Palgrave Macmillan

Mill, J S, 1890 [1861], *Considerations on representative government*, London: Longmans, Green

Miller, Z, 1981, 'The role and concept of neighborhood in American cities', in R Fisher and P Romanofsky (eds), *Communty organization for urban social change*, Westport CT: Greenwood Press, 3-32

Mohan, G and Stokke, K, 2000, 'Participatory development and empowerment: the dangers of localism', *Third World Quarterly*, 21, 2, 247–68

Mohan, J, 2011, *Mapping the Big Society*, Third Sector Research Centre, Working Paper 62, University of Birmingham, available at www. Birmingham.ac. uk/generic/tsrc/documents/tsrc/working-papers/ working-paper-62.pdf

Mohan, J, 2012, 'Commentary: geographical foundations of the Big Society', *Environment and Planning A*, 44, 1121–29

Morgan, K J, 2007, 'The polycentric state: new spaces of empowerment and engagement?', *Regional Studies*, 41, 9, 1237–51

MORI, 2004, *Rules of engagement? Participation, involvement and voting in Britain*, https://www.ipsos-mori.com/Assets/Docs/Polls/Rules%20 of%20Engagement%20Final%20Version.pdf

Morris, D and Hess, K, 1975, *Neighborhood power: The new localism*, Boston: Beacon Press

Mount, F, 2012, *The new few or a very British oligarchy: Power and inequality in Britain now*, London: Simon and Schuster

Mulgan, G, 2012, 'Government *with* the people: the outlines of a relational state', in G Cooke and R Muir (eds), *The relational state: How recognising the importance of human relationships could revolutionise the role of the state*, London: IPPR, 20–34

Mumford, L, 1954, 'The neighborhood and the neighborhood unit', *Town Planning Review*, 24, 4, 256-270

Murat, T and Morad, M, 2008, 'Democratic deficit, decentralisation and the quest for sustainable communities: a case study of Peckham community council', *Local Economy*, 23, 3, 136–51

NALC (National Association of Local Councils) 2015, *Devo-local: A white paper for empowering and strengthening local democracy*, London: NALC

NatCen Social Research 2013, *Evaluation of National Citizen Service*, available at http://natcen ac uk/our-research/research/evaluation-of-national-citizen-service-pilots/ (last accessed 18.11.2014)

Newman, I, 2014, *Reclaiming local democracy: A progressive future for local government*, Bristol: Policy Press

Newman, J, 2012, 'Making, contesting and governing the local: women's labour and the local state', *Local Economy*, 27, 8, 846–88

Newman, K and Lake, RW, 2006, 'Democracy, bureaucracy and difference in US community development politics since 1968', *Progress in Human Geography*, 31, 1, 44–61

NESTA and NEF, 2010, *Public services inside out: Putting co-production into practice,* London

Nisbet, R A, 1962 [1953] *Community and power* (first published as *The Quest for Community*), New York: Galaxy

Norman, J, 2010, *The Big Society: The anatomy of the new politics*, Buckingham: The University of Buckingham Press

Norris, P, 2002, *Democratic phoenix: Reinventing political activism*, Cambridge University Press

Oakeshott, M, 1962 [1947], *Rationalism in politics and other essays*, London: Methuen and Co Ltd

O'Brien, P and Pike, A, 2015, 'City deals, decentralisation and the governance of local infrastructure funding and financing in the UK', *NIESR* s233, R14-R26

Oldfield, A, 1990, 'Citizenship: an unnatural practice?' *The Political Quarterly*, 61, 2, 177–87

Owen, S, Moseley, M and Courtney, P, 2007, 'Bridging the gap: an attempt to reconcile strategic planning and very local community-based planning in rural England', *Local Government Studies*, 33, 49–76

Pacione, M, 1988, 'Public participation in neighbourhood change', *Applied Geography*, 8, 229–47

Page, EC and Goldsmith, MJ (eds), 1987, *Central and local government relations: A comparative analysis of West European unitary states*, London: Sage

Painter, J, Orton, A, MacLeod, G, Dominelli, L and Pande, R, 2011, *Connecting localism and community empowerment: Research review and critical synthesis for the AHRC Connected Communities Programme*, Durham: Durham University

Park, R, Burgess, EW and MacKenzie, RD, 1925, *The city*, Chicago: Unversity of Chicago Press

Parker, G, with Lynn, T, Wargent, M and Locality, 2014, *User experience of neighbourhood planning in England*, London: Locality

Parker, G, Lynn, T and Wargent, M, 2015, 'Sticking to the script? The coproduction of neighbourhood planning in England', *Town Planning Review*, 86, 5, 519–36

Parker, S, 2015, *Taking power back: Putting people in charge of politics*, Bristol:Policy Press

Parry, G, Moyser, G and Day, N, 1992, *Political participation and democracy in Britain*, Cambridge: Cambridge University Press

Pateman, C, 1970, *Participation and democratic theory*, Cambridge: Cambridge University Press

Pattie, C, Seyd, P, and Whiteley, P, 2004, *Citizenship in Britain: Values, participation and democracy*, Cambridge: Cambridge University Press

Peck, J and Tickell, A, 1994, 'Jungle law breaks out: neoliberalism and global–local disorder', *Area*, 26, 4, 317–26

Peck, J and Tickell, A, 2012, 'Apparitions of neoliberalism: revisiting "Jungle law breaks out"', *Area*, 44, 2, 245–49

Pelling, H, 1967, *Social geography of British elections 1885–1910*, London: Macmillan and Co Ltd

Pettit, P, 2012, *On the people's terms: A republican theory and model of democracy*, Cambridge: Cambridge University Press

Pike, A, 2006, *London – any place for parish councils?* Report for the Association of London Government, April

Pile, S, 1995, '"What we are asking for is decent human life": SPLASH, neighbourhood demands and citizenship in London's docklands', *Political Geography*, 14, 2, 199–208

Poole, KP and Keith-Lucas, B, 1994, *Parish government: 1894–1994*, London: National Association of Local Councils (NALC)

PNCB (Poplar Neighbourhood Community Budget), 2011, *The bid to be a pilot project*, London: Poplar HARCA

PNCB, 2013, *The Poplar Neighbourhood Community Budget*, London: Poplar HARCA

Pratchett, L and Wilson, D, 1996, 'What future for local democracy?', in L Pratchett and D Wilson (eds), *Local democracy and local government*, Basingstoke: Macmillan, 229–49

Prest, J, 1990, *Liberty and locality: Parliament, permissive legislation and rate payers' democracies in the mid-nineteenth century*, Oxford: Clarendon

Purcell, M, 2006, 'Urban democracy and the local trap', *Urban Studies*, 43, 11, 1921–41

Purcell, M, 2013, *The deep-down delight of democracy*, Oxford: Wiley-Blackwell

Putnam, R, 1993, *Making democracy work: Civic traditions in modern Italy*, Princeton, NJ: Princeton University Press

Putnam, R, 2000, *Bowling alone: The collapse and revival of American democracy*, New York: Simon and Shuster

Putnam, R, Feldstein, L and Cohen, D, 2003, *Better together: Restoring the American community*, New York: Simon and Schuster

Quintelier, E and van Deth, J W, 2014, 'Supporting democracy: political participation and political attitudes, exploring causality using panel data', *Political Studies*, 62, S1, 153–71

Raco, M, 2003, 'Governmentality, subject-building, and the discourses and practices of devolution in the UK', *Transactions of the Institute of British Geography*, 28, 1, 75–95

Raco, M and Flint, C, 2001, 'Communities, places and institutional relations: assessing the role of area-based community representation in local governance', *Political Geography*, 20, 585–612

Rao, N, 2000, *Reviving local democracy: New Labour, new politics?* Bristol: Policy Press

Reed, S and Ussher, K (eds), 2013, *Towards co-operative councils: Empowering people to change their lives*, The Cooperative Council's Network, available at www.empower.coop/Publications/Co-opcouncils.pdf

Reitzes, DC and Reitzes, DC, 1992, 'Saul D Alinsky: an applied urban symbolic interactionist', *Symbolic Interaction*, 15, 1, 1–24

Rhodes, RAW, 1988, *Beyond Westminster and Whitehall: The sub-central governments of Britain*, London: Unwin Hyman Ltd

Ridley, N, 1988, *The local right: Enabling not providing*, London: Centre for Policy Studies

Robson W, 1954 [1931], *The development of Local Government*, London, George Allen & Unwin

Rorty, R, 1979, *Philosophy and the mirror of nature*, Princeton, NJ: Princeton University Press.

Rose, G, 1971, *Local councils in metropolitan areas*, London: Fabian Research Series 296

Rose, M, 1986 [1972], *The relief of poverty 1834–1914* [second edition], Basingstoke: Macmillan

Rose, M, 2014, 'Negative governance: vulnerability, biopolitics and the origin of government', *Transactions of the Institute of British Geography*, 39, 2, 209–23

Rose, N, 1999, *Governing the soul: The shaping of the private self* [second edition], London: Free Association Books

Rowbothom, S, Segal, L and Wainwright, H, 2012 [1979] *Beyond the fragments: Feminism and the making of socialism*, London: The Merlin Press Ltd

Rowson, J, Broome, S, and Jones, A, 2010, *Connected Communities: How social networks power and sustain the Big Society*, London: RSA

Rowson, J, Mezey, M K and Dellot, B, 2012, *Beyond the Big Society: Psychological foundations of active citizenship*, London: Royal Society of Arts

Royal Commission on Local Government in England (Redcliffe-Maud) 1966–1969, 1969, *Volume 1 report*, London: The Stationery Office

RSA (Royal Society of Arts) City Growth Commission, 2014, *Unleashing metro growth: Final recommendations of the City Growth Commission*, available at www.citygrowthcommission.com/publication/final-report-unleashing-metro-growth/ (last accessed 13.7.2015)

Rustin, S, 2010, 'The rise of the parish council', *Guardian*, 1 December, www.theguardian.com/society/2010/dec01/parish-councils-gain-more-powers (last accessed 20.9.2013)

Rutherfoord, R, 2011, *The 2009–10 Citizenship Survey: Community action in England*, London: DCLG

Rutherfoord, R, Spurling, L, Abusby, A and Watts, B, 2013, *NCB pilot programme: Research, learning, evaluation*, London: DCLG

Saegert, S, 2006, 'Building civic capacity in urban neighbourhoods: an empirically grounded anatomy', *Journal of Urban Affairs*, 28, 3, 275–94

Sampson, RJ, 2012, *Great American city: Chicago and the enduring neighbourhood effect*, Chicago: Chicago University Press

Sandel, M, 1998, *Democracy's discontent: America in search of a public philosophy*, Cambridge, MA: Harvard University Press

Sandercock, L, 1998, *Making the invisible visible: A multicultural planning history*, Berkeley: University of California Press

Sandercock, L and Lyssiotis, P, (eds), 2003, *Cosmopolis II: Mongrel cities of the 21st century*, London: A&C Black

Savage, M, 1987, 'Understanding political alignments in contemporary Britain: do localities matter?' *Political Geography Quarterly*, 6, 1, 53–76

Savage, M, 2009, *The dynamics of working class politics: The labour movement in Preston 1880–1940*, Cambridge: Cambridge University Press

Savage, M, 2010, *Identities and social change in Britain since 1940: The politics of method*, Oxford: Oxford University Press

Schattschneider, EE, 1975 [1960], *The semi-sovereign people: A realist's view of democracy in America*, Boston MA: Wadsworth Cengage Learning

Schlossman, S and Sedlak, M, 1983, *The Chicago area project revisited*, A Rand note for the National Institute of Education, available at www.rand.org/content/dam/rand/pubs/notes/2005/N1944.pdf (last accessed 22.6.2015)

Schumpeter, J, 1976 [1942], *Capitalism, socialism and democracy*, London: George Allen and Unwin

Schutz, A and Miller, M (eds), 2015, *People power: The community organising tradition of Saul Alinsky*, Nashville, TN: Vanderbilt University Press

Scott, J, 1998, *Seeing like a state: How certain schemes to improve the human condition have failed*, New Haven, CT: Yale University Press

Scruton, R, 2006 [2000], *England: An elegy*, London: Bloomsbury

Seabrook, J, 1984, *The idea of neighbourhood: What local politics should be about*, London: Pluto Press

Seddon, J, 2014, *The Whitehall effect: How Whitehall became the enemy of great public services and what we can do about it*, Axminster: Triarchy Press

Shafique, A, 2013, *Enterprise solutions: New approaches to commissioning and public service mutuals: Lessons from co-operative councils*, London: RSA

Sharpe, LJ, 1970, 'Theories and values of local government', *Political Studies*, XVIII, 2, 153–74

Sharpe, LJ (ed), 1976, *Decentralist trends in Western democracies*, London: Sage

Shaw, CR, 1930, *The Jack-Roller*, Chicago: University of Chicago Press.

Shaw, CR and McKay, HR, 1931, *Juvenile delinquency and urban areas*, Chicago: University of Chicago Press.

Shaw, CR, McKay, HD and McDonald, JF, 1938, *Brothers in crime*, Chicago: University of Chicago Press.

Silver, H, Scott, A and Kazepov, Y, 2010, 'Participation in urban contention and deliberation', *International Journal of Urban and Regional Research*, 34, 3, 453-477

Sirianni, C and Friedland, L, 2001, *Civic innovation in America: Community, empowerment, public policy, and the movement for civic renewal*, Berkeley: University of California Press

Skeffington, A, 1969, *People and planning*, London: HMSO

Slay, J and Penny, J, 2014, *Commissioning for outcomes and co-production: A practical guide for local authorities*, London: The New Economics Foundation

Smellie, KB, 1946, *A history of local government*, London: George Allen and Unwin

Smith, G, 2009, *Democratic innovations: Designing institutions for citizen participation*, Cambridge: Cambridge University Press

Smith Institute, The (ed), 2014, *Labour and localism: Perspectives on a new English deal*, London: The Smith Institute

Stears, M, 2012, 'The case for a state that supports relationships, not a relational state', in G Cooke and R Muir (eds), *The relational state: How recognising the importance of human relationships could revolutionise the role of the state*, London: IPPR, 35–44

Stewart, JD, 1985, 'The functioning and management of Local Authorities', in M Loughlin, MD Gelfand and K Young (eds), *Half century of municipal decline 1935–1985*, London: George Allen and Unwin, 98–120

Stewart, JD, 2000, *The nature of British local government*, London: Macmillan

Stoker, G, 2004, 'New localism, progressive politics and democracy', *The Political Quarterly*, 75, 2, 117–29

Stoker, G, 2011, 'Was local governance such a good idea? A global comparative perspective', *Public Administration*, 89, 1, 15–31

Stone, CN, 2001, 'Civic capacity and urban education', *Urban Affairs Review*, 36, 595–619

Stone, CN, Henig, JR, Jones, BD and Pierannunzi, C, 2001, *Building civic capacity: The politics of reforming urban schools*, Kansas: University of Kansas Press

Study Group on Local Authorities, 1972, *The new local authorities: Management and structure* (Bains report), London: HMSO

Sturaker, J and Shaw, D, 2015, 'Localism in practice: lessons from pioneer neighbourhood planning in England', *Town Planning Review*, 86, 5, 587–609

Sustein, C, 2001, *Republic. com*, Princeton: Princeton University Press

Swyngedouw, E, 2004, 'Globalisation or "glocalisation"? Networks, territories and rescaling', *Cambridge Review of International Affairs*, 17, 1, 25–48

The Conservative Party, 2015, *Strong leadership, a clear economic plan, a brighter, more secure future*, London: The Conservative Party

The Labour Party, 2015, *Britain only succeeds when working people succeed. This is a plan to reward hard work, share prosperity and build a better future*, London: The Labour Party

The Liberal Democrats, 2015, *Stronger economy, fairer society: Opportunity for everyone*, London: The Liberal Democrats

Thompson, EP, 2009, *Customs in common*, London: The Merlin Press.

Tilly, C, 1999, 'Survey article – top down and bottom up', *The Journal of Political Philosophy*, 7, 3, 330–52

Tomaney, J, 2006, 'The idea of English regionalism', in R Hazell (ed), *The English question*, Manchester: Manchester University Press, 158–73

Tomaney, J, 2013, 'Parochialism: a defence', *Progress in Human Geography*, 37, 5, 658–72

Tomaney, J, 2014, 'Region and place I: institutions', *Progress in Human Geography*, 38, 1, 131–40

Tönnies, F, 1936 [1887], *Community and society*, Newton Abbot: David and Charles

Travers, T, 1989, 'The Threat to the Autonomy of British Local Government' in C. Crouch and D. Marquand (eds), *The New Centralism: Britain out of step with Europe?*, Oxford: The Political Quarterly Publishing Company and Basil Blackwell, 3-20

Travers, T and Esposito, L, 2003, *The decline and fall of local democracy: A history of local government finance*, London: Policy Exchange

Twelvetrees, A, 2008, *Community work* [fourth edition], Basingstoke: Palgrave Macmillan

von Hoffman, N, 2011, *Radical: A portrait of Saul Alinsky*, New York: Nation Books

Walker, D, 2002, *In praise of centralism: A critique of the new localism*, A Catalyst Working Paper

Walls, D, 2014, *Community organizing*, Cambridge: Polity Press

Ware, A, 2012, 'The Big Society and Conservative politics: back to the future or forward to the past?' *The Political Quarterly special issue on the Big Society*, 82, 82–97

Warren, MR, 2001, *Dry bones rattling: Community building to revitalize American democracy*, Princeton, NJ: Princeton University Press

Warren, MR, 2009, 'Community organizing in Britain: the political organization of faith-based social capital', *City and Community*, 8, 2, 99–127

Warren, MR and Mapp, L, 2011, *A match on dry grass: Community organizing as a catalyst for school reform*, Oxford: Oxford University Press

Webb, S and Webb, BP, 1920, *A constitution for the socialist commonwealth of Great Britain*, London: Longmans, Green and Co

Webb, S and Webb, BP, 1924 [1907] *English local government from the revolution to the Municipal Corporations Act: The parish and the county*, London: Longmans and Co

Webb, S and Webb, BP, 1963 [1922] *The development of English local government 1689–1835*, Oxford: Oxford University Press

Wellman, B, 1979, 'The community question: the intimate networks of East Yorkers', *American Journal of Sociology*, 84, 1201–31.

Wellman, B, Wong, RY, Tindall, D and Nazar, N, 1997, 'A decade of network change: turnover, persistence and stability in personal communities', *Social Networks*, 19, 27–50.

White, J, 2005, 'From Herbert Morrison to command and control: the decline of local democracy and its effect on public services', *History Workshop Journal*, 59, 73–82

White, S and Leighton, D (eds), 2008, *Building a citizen society: The emerging politics of republican democracy*, London: Lawrence and Wishart

Whitehead, M, 2003, 'Love thy neighbourhood: rethinking the politics of scale and Walsall's struggle for neighbourhood democracy', *Environment and Planning A*, 35, 277–300

Whiteley, P, 2012, *Political participation in Britain: The decline and revival of civic culture*, Basingstoke: Palgrave Macmillan

Wilks-Heeg, S, 2009, 'New Labour and the reform of English local government 1997–2007', *Planning Practice and Research*, 24, 1, 23–40

Williams, C, 2003, 'Developing community involvement: contrasting local and regional participatory cultures in Britain and their implications for policy', *Regional Studies*, 37, 5, 531–41

Wills, J, 2008, 'Making class politics possible: organising contract cleaners in London', *International Journal of Urban and Regional Research*, 32, 2, 305–24

Wills, J, 2009a, 'The living wage', *Soundings*, 42, 33–46

Wills, J, 2009b, 'Subcontracted employment and its challenge to labour', *Labor Studies Journal*, special issue on community unionism, 34, 4, 441–60

Wills, J, 2010, 'Identity making for action: the example of London Citizens', in M Wetherell (ed), *Theorizing identities and social action*, Basingstoke: Palgrave Macmillan, 157–76.

Wills, J, 2012, 'The geography of community and political organisation in London', *Political Geography*, 2012, 31, 114–26

Wills, J and Linneker, B, 2014, 'In-work poverty and the living wage in the United Kingdom: a geographical perspective', *Transactions of the Institute of British Geographers*, 39, 2, 182–94

Wilson, D, 1999, 'Exploring the limits of public participation in local government', *Parliamentary Affairs*, 52, 2, 246–59

Wilson, J, 2012, *Letting go: How Labour can learn to stop worrying and trust the people*, Fabian Ideas 632, London: Fabian Society

Wilson, R and Leach, M with Henman, U, Tam, H and Ukkonen, J, 2011, *Civic limits: How much more involved can people get?* London: Respublica

Wright, JSF, Parry, J, Mathers, J, Jones, S and Orford, J, 2006, 'Assessing the participatory potential of Britain's new deal for communities: opportunities for and constraints to bottom-up community participation', *Policy Studies*, 27, 4, 347–61

Wyler, S, 2009, *A history of community asset ownership*, London: Development Trusts Association

Yates, D, 1973, *Neighborhood democracy: The politics and impacts of decentralization*, Lexington MA: Lexington Books

Index

Note: Page numbers in *italic* type refer to figures and tables; page numbers followed by n. refer to footnotes.

Webb, B.P. 48, 49, 50, 55, 75n.6,
    76n.10
Webb, S. 48, 49, 50, 55, 75n.6,
    76n.10
welfare standards 25–6
Whole Place programme 100
Williams, C. 112n.5
Wilson, J. 26
working class 72, 80, 92

Y

Young, M. 63
young people, Tulse Hill focus on
    126–9
youth offending 173–4